GUERRILLA
SAVING

GUERRILLA SAVING

SECRETS FOR KEEPING PROFITS IN YOUR HOME-BASED BUSINESS

**Jay Conrad Levinson
and Kathryn Tyler**

JOHN WILEY & SONS, INC.

New York ➤ Chichester ➤ Weinheim ➤ Brisbane ➤ Singapore ➤ Toronto

Copyright © 2000 by Jay Conrad Levinson and Kathryn Tyler. All rights reserved.

Published by John Wiley & Sons, Inc.
Published simultaneously in Canada.

This publication is designed to provide accurate and authoritative information in regard to the subject matter covered. It is sold with the understanding that the publisher is not engaged in rendering professional services. If professional advice or other expert assistance is required, the services of a competent professional person should be sought.

Library of Congress Cataloging-in-Publication Data:

Levinson, Jay Conrad.
     Guerrilla saving : secrets for keeping profits in your home-based business /
Jay Conrad Levinson and Kathryn Tyler.
          p.   cm.
     Includes bibliographical references and index.
     ISBN 0-471-34542-3 (pbk. : alk. paper)
     1. Home-based business—Management.   2. Marketing.   I. Tyler, Kathryn,
1970-   . II. Title.
HD62.38.L48   2000
658'.041—dc21   99-43408
                                                                                   CIP

Printed in the United States of America.

10 9 8 7 6 5 4 3 2 1

I dedicate this book to Marvin and Shirley Resking,
who are the best savers in the history of my universe.

—Jay Conrad Levinson

For my husband, Jeff, whose consistent support inspired me
to start a book, and whose discipline helped me to finish it.

—Kathryn Tyler

CONTENTS

CONTENTS

CONTENTS

CHARTS

ACKNOWLEDGMENTS

We would like to extend our gratitude to the following home-based guerrillas, who shared their ideas and experiences with us: Anthony Applebaum, Jeff Berner, Lillian D. Bjorseth, Jane Bluestein, Tom Boothe, Brian Boyer, Barbara Brabec, Bonni Kogen Brodnick, Steve Carlson, Dan Cerveny, Gerri Detweiler, Kathy Dimond, Laurie Dry, Gary Dunn, Michael Dziak, Marc Eisenson, Bruce Falkenhagen, Gary Foreman, Michele Foy, Kristin Gibson, Melissa Giovagnoli, Scott and Shirley Gregory, Catherine Groves, Shel Horowitz, Jaclyn Jeffrey, Edith Flowers Kilgo, June Langhoff, Susan Lannis, Theresa Le, Neal Lubow, Jean MacDonald, Laura Martin-Buhler, Jonathan Miller, Ron Miller, Terry Morin, Vicki Nelson, Dan Poynter, Ron Renner, Peter Rogers, Diane Rosener, Marilyn Ross, Diana Shang, Al Siebert, Darla Sims, Gerald Sweitzer, Coleen Sykora, Wanda Urbanska, Cindy Van Gelder, Dave Wampler, Stuart Watson, Todd Weaver, Eva Webb, Ruth Ann Weber, Barbara Winter, Toni Yount-Klein, Marcia Yudkin, and Marilyn Zelinsky.

Also, we would like to thank the following experts and entrepreneurs whose advice greatly contributed to the book: Jim Amos, Alice Bredin, Dave Klavitter, John Knowlton, John Kremer, Judy Lawrence, Tom Ludwig, Randy Rabourn, Richard Tyler, Cherie Umbel, Cheryle White, and Karl and Dan at the Wixom, Michigan, post office.

Special thanks also goes to those who critiqued the book: Lisa Balderston, Mark Brady, Mike and Sheryl Campbell, Sharon Cebulski, Bob Clough, Helen Cothran, John and Kirstin Hensley, Dale and Deb Hodson, Brian Johnson, Mana Mahfoozi, Jeanette McGrigg, Glenn Nomi, Brenda Mashburn, Theresa Rubin, Rob Schwocho, Flora Tyler, TJ and Megan Tyler, Chrisann Weeks, and Mike Zabrocki.

We would also like to thank Mike Larsen, our agent, without whom there would be no book; Mike Hamilton, our editor at John Wiley and Sons, Inc., and his staff; and our families, who were patient and supportive throughout the researching and writing process.

INTRODUCTION

It is one thing to earn a lot of money. It is far more difficult to hold on to that money, waste not one cent of it, and spend wisely that which you do spend.

That means attending to details, taking the time to know which corners to cut, then learning how to cut them, right? Right on all counts. That is why this book points out the details, illuminates the corners which must be cut, and shows you with words and examples how to spend wisely and waste not at all.

When guerrillas think of economizing, they do not necessarily think of trying to save money. What they do think of is getting the absolute most from any money they have invested in marketing. Guerrillas have the wisdom to know that economizing has nothing to do with the cost; it has everything to do with results.

To be sure, guerrillas adopt a philosophy of frugality and thrift. They know well the difference between investing in something disposable, such as paper and accounting services and investing in something that is truly an investment, such as a telephone system or customer-tracking software—items that they would use on a daily basis. There is a big difference between these two types of expenses, so you will not be surprised to learn that guerrillas rarely waste their time and effort on relatively low-cost disposable purchases, but are willing to expend the time and energy to enjoy a large savings on an expense that is really an investment in disguise.

A key to economizing is to think not in terms of purchasing, but in terms of acquiring. That means you open your mind to trading, sharing, renting, modifying an existing item, or borrowing. It means possibly learning a few skills so that you can do rather than hire. For example, desktop publishing software enables you to save a ton of money usually paid to pros.

Guerrillas are also keenly aware of when it makes sense to hire a pro, knowing that amateurish marketing is an invitation to disaster. They might hire a highly paid professional designer to give their marketing items a powerful visual format, then use their own staff members or themselves to continue generating marketing materials that follow this same format. They learn from any consultant they hire.

By understanding that economizing does not mean saving money, but investing it wisely, guerrillas test their investments on a small scale before plunging headlong into any kind of marketing. They have no fear of failure, providing the failures are small ones, and know that even one success in ten tries means discovering a path to wealth and profitability.

They know in their hearts that money is not the key to happiness or success, but that enough of it enables them to have a key made. Real frugality is more about priorities and results than just saving money.

Guerrilla Saving gets right to the heart of frugality, examines closely the methods of achieving it—from bulk buying to batch faxing, from alternative furniture to computer shareware, from stamps to modems. Each tip within these pages helps you save the money you have worked so hard to earn, transforms you from a freespending entrepreneur into a penny-pincher of the guerrilla variety.

I know the true tales of frugal guerrillas will delight your mind, but I know even more that putting their principles into practice will delight your accountant.

Jay Conrad Levinson
Marin County, California

CHAPTER 1 FRUGALITY IS AN ATTITUDE

Frugality is a perspective from which guerrillas approach every spending decision, to look beyond easy, expensive solutions to problems, for more creative, low-cost answers. It is an attitude that is cultivated slowly, over time. A large part of saving money is getting into the habit of doing things inexpensively.

This book will help you save money on specific items, but the most crucial lessons to learn are the philosophy of frugality, and the importance of applying it in your home-based business. This chapter covers some of the principles of thrift so that you can understand the rationale behind our cost-cutting methods. Elsewhere in the book we have focused on the expenses most home-based businesses have in common, such as office supplies but, because every business is different, it is vital to use these principles to begin examining your own circumstances to determine where you can start saving some hard-earned cash.

WORDS OF WISDOM

You need to remember that frugal doesn't equal cheap.

—Barbara Winter,
author of *Making a Living Without a Job*

THE IMPORTANCE OF PARSIMONY

Before we start discussing *how* to save money, you need to consider *why* you might want to. Saving money in your home-based business has many advantages:

➤ You do not have to earn as much to keep your business solvent. Failure to turn a profit causes thousands of businesses to fold every year. If your overhead is low, you can keep operating even if you are just starting out or have seasonal lulls.

➤ You have the option of working less. For instance, Jay has been working only three days per week since 1971.

➤ You can accept projects that you enjoy that may not pay as well as others. When your expenses are few, you have the freedom to work when and on what you'd like.

➤ You can invest in expansion, improvements, or new markets. The less it costs to run your business, the more discretion you have for allocating funds in new areas or on new equipment.

➤ And, of course, you get to keep more of what you earn. The higher your profit margin is, the bigger salary you can take.

Evaluate all your options before doing anything. There is usually a way you can do it better or cheaper or get by with what you currently have.

—Todd Weaver,
Minstrel Music Network

SHOPPING 101

Two types of purchases exist in business: disposable purchases and investment purchases. Guerrillas recognize the difference between these two, and decide which category a purchase falls into before they buy.

Disposable purchases are goods or services that you will use once. Staples and pens are disposable purchases. Purchases you will reap the rewards of, or suffer the problems of, again and again are *investment purchases.* A telephone is an investment purchase because you will use it every business day. A telephone answering service is also an investment purchase, because a poor service may cause you to lose callers week after week, whereas a good service will impress your customers.

Paper could fall into either category, depending on how you plan to use it. Copier paper for internal use would be a disposable purchase, whereas letterhead stationery would be an investment purchase—an investment in your image.

Once you know whether a purchase is disposable or an investment, you can use that information to decide where to save money. If a purchase is an investment, you may be willing to spend a little more money for added features or slightly better quality. It is also worthwhile to shop around more, spending more time calling different vendors or driving to several stores. In contrast, disposable purchases should be bought at the lowest possible price with the least amount of effort. Therefore, you may want to drive to three stores to save $150 on a fax machine, but you would not want to expend that much effort to save 50¢ on sticky notes.

This point may seem obvious but, many times, consumers do not consciously contemplate whether an item is disposable or an investment before they buy. Instead, they rush, skimping on investment purchases and blindly spending too much on disposable ones.

Say, for example, you are considering Model X photocopier, which costs $400, and Model Z copier, which costs $475. All the features are identical except that Model Z can make enlargements. You buy Model X because it is cheaper, and think you have just saved $75. But, over the next two months, you make six visits to the local copy shop to make enlargements and spend $20 on each visit for a total of $120. According to this scenario, your decision to buy Model X cost you $45!

It is easy to see how equipment is an investment purchase, but do not overlook products or services that improve your image, such as a daily radio advertisement. Before you sign the check, you may also want to consider:

How Will This Purchase Increase My Profitability?   Sonoma, California, home-based photographic-supply consultant Laurie Dry asks herself this question before she buys anything. If it does not contribute to the bottom line, she seriously considers keeping the money in her pocket. Alice Bredin, author of *The Home Office Solution* and *The Virtual Office Survival Handbook*, says, "Whenever you're considering spending money, think about what would happen if you didn't spend it. Then try not to spend it. That way you avoid overbuying. Software is a good example, because software is an incredibly powerful tool, but many people buy software and don't use it."

When Do I Need This?   The most important thing to employ when shopping is foresight. Do not decide at 10 A.M. that you need a widget and buy it before noon. Think about it. The more expensive the item or the longer you will use it, the more you should think about it. Amy Dacyczyn, author of *The Complete Tightwad Gazette*, says you should buy something when not having it costs you money.

For instance, consider how much money you spend by not owning a fax machine. How much do you usually spend at the local copy shop sending or receiving faxes? If you spend $10 a month, it would take over two years to break even on the purchase of a fax. In the meantime, would that money be better spent somewhere else or earning interest in the bank? Moreover, will your faxing needs change in the foreseeable future? For example, you do not want to buy a fax machine to submit your work to a client and then, next month, when you get Internet access, decide to email your work instead.

Which Features Do I Need? Which Ones Can I Live Without?   You may need to track your usage for a month or so to really determine this. Using the previous copier example, if you had tracked your copying habits for a month, you may have discovered how often you made enlargements, how much you spent, and the importance of having that feature.

Where Can I Get This?   Notice we did not say, *Where can I buy this?* By thinking in terms of acquisition, not consumption, you become more creative in thinking about where to obtain the item free, or how you can modify something you already have to serve a new purpose. For example, Kathryn needed a way to organize business cards and telephone numbers without having to scroll through her computerized notes. Her first thought was, "I need a Rolodex." But, upon reflection, she realized the true need: organized telephone numbers. Instead, she found an old recipe box and some index cards. She writes the person's name or staples the business card to an index card, then files it alphabetically. A free solution!

How Much Am I Willing to Pay for This?   If you decide you need to buy something, it helps to have a ballpark figure in mind before you hit the garage sales or the stores and are swayed by bells and whistles. If you do not have any idea how much an item costs, you might need to do a little research. Study sales flyers and newspaper ads. Call for mail-order catalogs. Ask around at association meetings.

Learn to use your imagination more and your pocketbook less. The people who aren't in business a long time throw money at their problems. Those who are, are good problem solvers. Find imaginative ways to produce the goals you want. Figure out how to get the most mileage out of every dollar you spend.

—Barbara Winter,
author of *Making a Living Without a Job*

BREAK OUT OF YOUR COMFORT ZONE

Even after you hear about a cheaper source for office supplies or a less-expensive Internet service provider, you may be tempted to continue to use old vendors. It is human nature. We grow accustomed to patronizing the same businesses or doing things the same way. It is easy, comfortable, and requires no effort—but it can be costly. After all, you will not save any money by continuing to do things the same way and buying the same things from the same people.

To trim expenses, guerrillas regularly test new methods and suppliers. They stretch a bit. They get out the map to find the new print shop a friend recommended, or pick up the phone to call a new office-supply company for a catalog.

To make the process a little easier:

➤ Start small, with something relatively inexpensive or easily replaceable. Jean MacDonald, home-based owner of Well-Tempered Web Design in Portland, Oregon, recently tested a new Internet site that searches for the best price in computer equipment and accessories on the web. She was afraid to use the site to buy a $1,000 item and then discover that the recommended company was fraudulent. Instead, she started by buying ink cartridges for her printer and an adapter for her digital camera; both cost less than $20. The site worked out so well that she has decided she will buy more equipment that way.

➤ Research new vendors thoroughly. Ask for references or call the local Better Business Bureau to be sure the company has a clean record.

➤ Take advantage of complimentary trial offers. For example, Kathryn tested out an online electronic library service for a month for free before she decided to sign an annual contract. She wanted to see if the service would have the wealth of information she needed and if she would use it often enough to justify the price.

➤ Pay by credit card. If you are unhappy with the service or the supplier turns out to be less than reputable, you have greater leverage if you want to contest the charges.

It may take some time before a new technique or supplier becomes comfortable. Keep experimenting!

> The best price is not always the best value. Service,
> durability, and reliability are components of value.
>
> —Shel Horowitz,
> author of *Marketing Without Megabucks*

LEARN NEW SKILLS

Advertisements have convinced us that we must leave everything to the "experts." If we need our dog trained, we call a dog trainer. If we need a skirt hemmed, we call a seamstress. We, as a society, have become so specialized that we know how to do only one thing well, and we trade that skill for everything else we need. We are afraid to try a new task by ourselves, in case we make a costly mistake.

Many times, however, with the proper tools, guerrillas can do an even better job than the so-called experts. Why? Because we have a vested interest, we care more about the project than the person we are hiring. We know more about our own businesses. We know what we want done. And we are willing to take the time required to do it right. It is much more cost-efficient, in the long run, to become self-sufficient.

Home-based guerrillas, especially, need to learn how to be jacks-of-all-trades. Because we do not have the dozens of employees or the seemingly unlimited funds that big corporations have, we need to rely on our entrepreneurial spirit. Home-based publisher Jane Bluestein of Instructional Support Services, Inc. in Albuquerque, New Mexico, has discovered this first-hand. She has taken a half-dozen computer classes on page layout. Bluestein estimates the classes cost her approximately $1,000, but knowing how to do page layout has saved her at least $5,000 in typesetting fees. Now she can lay out her catalog and books by herself, so her savings will increase over time.

9

Many people are reluctant to learn a new skill. There is a large up-front commitment of time and, usually, money. However, guerrillas will view it as an investment. Home-based publishers Scott and Shirley Gregory of Bookhome Publishing in Navarre, Florida, caution entrepreneurs against cutting out personal growth when slashing expenses. They regularly attend seminars and buy books, magazines, and tapes to stay current with their industry—and their competition. To home-based business owners who say they cannot afford the time to read, the Gregorys say you cannot afford not to. Ask yourself how much will you save over the long haul by learning how to do something yourself. Consider not only the financial gain, but also the time, energy, and personal-enrichment benefits.

For example, by learning how to lay out pages for her books, Bluestein saves the time and energy that would be required for her to deal with a professional. She does not need to spend hours on the telephone describing what she wants. It also gives her the freedom to make alterations without incurring additional costs if she changes her mind along the way. Finally, she has increased her knowledge which, even if she decides to use a professional typesetter in the future, will help her to make good design decisions.

Community colleges, government agencies, and adult education programs are fabulous resources for learning new skills. If you cannot locate any classes in your chosen subject, ask yourself where can you find people who are willing to share their knowledge. Hire a consultant to share information or advice with you. A couple of hours of consulting fees could save you a lot more money you may waste on mistakes. When home-based newsletter editor Edith Flowers Kilgo started *Creative Downscaling* in Jonesboro, Georgia, she paid a couple of newsletter publishers for consulting advice, and felt it was money well-spent. "I could only afford an hour with each one but what they told me saved me tons of money." She suggests, "If you can only afford one hour, so be it. Make a concise list of questions—and talk fast." Before you hire outside help, Ron Miller, home-based owner of Advantage Northwest, a custom machining and fabrication company in Hillsboro, Oregon, recommends having a clear idea of what you need help with and conveying that to a consultant.

John Kremer, author of *1001 Ways to Market Your Books,* says, "It pays to get the advice if it's necessary. But if you're networking properly, you probably won't have to pay. You can get the advice you want free." Oftentimes, more experienced guerrillas are eager to give advice to novices. Look for organizations, or ask around in your network of friends and family for individuals who have mastered the skill you want to learn. You may be able to pick their brains for free. Gerri Detweiler, a home-based financial consultant, speaker, and author of *The Ultimate Credit Handbook,* from Woodbridge, Virginia, says she learned a lot about public speaking from members of the National Speakers Association.

Frequently, the most crucial part of doing a professional-looking job is not the knowledge required, but the tools. Study the tools the professionals use. How much do they cost? Are there one or two that can perform the majority of the tasks you need? How much does it cost to rent them? If you bought them, would you use them more than once? For example, in order to lay out her work, Bluestein needed to buy a scanner and desktop publishing software. The initial investment was probably close to what a professional typesetter would charge for one job. However, now she possesses the skills and tools required to do a professional-looking job whenever she likes, with no added investment. It is a mistake to skimp on the tools because they are usually the key to polished results.

We are not saying that you should never call an expert or consult a professional. There is nothing more detrimental to your business than sloppy, amateurish work. A smeared logo or an incomprehensible brochure will undoubtedly cost you more in rework and damage to your image than they will save.

However, do not just hand over every task to an expert without first determining if you can learn how to do the job yourself, particularly if you think you might like it. And, if you decide that it is too expensive to learn or you cannot find a teacher, contract a professional, watch how he does it, and learn something, so that the next time maybe you can do part or all of the job yourself.

The ability to do things yourself is a huge money saver and it's not that hard. A big mistake is hiring other people to do things that you could do yourself. Make use of your time; learn how to do your own typesetting, how to do your own web site. Picking up a book on how to code in HTML is no more difficult than learning a new word-processing program. People are too often scared to try something new.

—Steve Carlson,
Upper Access Books

GET ORGANIZED

When was the last time you lost something? How long did it take you to find it? Did you *ever* find it? It is particularly important for home-based guerrillas to be organized, because of the tendency for work and home life to blend together. Crayons get mixed with highlighter pens. Office-supply catalogs lounge alongside copies of *Lands' End* and *Eddie Bauer*. In a traditional office, when you cannot find something, you only need to search one or two rooms. In a home office, when you cannot find something, you start in the office and then move to the rest of the house and, possibly, to the car.

Losing things is expensive. It costs money in lost work time and rework if you cannot find what you want. It also costs money when you buy more of what you already have but cannot find. For instance, when Kathryn moved her office from one spare bedroom to another, she lost a lot of things in the process. Even though she was only moving ten feet, everything got boxed and put in the basement until she had time to organize it. The problem was, as you can imagine, she never set aside time to organize it and she kept trekking downstairs to look for things. When one deadline loomed, she lost two hours combing through boxes for plain manila envelopes. She finally bought more at the office supply store, even though she swore she had a brand new box . . . somewhere.

If a purchase is going to make you more organized or save you significant amounts of time, it is usually worth the cost. Kathryn kept her files in cardboard boxes for three years. That worked for a while but, as she continued to accumulate research and copies of her work, the number of boxes quadrupled. Although they were a frugal solution, she eventually decided it was cheaper to buy a filing cabinet than to keep losing work time and energy shuffling papers and lifting boxes.

If you need help getting organized, it is usually because you have too much stuff to begin with. Start by throwing out the junk you do not use, or donate it to charity and take a tax deduction. To assist you in your dejunking quest, we strongly recommend reading *Clutter's Last Stand* by Don Aslett.

Another way to become more organized is to create systems for everything you do regularly in your business. Organizational failures occur when you leave things to chance. You need systems for tracking appointments, returning telephone calls, placing orders, replying to email, storing information that needs to be acted upon, updating web pages, backing up computer files, and so on. For example, Jay answers his email immediately to keep it from piling up.

MANAGE TIME, MANAGE MONEY

Home-office expert Alice Bredin says, "A few habits really differentiate the productive home-based business owners from those that seem to be struggling. One is the focus on viewing time as money. What I mean by that is a business owner who is continually asking himself, every few hours, 'Am I doing something that is going to earn me money? Move my business forward?' "

Home-based professional organizer Susan Lannis, owner of Organization Plus from Clackamas, Oregon, says that most people view their day as having two parts: committed time, such as appointments, and allocated time, time that has been mentally set aside to work on a specific project. However, Lannis says, we must also remember to plan our day to include time for routine tasks, such as eating lunch, answering email, and returning phone calls.

Lannis says that how you approach *committed time*—time when you are committed to another person, such as a meeting—is crucial to good time management. She says each meeting actually has five parts. First, there is the time to prepare for the meeting, to gather what you need to take. Second is the time to get to the meeting, the travel time. Third is the meeting itself. Fourth is the time to return from the meeting. And, fifth, is the oft-forgotten element: the time to debrief. This means the time to accomplish the things you agreed upon during the meeting. If you omit this last step, much of your meeting time is wasted, because you fail to act on the decisions you made.

Lannis gives the example of a meeting with your accountant. The meeting itself will last two hours, but it will require a half-hour to gather the papers you will need to give her. You also need to figure in a half-hour when you return, to find additional papers she asked for during the meeting, research answers to questions she had, and mark quarterly filing periods in your datebook. Finally, you have the twenty-minute drive to and from the appointment. Lannis notes that you should really allot an extra ten minutes both ways as a "buffer zone." Allowing a buffer zone around appointments allows for traffic jams and other unforeseen delays. Thus, a two-hour appointment has suddenly become a four-hour appointment! Accepting how long an appointment or meeting is going to take is sometimes difficult; we like to fool ourselves into thinking we can accomplish forty-eight-hours' worth of tasks in a twenty-four-hour day. However, determining the actual time required for an appointment or project and scheduling appropriately results in less haste and reduced stress.

In *The Art of Time*, author Jean-Louis Servan-Schreiber tells a story about a doctor who always ran late. He instructed his nurse to schedule his appointments thirty minutes apart when, in actuality, he spent about forty-five minutes with each patient. Instead of determining how long he spent with each person and then scheduling accordingly, he ran late every day for twenty years. How much easier it would have been for everyone if he had just accepted that he could only see ten patients a day, instead of trying to cram in sixteen. How much stress and backtracking he could have saved his patients, nurse, receptionist, and himself. Are you like that doctor? Giving yourself enough time to complete a job saves anxiety but, equally important, it saves money in rework and lost clients.

One of the biggest obstacles to organization and good time management is a failure to realize how long an activity takes, or misjudging what Lannis calls *allocated time*. For years Kathryn wrote articles without any idea of how long it took her to complete them. She simply started when she got the assignment and finished by the deadline. She eventually realized it would be beneficial to know exactly how much time she needed. So, immediately after she received one assignment, she started to keep a log, documenting every moment she spent on the article and what she was doing. Now she knows how much time to budget for each step of a project.

Furthermore, she has used the information to compute her equivalent hourly wage. Many home-based guerrillas are paid by the job, not by the hour, so it is especially important to know how much time it takes to complete a project. This prevents underbidding a job by underestimating the amount of time required to do it. Artists, in particular, may find it difficult to place a dollar value on their work, because it is difficult to benchmark their work with that of other artists, since every piece of art is unique. For example, Ruth Ann Weber, home-based owner of It's Something Special, a company that sells hand-painted furniture and offers painting classes in Jackson, Michigan, found it was crucial for her to know the cost of materials and how many hours she spends painting a piece of furniture in order to price it so that she makes a profit.

Calculating your hourly wage also yields the knowledge necessary to make decisions about time-saving purchases. For instance, if you know you earn $25 an hour, and you waste two hours a day driving to the post office, waiting in line, and driving home again, you can conclude that every postal excursion costs you $50 in lost work time. If you bought a postal scale, you would not need to drive to the post office. The scale may cost $30, but you recoup more than that in just one work day. If you did not know your average hourly wage, you might resist buying a scale because you mistakenly believed it was cheaper to just go to the post office. One caveat: Just because something saves time does not mean it is worth buying. The product or service must save more in potential paid work time than it costs.

Lannis says home-based guerrillas hold three job titles—Owner, President, and Worker—and need to organize their time accordingly. She says the Owner's job is to determine the company's goals and overall vision. This activity takes one day per month. The President's or Manager's job is to market, schedule work, manage cash, and do accounting. This role requires one day per week. The rest of the time is devoted to the Worker's job, the work for which we are paid. Lannis asserts that most home-based guerrillas have no trouble with the Worker's job, but often fail to allow time to accomplish the other two roles, which results in falling behind or working weekends and nights. She said when she started to block out time for the other two jobs, she felt on top of her business. Now she reserves every Monday for managerial tasks and the last Friday of the month for planning.

By making time for routine tasks, we can get a more realistic picture of our schedules. Says Lannis, "You need to figure out how much of your day is gone before you start. For instance, if your routine tasks take an hour, you can only commit and allocate seven hours a day. This keeps you from overallocating and overcommitting."

When you become more aware of your time and how it relates to your income, you may also discover that your business has seasons. For example, many businesses find they have a slowdown during December or the week between Christmas and New Year's. If you know when your peak and off-peak periods are, you can plan your time to take advantage of them.

The end of December and the first few weeks of January are the slow time for Peter Rogers, a home-based professional location photographer from Chino Hills, California. "I don't worry about it anymore," he says, "because I know business will be booming in a couple of weeks. Experience brings you the ability to look beyond the down times. I just accept it as an assigned vacation. You can fight it or you can roll with it."

TIP! *Select services or vendors based on location. For instance, home-based environmental consultant and oil engineer Bruce Falkenhagen, who lives in the small community of Nipomo, California, must drive up or down the coast for almost every service he needs. Thus, he selected a bank based on which one had branches both north and south of him, so that he could combine making deposits with any other errand. Batching errands is a great way to save time and gas money.*

MAKE GOOD USE OF WHAT YOU HAVE

It is said that humans only use about 10 percent of their brains' capacity. The same thing can often be said about office equipment. Many of us only use a small fraction of the features available on the equipment and computer software we own, because we do not know what we have or how to use all of it.

How can you get more out of your investments?

➤ As soon as you buy something, spend several hours familiarizing yourself with all of the features while you are still enthusiastic about the novelty of it.

➤ Read the manual. For some reason, many of us refuse to read directions. Perhaps it is because we are afraid that asking for help is weak. But unfortunately, most machines are not user-friendly. To learn how to operate many machines, you need someone to show you, or you need to read the instructions.

➤ Use "Help" buttons in computer software. Many programs contain step-by-step instructions on how to complete tasks, visual demonstrations, and answers to frequently asked questions (often called FAQs).

➤ Ask questions. If you worked in a traditional office, you would have many co-workers around to help with everyday problems, such as how to create datatables in a word-processing program. As a home-based guerrilla, you need to develop alternative support systems. When faced with a challenge, ask around. Ask friends, family members or vendors, or find a user group on the Internet.

➤ Visit manufacturers' web sites and call helpline telephone numbers. Most companies offer assistance to customers using their products.

➤ Consider taking a class. It is not unreasonable to spend money learning how to use a computer software program, especially if it is complicated. After all, if you do not know how to use it, you will not use it, and the money you spent on it will be wasted.

➤ Call in a consultant. If you are paying a professional to do a job that your computer could do if properly programmed, it may be worthwhile to pay a consultant for a one-time visit. Have a professional set up the system and teach you how to use it. For example, are you employing an accountant to do your bookkeeping? Could you automate it and save money? Michele Foy, home-based owner of Dynamic Alternatives, a computer and general management consulting firm in Highland Park, Illinois, says that a well-designed computer system can do many repetitive tasks and save small businesses a lot of money. She adds that most businesses can reduce their manpower using the equipment they already own.

Instead of buying something new to solve your problem, go shopping in your office. Maybe there is a software program that came with your computer that will suit your purposes. Or perhaps your modem has fax capabilities. It is wise to familiarize yourself with what your equipment and software have to offer. You have already paid for it, you may as well see what you've got!

> *Save time in meetings by not meeting! Before scheduling a meeting, see if you can accomplish your goals via email, fax, or telephone. Author Alice Bredin says that many people "over-meet," cheating themselves out of work time. June Langhoff, author of* Telecom Made Easy, *says that she encourages her clients to teleconference instead of meet face-to-face. Though teleconferencing costs about $10 to $20 per participant per call, it is a bargain if you have to spend that in gas (or airfare) and lost work time. If you must meet face-to-face, Bredin recommends a breakfast or coffee-break meeting, as opposed to a lunch meeting, because it will be less costly.*

TIP!

REAP DIVIDENDS FROM KINDNESS

On the surface, being nice does not seem to have anything to do with saving money. However, if you have ever watched a barn raising, you know that having friends saves time and money. Guerrillas with support systems rely on friends for services instead of paying for them. Networking, mentoring, sharing, karma, call it what you will, being pleasant and helping others when you can will help you.

Of course, your kindness or eagerness to help others must be sincere. If you give looking to receive, the alliance will backfire. The keys to scratching others' backs are:

➤ When asked, give generously. Guerrillas who freely share information position themselves as experts in their fields.

➤ If a person does not ask for help, offer.

➤ Take names, addresses, and phone numbers. Have a system for storing contact information that makes it easy to find people again.

➤ Keep in regular contact. Do not misunderstand: Do not send weekly communiqués if you have nothing to say. But, if you stumble upon a newspaper article on a topic of interest to an acquaintance, fax it. Or, if you have new information to share about a subject you have previously discussed, call. If you do not communicate regularly, you will lose touch with one another.

➤ Make it easy for others to contact you. If you move, send a change-of-address card to every person with whom you have done business. Answer telephone calls and email promptly.

Wanda Urbanska, co-author of *Moving to a Small Town* and co-owner of Levering Orchard in Mount Airy, North Carolina, emphasizes the importance of community. She says that she tries to help out new businesses whenever she can, and she has reaped the rewards of that generosity in one way or another. For example, she offered a new neighbor the use of her copy and fax machines. Later, he produced a videotape for her for free. By the way, Urbanska has one home-based business and another which is not. She and her husband run an orchard at home, and she has an office downtown for her writing and publishing projects. It is noteworthy, though, that Urbanska does not pay rent on her outside office. The elderly man that owns it lets her use it for free! "You have to keep giving back. It's very much that kind of economy. Take time to create a web of community; one of the offshoots is saving money, but that's not the reason you're doing it."

Ask for what you want. When you need something, tell people you are looking for it. You might be surprised where the savings will come from. I made a casual comment to a neighbor that I was in need of a copier, and I ended up with a one-month-old $1,800 copier for $200.

—Susan Lannis,
Organization Plus

INVEST IN YOUR HEALTH

Many home-based guerrillas we spoke with emphasized the importance of spending money on things that improved their physical and mental health. When you are self-employed, you do not get paid sick days. No one picks up the slack while you are in bed with the flu. The bottom line is: Guerrillas cannot afford to be ill. Therefore, it is crucial to stay healthy, even if that means spending a little money on prevention.

For instance, Gerri Detweiler bought a headset, an ergonomically correct keyboard, and voice-recognition computer software. Though these tools cost her a few hundred dollars, they save her untold amounts in doctors' bills and discomfort due to arm and shoulder strain. Detweiler views such tools as investments in increasing her productivity and decreasing her work time. Several of the home-based guerrillas mentioned voice-recognition software as one of the keys to their high productivity.

It is wise to buy tools that will help you be more productive or will reduce the toll on your body. As one business owner said, if you worked for someone else, you would complain to your employer if the office were too hot, cold, or otherwise uncomfortable. You should not live with poor working conditions just because you are self-employed. The more time you spend at work, the more important it is for you to be at ease. That does not mean you have spend $5,000 on an air-filtration system, but you may want to get a fan or air-conditioning, even if you only use it a couple of weeks per year.

Moreover, take the time to get enough sleep, exercise, and eat right. Skipping lunch will catch up with you in lost productivity. Create rituals that nurture your mental and physical health, such as taking a morning walk or quitting at a regular hour. For instance, home-based editor of *Workers on Wheels* Coleen Sykora and her husband, Bob, eat breakfast in a restaurant every day. It gets them up, dressed, and out of the house early, and they have a good, solid meal to start the day. "Even though it would be a whole lot cheaper to fry eggs and cook oatmeal, it's not the same," she says. "We need that time together to do our best job."

Home-office expert Alice Bredin says, "Good health is critical to avoiding one of the greatest pitfalls: burnout. One thing I see is a business owner who starts out with creative energy and excitement and quickly deteriorates into someone who isn't getting that much done in a day even though they're working all the time. People think the path to success is to work like crazy. The path to success is to work hard, but take enough breaks."

To avoid burnout, you need to get out of the house. Get some fresh air, see people. "It's important to replace the interaction you used to have in an office. We get energy from other people. Set up two lunch meetings every week," suggests Bredin. She also recommends taking an occasional half-hour afternoon nap. "Many of the most successful people—Eleanor Roosevelt, Winston Churchill—recognize the fact that you can't expect to run at full throttle without getting a nap."

Beginning home-based business books often warn against keeping "banker's hours." They offer strategies to get you out of bed in the morning and keep focused on work, instead of household chores or other diversions. However, we have found the bigger obstacle for most home-based guerrillas is not going to or staying at work but, rather, knowing when to stop.

Workaholism can be a greater danger for home-based entrepreneurs than for traditional professionals or even entrepreneurs with businesses outside the home. Why? By working at home, you are never away from work. For some people, there is nothing to stop them from working every waking moment. That is why it is important to recognize this potential pitfall early, and take steps to prevent it. Home-based publisher Jane Bluestein designed her home office in the basement. When she gets off work, she goes upstairs and shuts the door. Though it is a small feature, she likes the physical separation the door creates.

It is important to create a balance between your work life and your home life. If you work eighty hours one week and twenty hours the next, your health and business will suffer. When you crash, marketing stops, calls are not returned promptly, and email goes unread. Crashing looks poor to your customers. Sprinting may work in the short term, but it is not how you want to run your business on a regular basis. It costs more to overcome a marketing gap or a loss of presence in the field than it does to keep a consistent, manageable image.

Try to set regular business hours. The temptation of working all the time is always there. But it's important to have a regimented schedule of some sort. This is when I'm working and this is when I'm not working. Otherwise, your work becomes your life, and what's the point?

—Jonathan Miller,
Reunited, Inc.

MODERATION IN ALL THINGS

If you do something regularly, a little bit at a time, it will be much more manageable than if you let it go, with the thought of doing it all at once later. For example, filing a half-dozen papers a day takes only a few minutes. But if you drop all paper into a to-be-filed in-box with the intention of doing it later, it will take much longer to scale the mountain. Why? First, you must surmount the mental baggage: "Oh my gosh, that will take me *forever.*" Second, you must find a block of several hours of uninterrupted time. Therefore, you let it go until the problem gets so bad that it causes your primary tasks to suffer ("I can't find the papers I need for my presentation today").

The problem is that most of the things that fall into the investment category are things Stephen Covey, author of the *7 Habits* series, calls *quadrant two* activities, meaning they are important, but not urgent. Because home-based guerrillas often work alone, they find themselves in the role of firefighter too often, unable to douse the flames long enough to refill the water tanks. It is vital, however, to make the time to accomplish these goals—exercise, file, invoice, plan, read, and so on—because, otherwise, we will find ourselves facing a wall of fire without water.

Instead of waiting until you have a large block of time—which will never happen—do a little bit. Plan one part of your marketing strategy. Take a short walk around the block. File two papers. Read one magazine article. Three minutes of action now is better than three hours of intention later.

23

THE HOME-COURT ADVANTAGE

"Being self-employed and working from home seems like a new trend, but 100 years ago, 90 percent of us were self-employed and worked from home. We lived and worked on farms, druggists lived upstairs from their pharmacies . . . ," says Jeff Berner, home-based author of *The Joy of Working from Home: Making a Life While Making a Living,* from Dillon Beach, California. "I want people to know that working independently, in the spirit of community, is the traditional American thing to do."

Not only is it patriotic, it is economical. You can take comfort in the fact that, as a home-based guerrilla, you are already saving large sums of money. You do not have to pay rent for office space. If you own your home, you are building equity with every mortgage payment. You may have renovated your house to accommodate your office, which will increase its market value when you sell. You may be living in a more inexpensive area than you would if you were commuting to a job. And, by not having to commute, you are saving money on transportation. You probably do not eat in restaurants as often as you would if you worked elsewhere, and you probably spend less on business attire.

Perhaps you spend less on child care than you would if you had to go to a traditional office. Most times, working from home drastically reduces or eliminates the need for outside child-care providers. Kathryn's young son goes to a neighbor's home for only a few hours a week. Ron Renner, home-based owner of Geppetto's Woodworking in Vancouver, Washington, says his home-based business has allowed him to raise his son without ever using a babysitter. Some guerrillas may be able to work while their children are in school.

In fact, you are saving money in hundreds of little ways by integrating your work life into your home life. The home-based guerrillas we interviewed listed many benefits about working from home, but the advantage they cited most often was that they are able to make good use of their time. When they have a few moments of down time between clients, they can throw in a load of laundry. They can walk the Labrador during their lunch break and be home when the plumber gets around to fixing the shower, without sacrificing a whole day of work. They save time and life energy—energy that can be reinvested in their businesses.

For instance, Eva Webb, home-based owner of The Income Tax Store, a tax preparation service in Sayetteville, Georgia, describes her transition from the traditional corporate world to working at home: "When I retired early from my job with the Department of Defense, I took a salary reduction of $22,500 a year. I was really worried that our lifestyle would change drastically and we would have to eat beans every day. But I can't tell a difference in our lifestyle at all, except that I watch what I spend more carefully. By working at home, I save on gas, clothes, dry cleaning, car insurance, and food (no eating out at work or very little at home). I have time to do my own housework, yardwork, and home maintenance and don't have to pay for these services anymore. I have the time to shop for bargains. I can wear casual clothing and feel relaxed all the time. I can arrange my schedule however I want. I get much more rest, and I'm doing what I enjoy. Working in this stress-free environment has also saved numerous doctor bills."

What Eva Webb discovered, and you probably have, too, is that by deciding to be home-based, you are saving in many ways that are difficult to quantify. So, congratulations, you are already well on your way to becoming a guerrilla saver!

CHAPTER 2

PENNY-PINCHING ON PENS, PAPER, AND PAPER CLIPS

Pens, paper, paper clips, and other office supplies are the cornerstones of many home-based businesses. Though they do not cost a lot individually, they are items you buy repeatedly and use in large quantities, which means there is potential for huge savings.

For instance, if you add up the amount of paper you use in a month, a 50¢ difference between the name brand and the generic brand may save you $50 or more per year. That is why it is especially important to examine these expenses regularly and to keep looking for cheaper sources. Do not overlook places where you can save a few dollars or cents—it adds up! Moreover, it keeps you in a frugal frame of mind.

PRESTAMPED ENVELOPES AND POSTCARDS

Consider buying envelopes and postcards from the post office. For 3¢ to 13¢ more than postage (depending on the quantity ordered), you can buy

Think ahead. Watching your supply level is important. When you get yourself in a bind, you end up paying a premium at the local stationery store.

—Michele Foy,
Dynamic Alternatives, Inc.

stamped envelopes preprinted with your return address. For example, a box of 500 costs $176.40 plus $5.20 shipping and handling (36¢ each, or 3¢ more than postage alone). Envelopes from a printer cost about 15¢ each—and that does not include postage. That is a savings of 12¢ per envelope! Preprinted, stamped envelopes also save time because you do not need to type a return address or affix stamps. The drawbacks are you cannot choose the ink color, pica, or typestyle—all envelopes come in black, eight-point Helvetica type—which means they may not match your letterhead. Orders take three to four weeks to arrive.

Prestamped, blank stationery is an even better deal. For the same price as postage or a penny more, you can buy stamped, blank envelopes (33¢) and postcards (21¢). For more information, contact your local post office or

Philatelic Fulfillment Service Center
United States Postal Service • PO Box 419208 • Kansas City, MO 64141
phone: (800) 782-6724 • fax: (816) 545-1212
web site: http://www.usps.gov

An alternative to preprinted envelopes is a rubber stamp. Depending on the nature of your business, this can be an inexpensive alternative. Laura Martin-Buhler, home-based editor of *The Gentle Survivalist* newsletter, from St. George, Utah, finds that a rubber stamp is convenient because she can also use it to endorse checks. Edith Flowers Kilgo, editor of *Creative Downscaling,* uses a rubber stamp to create her own reply envelopes. She buys 360 envelopes for $1 at a dollar store and then stamps them with her address while talking on the phone or watching

TV. "Stamping envelopes is boring, but I save tons of money by not having a printer do this," says Kilgo. "Not every company could get by
with this but, because we are a frugality publication, this approach actually gets the requester's attention and makes them believe we know
about frugality."

> **TIP!**
>
> *Marc Eisenson, home-based co-author of* Invest in Yourself, *editor of* The Pocket Change Investor, *and publisher of* Good Advice Press *in Elizaville, New York, gets all of his paper clips for free from the bank. His bank collects so many that Marc says, "They must keep them in a fifty-five-gallon drum," and adds that the tellers at his bank have always been happy to give him all he wants, just to get rid of them!*

SHIPPING SUPPLIES

The post office is also the best place to find free shipping supplies,
including overnight and Priority Mail envelopes and boxes, rubber
bands, mail trays, mail bins, and mail sacks. Steve Carlson, home-based
publisher of Upper Access Books in Hinesburg, Vermont, recommends
buying packing boxes from a precycler, a company that gets boxes from
corporations that did not use them and resells them for next to nothing.
"We spend a penny on a box that would have cost us a dollar if we
bought it retail," says Carlson. "Of course, the disadvantage is you have
to use what sizes are available. But a small company doesn't have to be
as systematized as a big company with a packing room of 100 people. If
another box becomes available, you adapt."

Moreover, Carlson never buys packing materials. Instead, he reuses
packing peanuts he receives, or uses free sources, such as the ends of
newsprint rolls. Dave Wampler, home-based owner of Simple Living
Network, an online company from Trout Lake, Washington, that sells
products that help others live a more conscious, simple, healthy, and
restorative lifestyle, has a paper shredder that he uses to destroy all junk
mail. He uses the resulting confetti as free packing material.

TIP! *Shel Horowitz, author of* **The Penny-Pinching Hedonist,** *gets all the pens he can use free from trade shows that he attends.*

COPIER AND PRINTER CARTRIDGE RECYCLING SERVICES

Cartridges in copiers and laser and ink-jet printers contain a tube or bladder that holds the toner or ink. In most copiers and printers, the cartridge can be recycled and the bladder refilled several times, for about $50 each time. A new, original equipment manufactured (OEM) laser printer toner cartridge costs $75 to $100, so refilling can save you quite a bit of money, depending on how many cartridges you use.

Recycled cartridges may be remanufactured or recharged. *Remanufactured* means the cartridge was cleaned, the worn parts were repaired or replaced, and the toner was refilled. *Recharged* usually means that only the toner was refilled. Most laser toner cartridges can be remanufactured many times, monochrome ink-jet cartridges usually can be remanufactured ten to twelve times, and tricolor ink jet cartridges usually can be remanufactured three to six times.

Recycling companies claim that remanufactured cartridges produce blacker blacks and more printed pages than new cartridges because remanufacturers add 10 to 30 percent more toner than OEMs. This is difficult to test, because it would require printing thousands of pages but, even if they have equal print quality and print the same number of pages, it is still much cheaper to use a recycled cartridge than a new one. Besides saving money, recycling cartridges is environment friendly. Each cartridge requires half a quart of oil to make and can be manufactured with up to four pounds of nonbiodegradable materials which, if not recycled, will end up in a landfill.

Remanufacturing services vary widely, so choose a service carefully. There are no legal standards that cartridge remanufacturers must meet. If the company does not do a quality job, the cartridge may fail and possibly cause damage to your printer. This may be one reason why printer manufacturers discourage the use of remanufactured ink jet and toner cartridges. When we spoke with a Hewlett-Packard (HP) representative about remanufactured cartridges, he said HP does not remanufacture cartridges. (They do accept empty cartridges for recycling, and then make a donation to charity.)

Some OEMs claim that using remanufactured cartridges will void your printer's warranty, but remanufacturers refute this. They say this practice is illegal, according to the Sherman and Clayton Anti-Trust Act, which states no manufacturer is allowed to limit a warranty based on the customer using only that manufacturer's supplies or service, but you may have trouble enforcing that if your printer requires warranty work.

Cheryle White, executive editor of *The Cartridge Recycling Magazine* in Las Vegas, Nevada, says she has been using remanufactured cartridges since 1989 and has never had a problem with them. She says that it is "highly unlikely" that a printer cartridge would damage the printer and she, personally, has never seen it happen. Publisher Marc Eisenson agrees and says that he has used hundreds, if not thousands, of recycled cartridges and has never had a serious problem.

Lillian D. Bjorseth, home-based speaker, trainer, and author of *Break-through Networking: Building Relationships that Last*, from Lisle, Illinois, uses remanufactured cartridges and is pleased with them. The one time she had a problem with a cartridge, the remanufacturer immediately came to replace it, and gave her a discount because she had ruined a few pieces of her linen bond stationery.

In deciding whether or not to buy remanufactured cartridges, you should remember that printer manufacturers make quite a profit selling new cartridges. Some manufacturers even use recycled parts in their new cartridges (check the box for words like "made from new and recycled materials"). If your printer is no longer under warranty, the cost savings may be worthwhile.

Some remanufacturing services deliver, while others work strictly by mail. You may or may not have to pay shipping charges. The local service we use delivers within one business day free (same-day service costs $5), which saves us time and gas.

If you decide to try a cartridge-remanufacturing service, look for one that guarantees workmanship or refunds your money. To find a service, look under "Computer Repair and Service" or "Laser Printer Supplies" in the *Yellow Pages,* or look on the Internet. *The Cartridge Recycling Magazine* maintains a web site with recycler names and addresses sorted by zip code at http://www.tcrm.com. When you contact a service, ask for references.

Here are a few mail-order remanufacturing services:

RDS Recharging Systems
29 Vassar Road • Poughkeepsie, NY 12603
phone: (800) 344-9951 • fax: (914) 462-4610
web site: none listed

Laser Recycling Company
12223 West 87th Street Parkway • Lenexa, KS 66215-2811
phone: (913) 599-3337 • fax: (913) 894-8997
web site: http://www.laserrecycle.com

Quill Corporation
PO Box 94080 • Palatine, IL 60094-4080
phone: (800) 789-1331 • fax: (800) 789-8955
web site: http://www.quillcorp.com

When the print quality from your printer cartridge begins to fade, remove the cartridge and shake it vigorously over a wastebasket. This will redistribute the remaining toner, and extend the life of the cartridge.

DO-IT-YOURSELF INK-JET PRINTER CARTRIDGE KITS

If you are handy, you can also buy kits to refill ink-jet printer cartridges yourself. There are two types: injection and click in. An ink-jet cartridge kit costs about $21 to $27 and contains three refills. However, White cautions that the injection kits can be extremely messy. Also, if you do it yourself, you have no way of cleaning the parts, which means that there is a greater likelihood of printer failure as a result of clogged parts. A remanufacturer would clean the parts, but most do-it-yourselfers do not have the knowledge or tools to do this. If you decide to use an injection kit, be careful not to insert the needle too far into the bladder, as you may puncture it.

Click-in ink-jet refills, on the other hand, are fairly straightforward and relatively clean. Diane Rosener, home-based editor of *A Penny Saved* newsletter, from Omaha, Nebraska, says she has not had any problems refilling hers. If you want to try an ink-jet refilling kit, they are available from discount office-supply stores and the remanufacturing services listed earlier.

Use nondisposable items whenever possible. This helps save the environment as well as your money. For example, Theresa Le, an independent contractor with a direct-selling cosmetic company from San Jose, California, uses washcloths in her product demonstrations instead of disposable facial tissues, and then launders them between customers.

SELLING EMPTY CARTRIDGES

Even if you decide against *buying* a remanufactured cartridge, you should consider *selling* your empty ones. First, it saves the environment, because all that plastic does not end up in a landfill. Second, it can earn you as much as $20 each. If you run a business with regular access to empty cartridges, such as an office-cleaning company, it may be quite lucrative. Chart 2-1 illustrates what remanufacturers are currently paying for empty cartridges.

CHART 2.1 Market Price for Empty Cartridges

EMPTY CARTRIDGE	MARKET PRICE PER CARTRIDGE
HP Series 4000	$20
HP Series 5L	$10
Xerox XC	$7
Sharp Fax Cartridges	$3
HP 51645A (Ink Jet Cartridges)	$2

Cheryle White says the type of cartridges in demand fluctuates but, typically, the newer printer cartridges are at a premium. Depending on how many empty cartridges you have, you may or may not have to pay shipping. For instance, Nashua Corporation pays shipping for fifty or more empty cartridges; the minimum the company accepts is five. Call remanufacturers to get a current quote.

Nashua Corporation
44 Franklin Street • Nashua, NH 03060
phone: (800) 333-3439 • fax: (603) 880-2477
web site: http://www.nashua.com

Some people may be squeamish about dumpster diving, but it can be a good source of free supplies. Brian Boyer, home-based owner of Collectorshop, an online supplier of imported CDs, and author of The Slacker's Handbook, *from Arlington, Illinois, says he salvaged several boxes of envelopes from the recycling bins at his school. He places labels over the return address and reuses them. As a result, he has not had to buy envelopes for over five years!*

SAVING RESOURCES

High-quality twenty-pound, 25 percent cotton-bond watermarked paper stands up well to handling and projects a professional image. However, it costs $15.46 a ream, almost eight times as much as photocopier paper ($2 per ream). It makes sense, then, to reserve the good stuff for outgoing correspondence only. When printing drafts, use plain copier paper.

(Remember to take the high-quality paper out of the printer when you are finished.)

Author Lillian D. Bjorseth prints on both sides of every sheet of paper except when she is printing outgoing correspondence. Some printers jam when you try to reuse paper, but Bjorseth says the key is to keep like paper together. In other words, do not mix twenty-four-pound paper with twenty pound, or linen bond with plain copier paper.

Another way to reduce paper consumption is to use your computer's print preview, grammar-check, and spell-check options. Learn to edit on the screen as much as possible. Then, you can print one final rough draft to proofread. It is always smart to proofread one hard-copy draft, as some typographical errors can slip by you on the screen. For instance, if you write "form" and you meant to write "from," spell check will not catch it.

Home-based fashion designer Diana Shang, from San Pedro, California, reduces her paper usage by storing as much information in the computer as possible, so that she does not need to have paper around, except for her drawings.

If you regularly shop at a discount office-supply store, get on its mailing list. Oftentimes, stores send coupons and information about promotional events to regular customers. For instance, Kathryn received a $15 coupon toward any purchase at Staples in the mail. For the coupon and $1, she bought a box of ballpoint pens, one ream of copier paper, one box of jumbo paper clips, a highlighter pen, and a month-at-a-glance calendar!

RECHARGEABLE BATTERIES

Almost everyone knows that rechargeable batteries are better for the environment, but how much do they really save? As much as 16¢ per hour of use. And are they worth the extra trouble involved in recharging? Yes.

35

Rechargeable batteries come in two types: nickel cadmium (NiCad) and alkaline. Though they function similarly, the two systems are completely different and should never be interchanged. NiCad batteries, such as Eveready, must be charged prior to the first use, whereas alkaline batteries, such as Rayovac Renewal, are 100 percent charged when you buy them. How long does it take to recharge batteries? Usually, three to five hours.

Another difference is that alkaline batteries gradually lose rechargeable power, meaning the first time you charge them they will hold 100 percent but, with each consecutive charge, they hold less. Alkalines can be recharged about twenty-five times. NiCad batteries hold the same amount of charge over the life of the battery, but they hold less than disposables.

Rechargeables have a higher initial cost, because you must buy the recharger, but, unlike disposables, you can use them over and over again, which lowers the cost per use. For example, Eveready rechargeables can be recharged up to 500 times. In our area, we found that 4 AA size batteries cost about 1¢ per hour of use as opposed to 9¢ to 16¢ per hour of use for disposables.

Home-based business professional Cindy Van Gelder, former editor of *Keep Your Cash* newsletter, in Holland, Michigan, uses rechargeable batteries for almost everything, and recently noticed that her post office was using them in its scales. She appreciates the environmental friendliness of rechargeables. Van Gelder points out that NiCad rechargeable batteries contain small amounts of mercury, which means they should be taken to your city's hazardous-waste collection. Alkaline batteries contain minuscule amounts of mercury and are safe to toss into the regular trash in most communities. Disposable batteries now contain insignificant amounts of mercury, and can be disposed of in the normal trash in many cities, but the casings still add to landfills more than rechargeables. Why? Because you use and dispose of many more.

Despite their advantages, rechargeables do hold less power than new batteries, so guerrillas will want to consider when and where the batteries will be used. A brochure by Eveready Battery Company, Inc. entitled, "Rechargeable Batteries & Chargers Make Sense!" cautions against using rechargeables for smoke detectors or infrequently used devices, probably because rechargeables do not store well. In contrast, disposables can be stored for up to five years and still deliver power.

Thus, we suggest you use rechargeables when reliability is not crucial. For instance, we will use rechargeable batteries in our tape recorders when we are dictating, but we use only new disposable ones when we are interviewing someone. We cannot risk losing power during an interview, but we do not mind changing batteries when we are working by ourselves.

And, as with many money-saving tactics, to use rechargeables you will need to plan ahead because recharging takes several hours. We keep two plastic bags, one labeled "bad" and the other "good," in the drawer. When the bad bag gets full, we set up the recharger. Because we have enough batteries to rotate, we are never caught without charged batteries.

Be willing to look for the best supplier for individual items.

—Shel Horowitz,
author of *The Penny-Pinching Hedonist*

MAIL-ORDER OFFICE-SUPPLY COMPANIES

Mail-order office-supply companies usually have a wide selection, particularly of hard-to-find items. They are also convenient, because they deliver to your door, which saves gas and time. Mail-order companies can offer low prices, because they do not need to pay high rent in a strip mall and can sell their products nationally. Guerrillas who live in rural areas, where shopping choices are limited to stationery and department stores, will probably save the most money using mail order.

The disadvantages to mail order are that you cannot touch the merchandise before buying to determine if it meets your business needs and, sometimes, you have to buy in large quantities. Also, some mail-order companies tack on shipping and handling or other fees, such as small order processing charges. Many companies will waive shipping and handling charges if you order more than $50 worth of supplies, so you will want to wait until you need that much.

Listed here are several mail-order companies you may want to check out. Call for a free catalog, and compare the prices to the stores in your area. Remember to compare each item you buy individually; one source rarely has the best price on everything.

Chiswick Trading, Inc.

33 Union Avenue • Sudbury, MA 01776-2267
phone: (800) 225-8708 • fax: (800) 638-9899
web site: none listed

Products: Labels and packing supplies, including recloseable plastic bags, padded mailing envelopes, and videotape mailers.

Shipping & Handling: You pay, regardless of the size of your order. And, if your order totals less than $50, you also have to pay a $3 processing charge.

Guarantee: Money back for any product within thirty days.

Hours: Monday–Friday, 8 A.M.–8 P.M., Eastern time. Saturday 9 A.M.–5 P.M., Eastern time.

Comments: Catalogs are in color with clear pictures and easy-to-understand price charts. The table of contents is easy to use, but the catalog does not have an index.

Fidelity Products Company

5601 International Parkway • Minneapolis, MN 55440-0155
phone: (800) 326-7555 • fax: (800) 842-2725
web site: none listed

Products: Shipping and storage products, as well as a full line of graphics supplies, like art pens, portfolio cases, and presentation easels.

Shipping & Handling: You pay. The operator determines shipping and handling charges at the time of your order.

Guarantee: The company will refund your money (including the original shipping costs) and pay return shipping on any product for thirty days.

Hours: Monday–Friday 8 A.M.–7 P.M., Eastern time. Saturday 9 A.M.–3 P.M., Eastern time.

Comments: The catalog has color pictures, but tiny print. Also, it is difficult to find what you are looking for because there is no table of contents, and the index is in the middle of the catalog instead of at the end.

Grayarc
PO Box 2944 • Hartford, CT 06104
phone: (800) 243-5250 • fax: (800) 292-4729
web site: none listed

Products: Labels, forms, stationery, shipping supplies, and a limited amount of common office supplies. The company also prints your company's logo on promotional items, such as mugs, pens, shopping bags, and key chains.

Shipping & Handling: Free to the contiguous forty-eight United States if you pay in advance.

Guarantee: Refunds your money at any time for any reason and will also reimburse you for return postage.

Hours: Monday–Friday 8 A.M.–6 P.M., Eastern time.

Comments: The catalog is in color with easy-to-read price charts. Many of the personalized items require a minimum order of 250. There is no table of contents. The index is color-coded by category which, instead of being helpful, makes it more difficult to find what you want. For instance, to find markers you would need to look under the right category, "Office & Warehouse Supplies," and then alphabetically for *M*.

OfficeMax
3605 Warrensville Center Road • Shaker Heights, OH 44122-5203
phone: (800) 788-8080 • fax: (800) 995-9644
web site: http://www.officemax.com

Products: Over 7,000 office supplies, computers, software, electronics, and furniture.

Shipping & Handling: Free next-business-day delivery within delivery area with a minimum order of $50. Under $50, costs $12 to ship. Delivery area determined by proximity to stores.

Guarantee: If you find an identical item advertised by any other office products superstore for less within seven days of your OfficeMax purchase, OfficeMax will match their price and give you a credit for 55 percent of the difference, up to $55. Satisfaction guarantee states that the company will refund your money if you return the item in the original packaging with a receipt within thirty days.

Hours: Twenty-four hours a day, seven days a week.

Comments: The catalog has a color-coded table of contents that is fairly easy to use, and an alphabetical index. The catalog is in color and contains photographs of all of the products. Sprinkled liberally throughout the catalog are helpful "MaxFacts"—explanations of the products, tips on finding the best product for your needs, and pithy business advice. For example, "D-ring binders hold up to 50 percent more paper than round-ring binders." The worst thing about the OfficeMax catalog is the prices are not listed for many of the products. Instead, it says "CheckMax," which means you are required to call or go to the store to obtain the price because it "frequently fluctuates," and then they can supposedly "give you the best value." This is annoying and defeats the purpose of mail-order convenience.

Penny Wise Office Products
6911 Laurel Bowie Road, Suite 209 • Bowie, MD 20715
phone: (800) 942-3311 • fax: (800) 622-4411
web site: none listed. Have your modem dial (800) 752-3012.

Products: A large selection of office products.

Shipping & Handling: Free delivery within the continental US on orders over $25—a significantly lower minimum than most mail-order companies—except on furniture, computer software, and custom imprinted merchandise.

Guarantee: The company has a low-price guarantee: If you find the same item for less, Penny Wise will match the price. Return shipping is free.

Hours: Monday–Friday 8 A.M.–8 P.M., Eastern time. Saturday 9 A.M.–3 P.M., Eastern time.

Comments: With the sales flyer, we received a coupon for $5 off our first order of $25 or more. If you order via computer, you can take an additional 3 percent off of the price. Penny Wise sends a small promotional catalog containing the 1,000 most commonly ordered items, and then sends a larger 20,000-item catalog after your first $25 order. The color promotional catalog has a clear index, but no table of contents. The pricing charts can be confusing, because the company shows the "List Price" alongside their price. There is a $25 minimum order. One advantage of Penny Wise is that you do not need to buy in as large quantities as you do with most mail-order office-supply companies. For instance, you can buy one ream of paper or one box of paper clips, if you wish, instead of being forced to buy ten. Many home-based business and industry associations offer discounts to Penny Wise as a benefit of membership (see Appendix A).

Quill Corporation
PO Box 94080 • Palatine, IL 60094-4080
phone: (800) 789-1331 • fax: (800) 789-8955
web site: http://www.quillcorp.com

Products: A comprehensive office products catalog, and several specialty catalogs, including one solely for desktop publishing supplies. You can also receive Quill's catalog on CD-ROM free.

Shipping & Handling: Free on most orders over $45 in the contiguous forty-eight states. You have to pay shipping charges if you order equipment, such as a computer, or if you want rush next-day service. Quill charges a $2.50 small-order processing charge for orders under $20.

Guarantee: Money back. Accepts returns for ninety days (thirty days for computers, software, and peripherals). Kathryn ordered a recycled printer cartridge from Quill online and the cartridge turned out to be incompatible with her printer (hers was an HP LaserJet 4ML, the cartridge was for HP LaserJet 4M). When she called to return it,

41

the operator was exceptionally friendly. The operator said her account would be credited for the full amount, and to simply donate the cartridge to a nonprofit organization. The whole transaction took less than five minutes.

Hours: Monday–Friday 8 A.M.–9 P.M., Eastern time. Saturday 9 A.M.–3 P.M., Eastern time.

Comments: We received a coupon for 20 percent off our first order. And Quill advertises several special sales. For instance, if you buy twelve rolls of Scotch tape for $16.68, you get a five-pack of colored Post-it Notes free. (The Penny Wise catalog lists those two items at a total of $19.13—a savings of $2.45.) Quill has its own line of office supplies that are guaranteed and cheaper than name brand. With our first order, we received several samples of Quill brand supplies, and we were pleased with them. Though the printed catalog is in color and has easy-to-understand pricing, it is very poorly organized. For instance, copier paper is featured in the catalog in three separate places, which makes it difficult to compare. The table of contents is equally perplexing. For example, it lists these color-coded divisions: Recycled Products, Desktop Publishing Supplies, Custom-Printed Supplies, and Shipping Supplies Plus Mailroom, Breakroom & Janitorial. Where would you look for envelopes? We did not know either. As it turns out, the answer is all of the above.

RapidForms

301 Grove Road • Thorofare, NJ 08086-9499
phone: (800) 257-8354 • fax: (800) 451-8113
web site: http://www.rapidforms.com

Products: Stationery, labels, printed postcards, desktop publishing supplies, imprinted promotional items (i.e., mugs and sweatshirts), and a limited amount of office supplies. The company has a good selection of stock logos from which to choose.

Shipping & Handling: Free if you prepay by check or money order (this discount does not apply to orders paid by credit cards).

Guarantee: Unconditional money back.

Hours: Monday–Friday 8 A.M.–8 P.M., Eastern time. Saturday 8 A.M.–12 noon, Eastern time.

Comments: A color catalog with a mixture of photographs and drawings. Pricing charts are complex. Many of the charts contain the prices for several different items, such as ink-jet labels, laser labels, designer laser labels, and removable adhesive laser labels, as well as the quantities and prices of each. There is an alphabetical index, but no table of contents.

Staples, Inc.
8 Technology Drive • PO Box 5173 • Westborough, MA 01581
phone: (800) 333-3330 • fax: (800) 333-3199
web site: http://www.staples.com

Products: A wide assortment of office supplies, equipment, and furniture.

Shipping & Handling: Free next-day delivery on orders over $50 within local delivery area (if under $50, delivery costs $10). Delivery areas are determined by the store nearest you. Call for store locations.

Guarantee: Money back within ninety days of purchase (fourteen days for computers, thirty days for software). They will pick up the returned items.

Hours: Monday–Friday 8 A.M.–midnight, Eastern time. Saturday 9 A.M.–9 P.M., Eastern time. Sunday 11 A.M.–8 P.M., Eastern time.

Comments: The catalog is in color with photographs of every product and easy-to-understand pricing. The index is alphabetical and easy to use. There is a table of contents that is color-coded and clear. This is one of the most well-designed catalogs we have seen. The only drawback is, for some items, such as the copier paper, no prices are listed. Instead, it states, "Call for low delivery price," which is inconvenient.

Viking Office Products
13809 South Figueroa Street • PO Box 61144 • Los Angeles, CA 90061-0144
phone: (800) 421-1222 • fax: (800) 762-7329
web site: http://www.vikingop.com

Products: Over 10,000 office products.

Shipping & Handling: Free on orders of $25 or more ($2.83 on orders less than $25).

Guarantee: Credit or refund on any item within thirty days.

Hours: Twenty-four hours a day, seven days a week.

Comments: Viking sends a promotional catalog, and will send a larger one containing 8,000 office products if you ask. The promotional catalog is in color, but does not have an index or a table of contents. Moreover, the prices in the catalog are deceiving. For example, the large print advertises copier paper at $1.99 per ream, but the small print states that you are required to buy ten reams (one carton), so the actual price is $19.90, and there is a limit of five cartons per customer.

Wholesale Supply Company
PO Box 23437 • Nashville, TN 37202
phone: (800) 962-9162 • fax: (800) 962-4FAX
web site: http://www.wholesalesupply.com

Products: A moderate selection of the most commonly used office supplies and some low-tech equipment, such as calculators and adding machines.

Shipping & Handling: You pay. There is a minimum $25 order.

Guarantee: No questions asked if the product is unused and it is returned within thirty days of purchase. If the error is the company's fault, it will reimburse you for shipping.

Hours: Monday–Friday 8 A.M.–8 P.M., Eastern time.

Comments: The catalog is completely in black-and-white drawings, so you have to look closely at the products to ensure you are ordering the right color and size. The prices, though, are clearly displayed. Some of the products are listed as "Name Brand," but the brand will vary based on the market price at the time of your order. There is no index or table of contents.

Chart 2-2 is a cost comparison of ten of the most commonly purchased office products from the mail-order companies that carried all of those items. Chiswick Trading, Fidelity Products, Grayarc, and RapidForms do not carry all of the ten items we selected, so they are not listed. And, unlike Staples and OfficeMax, Office Depot does not have a catalog, so it too, has been omitted.

It was difficult to compare apples to apples, even though we selected common brand names because all of the catalogs do not carry the same brands. In such cases, we tried to choose items of comparable quality. A guerrilla, of course, would not buy the name brand if the generic brand were cheaper and of similar quality.

CHART 2-2 Mail-Order Office-Supply Comparison

ITEM	OFFICEMAX	PENNY WISE	QUILL	STAPLES	VIKING	WHOLESALE
Plain 20-pound 8½" × 11" copier paper (5,000 sheets)	$19.99	$29.90	$37.90	$22.99	**$19.90**	$23.99
3M Post-it Notes (12)	**$3.99**	$5.88	$7.19	$7.25	$5.99	$8.64
3M 3.5" DS/HD diskettes (10)	$6.99	$6.95	$6.10	$6.99	**$4.90**	$4.99
#10 envelopes (500)	**$4.29**	$6.49	$5.49	$10.99	$4.59	$5.99
Brown kraft 28-pound 9" × 12" clasp envelopes (100)	**$4.19**	$5.99	$8.99	$4.99	$4.99	$4.99
Paper clips (1,000)	$2.90	$1.14	$1.49	$1.39	**$0.89**	$0.92
Papermate pens (12)	$1.09	$0.95	$1.09	$1.09	**$0.79**	$0.96
Highlighters (12)	$5.99	$5.06	$5.79	$5.69	$5.88	**$3.99**
Avery labels (3,000)	$22.99	$21.39	$26.96	$21.55	$29.69	**$18.87**
Manila file folders letter-size (100)	$3.59	$4.69	$4.99	$6.88	**$2.99**	$3.99
Subtotal	**$76.01**	$88.44	$105.99	$89.81	$80.61	$77.33
Shipping	**Free**	**Free**	**Free**	**Free**	**Free**	$5.99*
Total	**$76.01**	$88.44	$105.99	$89.81	$80.61	$83.32

*Approximate shipping costs for UPS ground service from Nashville to Detroit. The lowest price is in **bold**.

Another difficulty is that the catalogs often sell items in vastly different quantities, which can greatly affect price. For example, it may take you years to use 10,000 paper clips, but that is the minimum purchase for some companies. We suggest you use the chart as a rough guide. Guerrillas will want to create their own charts of the items they purchase most often.

TIP!

Regular visits to garage sales and flea markets can yield amazing bargains. Coleen Sykora, home-based editor of **Workers on Wheels** *newsletter, says she has found good deals on general office merchandise at auctions. For instance, she bought three boxes of 500 envelopes, a total of 1,500 envelopes, for $1. She notes, "You can't rely on those kinds of deals, but they sure are nice when you find them."*

DISCOUNT OFFICE-SUPPLY SUPERSTORES AND WAREHOUSE CLUBS

Stationery stores are becoming a thing of the past. Discount office-supply superstores, such as Staples, OfficeMax, and Office Depot, offer larger selections and lower prices. Look for store brands, and be sure to apply for business discounts.

Warehouse clubs, such as Sam's Club and Costco, also sell small amounts of office supplies in bulk at a discount. Though they require an annual membership fee (about $35), the cost may be worthwhile for guerrillas who buy a lot of supplies or use the membership to purchase other household items (i.e., toilet paper). To determine if you would benefit from a membership, ask for a free day pass. This will allow you to compare prices. Estimate your approximate savings on office supplies and anything else you would buy, then deduct the membership fee. If you still save, consider joining.

One way to compare prices is to use what author Amy Dacyczyn calls a "price book." In her book, *The Complete Tightwad Gazette*, Dacyczyn uses a three-ring binder to keep track of the food prices at different grocery stores. She writes the store, brand, size, and unit price for an item on a sheet of notebook paper and alphabetizes them. We adapted her idea to track prices on labels, envelopes, paper clips, and so on at different office-supply sources. By maintaining a log, we recognize bargains, like the day Kathryn found watermarked, 25 percent cotton-bond envelopes on sale for $2.00 per box instead of $5.99. She bought the whole shelf. Chart 2-3 illustrates a sample page of our price book.

Gary Foreman, home-based editor of *The Dollar Stretcher* newsletter, uses a similar system that he learned when he was a purchasing department manager. He keeps a "buy card," which lists what he bought, when he last bought, whom he bought it from, what he paid, and other quotes he got. This system has added advantages because, at a glance, he can see the quantities he buys and how long they last. These can be important factors in determining how much to buy in the future, if, for instance, the price of paper drops dramatically. (Paper prices can fluctuate by as much as a dollar or two within weeks because of the current supply of postconsumer waste paper.)

To make comparison shopping easier, Michele Foy, home-based owner of Dynamic Alternatives, a computer and general-management consulting firm in Highland Park, Illinois, keeps a catalog library. When a new catalog comes in, she adds it to her file, and tosses the old one.

CHART 2.3 Price Book Paper Comparison

20-POUND, 8½" x 11" WHITE COPIER PAPER				
STORE	BRAND	SIZE	PRICE	PRICE/UNIT
Staples	Staples Brand	case	$22.99	$2.30/ream
	Staples Brand	ream	$2.89	$2.89/ream
	Hammermill Unity	case	$25.99	$3.49/ream
OfficeMax	generic	case	$21.79	$2.18/ream
	Georgia Pacific	ream	$4.99	$4.99/ream
Office Depot	generic	case	$19.99	$2.00/ream
Sam's Club	generic	case	$19.99	$2.00/ream

BULK BUYING

Stocking up once a month saves gas and time, and you will not run out of paper the night before a deadline. Also, when you buy in bulk, the per-unit cost drops. For example, one dozen ball-point pens cost $1.09, but six dozen cost $5.94 (99¢ a dozen). The best time to buy office supplies is in August, September, and October during the back-to-school sales. Buy enough to last you until the next sale. Diane Rosener, home-based editor of *A Penny Saved* newsletter, in Omaha, Nebraska, also recommends scouring the clearance bins after the back-to-school rush is over. According to Rosener, other times office supplies go on sale are the beginning of the year and around April 15th.

One caveat: Some items lose their usefulness if stored improperly or for too long. For instance, envelopes—if they are stored in a humid climate or on a damp floor—can stick closed, rendering them useless. Kathryn had to toss out a whole box of manila envelopes because she stored them underneath her desk, where water had leaked in from outside.

Judy Lawrence, author of **The Budget Kit** *and a financial counselor, from Albuquerque, New Mexico, recommends bulk buying with another home-based guerrilla. That way, both of you can get the lowest unit price without having to use 100,000 staples by yourself.*

3 FRUGAL PHOTOCOPYING, PHOTOGRAPHY, AND PRINTING

Home-based guerrillas do not have traditional stores in which to showcase their wares. Thus, they often rely on printed materials—stationery, catalogs, newsletters, and the like—to sell their products and services. Many times, these printed materials are the foundation upon which customers form their first impressions. So, professional-looking documents are important. However, custom-printed materials can be outrageously expensive. The keys to saving money are: Keep documents simple, shop around, and do not buy more than you need.

PHOTOCOPYING

COPY SHOPS VERSUS COIN-OPERATED MACHINES

Generally, the cheapest places for photocopying are the copy shops such as Kinko's; Mail Boxes, Etc.; Staples; and OfficeMax (about 5¢ a page, though you can find them for as little as 1¢ each). However, even among these sources, you may find discrepancies. Scout out the cheapest. Also, be aware that some stores charge more when the staff makes the copies than when you serve yourself.

When possible, avoid making copies on coin-operated machines that you find at the library, post office, and grocery stores. At these locations, copies can cost as much as 25¢ each! Once, Kathryn realized she was spending 10¢ a copy at the library to reproduce a few pages out of a book. She checked out the book and walked around the corner to the copy store where she paid 6¢ a copy—an instant savings!

> *If you are in a hurry and need to make copies on a coin-operated machine, set the parameters to "legal size." This gives you more space on the copier and, oftentimes, you can get two pages of a book on one sheet. Thus, you get two copies for the price of one!*

COPY SALES, COUPONS, AND FREQUENT-BUYER CARDS

Keep an eye out for copy sales and coupons. Sales on photocopying are common in areas where there is a lot of competition. For instance, a Mail Boxes, Etc. store near Kathryn has a Customer Appreciation Month. During the month of October, all white paper copies cost only 2¢ each. When possible, Kathryn saves her copying for this time.

Laurie Dry, a home-based consultant who sells photographic supplies, says that a local copy store has a standing discount every Thursday and Friday night of 4¢ a copy. Dry copies her newsletter on one of those nights. If you do a lot of regular copying, Dry also recommends talking to the owner to negotiate a deal that guarantees a certain amount of copying volume per month in exchange for a reduced rate. If you do a high volume of copying, look into discounts. Many shops offer discounts for copies made in batches of 100 or more.

In addition, ask about frequent-buyer cards. Some stores sell a card good for a specific number of copies, usually 100 or 1,000, in exchange for a lower rate per copy. This is a good deal if you are 100 percent certain you will use the card. If you do not use it, it is as if you gave the store your money for nothing. For instance, Kathryn bought a similar card for faxes and, before she used up the punches, she bought a fax machine. The store refused to give her a refund on the remaining faxes. If there is any doubt about whether you will use the card, do not risk losing several dollars to save a few pennies.

Finally, look for copy coupons. A while ago, Raisin Bran cereal boxes had a coupon for two-for-one copies at Mail Boxes, Etc. When Raisin Bran went on sale, Kathryn bought a bunch (using cereal coupons). The copy coupons did not expire for one year and she collected quite a few, so Kathryn saved 50 percent on all of her copying for the whole year!

Other places to look for coupons include: mailbox circulars, local newspapers, and in-store flyers. Edith Flowers Kilgo, editor of Creative Downscaling, says in areas where OfficeMax and Office Depot compete, you can find 1¢ to 2¢ copy coupons in the Sunday supplement.

You can get free photocopying at many libraries if you are copying reference materials. Because reference materials are not available for check out, many libraries offer this service. Ask the reference librarian.

PHOTOGRAPHY

Home-based guerrillas occasionally need pictures taken, either of their products or themselves, for marketing purposes. However, a professional photographer can charge hundreds of dollars for the photo shoot, then more money for each print.

SAY CHEESE!

If you are lucky enough to have a photographer in the family, ask him or her to shoot pictures for you. If you do not know any professionals, ask around for amateur volunteers. Most people can capture one good-looking shot if they have a decent camera and take enough rolls of film. If you need a portrait, instruct your photographer to take the picture vertically and focus on your chin. The most important thing is to take a lot of pictures—several rolls, if you can.

If you need to buy a new camera, consider mail-order sources, which can be found in photography magazines. If you know what you want, mail-order companies are much cheaper than local stores. For example, a local store sells a Canon Rebel G equipped with lens, neck strap, and flash for $370, whereas mail-order sources sell the same thing (including shipping) for $320. However, Peter Rogers, a home-based professional location photographer from Chino Hills, California, warns that some mail-order camera equipment companies do a bait and switch. They advertise one price then, when you call to order, they ask if you want a "USA warranty," which costs $30 or so extra. However, Rogers says that he has been using mail order to purchase equipment and film for years and that, in the past few years, such mail-order tricks seem to be on the decline. For mail-order camera equipment, Rogers recommends:

Camera World of Oregon
700 NE 55th Avenue • Portland, OR 97213-3150
phone: (800) 695-8451 • fax: (503) 205-5901
web site: http://www.cameraworld.com

Jeff Berner, home-based author of The Joy of Working from Home: Making a Life While Making a Living *and a professional photographer, says film at camera stores is much cheaper than at drugstores: "Buy it by the dozen, and put the unused rolls in your refrigerator," for optimum storage.*

PROFESSIONAL PHOTOGRAPHERS

If you prefer to leave it to a professional, photographer Peter Rogers recommends finding a photographer through referrals. "Professional photography can be a big investment, so don't leave it to chance," says

Rogers. "Your best option is to ask colleagues if they have had any experience with photographers. This might save you research time and make you more comfortable with your selection."

If you do not know anyone who has used a professional photographer, Rogers suggests looking at catalogs or brochures with photographs that appeal to you, then contacting the company to ask who took the pictures. Another option: Ask at a photo lab. "They deal with photographers on a daily basis and can be a great source for recommendations," says Rogers. "But it must be a true full-service custom lab, not Bob's one-hour photo lab and gas station."

Once you find a couple of professionals, how do you evaluate them? Rogers recommends asking these questions:

➤ Have you photographed this type of product before?

➤ How much would you charge for this job? Does that include the cost of materials (film and processing)? If not, how much are materials?

➤ Do I get to keep the negatives or transparencies (most printers prefer photographs on transparency film for better reproduction quality)? If not, how do I go about securing ownership of these pictures for future projects?

➤ Do you have a portfolio of images I can review?

One money-saving tip Rogers recommends is to find an experienced photographer who does not have his own studio. A home-based professional photographer may charge less than a photographer with the same amount of experience who owns a studio, because the studio photographer has to charge enough to cover his overhead.

How much do professional photographers charge? It depends on the photographer's experience and where you live, but most charge an average of $500 to $2,000 per day, plus materials. Rogers says another trick for saving money is to use a professional from outside a metropolitan area. For example, a professional photographer with twenty years of experience in Chicago will most likely charge more than a professional with the same experience in Moline, Illinois. If you live in a big city and need to do a large photo shoot, it may be worthwhile to find a professional photographer based outside of the city.

If all you need is a head shot for a promotional piece, such as a press release, you may pay upwards of $300 with a studio photographer. A less expensive alternative is to have your picture taken at a photo-processing lab. We are not talking about a passport photo machine. Some full-service custom photo labs have photographers that can shoot a roll or two of film for you on site. Home-based Gerri Detweiler, lecturer and author of *The Ultimate Credit Handbook,* got publicity photos taken at a local photo shop for $25 and was very pleased with the results.

MODELS

A few home-based guerrillas, such as clothing designers, need models to display their products for photographs. Though using friends and family members is an inexpensive option, it is likely that their inexperience will show, says home-based professional location photographer Peter Rogers. "Amateur models usually appear stiff and awkward in front of a camera," says Rogers. "This can be distracting to consumers looking at your catalog." Professional models know how to display the product in the most flattering way. For instance, professionals know how to pose so that the fabric on a garment hangs correctly. A professional model in conjunction with a photographer will choose the correct angles and poses to highlight the clothing. "Experience in front of a camera will always show," says Rogers. Thus, he recommends using professional models whenever possible.

Some professional photographers have access to models, so when you contract with a photographer, ask to see modeling cards of his favorite models. If the photographer does not have model recommendations, you will need to contact a modeling agency. Models often charge as much or more than the photographer. How much should you expect to pay? Most agencies charge from $125 to $500 an hour for a model. One way you may be able to save money on a model is to contact local modeling schools. "Although a student's experience level is minimal, the models in training will give a good effort for a very reasonable price," says Rogers.

DEVELOPING

Most professional photographers arrange for developing and deliver the prints or transparencies to you. If you take the photographs yourself, however, you will need to have them developed. If the highest print quality is crucial, such as in a catalog, we recommend finding a full-service custom photo lab like the professionals use.

In some cases, you may want to check out mail-order film processing companies. Coleen Sykora, home-based editor of *Workers on Wheels,* a newsletter for RVers, uses York Photo Labs for the pictures in her publication. The company charges $3 plus $1 shipping and handling to process a roll of twenty-four-exposure 35 mm film into single $3\frac{1}{2}'' \times 5''$ prints. A computer disk costs $5.95 per roll, plus the cost of film developing.

York Photo Labs
PO Box 500000 • Parkersburg, West Virginia 26102-9499
phone: (304) 424-YORK • fax: (304) 420-5600
web site: http://www.yorkphoto.com

> *If you regularly need photography for your web site, you may want to consider investing in a digital camera. Though they are expensive (about $700), you can see the picture instantly and delete it if you are unhappy with it. This saves time and eliminates a lot of wasted film and developing costs. Digital cameras are best for Internet use, because the quality is not as good as film.*

REPRINTS AND COPYRIGHTS

Reprints from a professional photography studio can be extortionate. Because the studio usually holds your negatives hostage, it can charge an outrageous amount for reprints—$20 each or more for an $8'' \times 10''$! Look for a professional photographer who will allow you to keep the film, so you can take it to the photo lab whenever you need prints made. John Kremer, author of *1001 Ways to Market Your Books,* recommends asking the photographer upfront to sign an agreement that states you own the copyright.

Professional location photographer Peter Rogers says that whether he gives the film to the client or not depends on "the nature of the assignment and its ultimate usage. But customer possession of the film is always negotiable. You can ask the photographer to build unlimited/ exclusive usage of the photos into the overall day rate he will charge to complete the assignment." Therefore, ask your photographer what his policy is, and negotiate an agreement before the flash goes off.

Once you have your film, get a commercial photo lab to make reprints. Do not overlook out-of-town labs. Though you may have a slight delay due to shipping, if you can wait, you can often garner a better deal than you can obtain locally. For instance, Ornaal Image Works in New York charges $18.75 plus shipping for twenty-five black-and-white 5" × 7" glossies.

Ornaal Image Works
24 West 25 Street • New York, NY 10010
phone: (800) 826-6312 • fax: (212) 463-8466
web site: http://www.ornaal.com

ABC Pictures
1867 E. Florida Street • Springfield, MO 65803-4583
phone: (417) 869-3456 • fax: (417) 869-9185
web site: http://www.abcpictures.com

STOCK PHOTOGRAPHY, PHOTO CD-ROMS, AND FREE PHOTOS

Another alternative to using a professional photographer on assignment is to use stock photography, photo CD-ROMs, or free photos downloaded from the Internet. *Stock photographs* are generic photographs to which companies sell one-time or all rights. The cost of a stock photograph depends on its subject matter, intended distribution, size needed, and rights purchased, but average about $150 for one-time rights. Photo CD-ROMs are collections of thousands of images sold for a flat fee of about $200.

Kristin Gibson of Gibson Associates, a home-based marketing communications firm in Weston, Connecticut, regularly uses both stock photography and photo CD-ROMs in creating marketing materials for her clients. She explains the advantages and disadvantages: "If you purchase a stock photo, you have to contract for the usage. If you purchase a photo CD, you have unlimited usage. One problem with photo CDs is you don't have exclusive usage so, six months down the road, you could see the image everywhere." She recommends using photo CDs in documents that have a limited life, such as in an event brochure or a direct-mail piece. She also suggests buying the newest CDs, so that you are among the first to use an image. You can find photo CD-ROMs in any computer software store. For information on stock photographs, contact professional photographers (many sell stock images in addition to working on assignment). Stockphoto at http://www.stockphoto.net serves as a clearinghouse for professional photographers selling stock photographs in their inventories. Or, look for stock photography companies, such as:

The Stock Market Photo Agency
360 Park Avenue South, 16th floor • New York, NY 10010
phone: (800) 999-0800 • fax: (212) 532-6750
web site: http://www.stockmarketphoto.com

You can also find free photographs on the Internet, but most sites prohibit commercial use. However, one site we found that allows you to use its free photographs for commercial use (with limited exceptions) is http://www.zettweb.com/grab-a-picture/index.html.

PRINTING

Depending on your business, printed materials can be vital or just superficial. However, every home-based guerrilla needs printed materials, even if only letterhead and business cards. And, since you work at home and are less likely to host clients in your office, your printed materials carry a stronger impression. You want to present a professional image without spending a fortune.

Home-based publishers Scott and Shirley Gregory of Bookhome Publishing in Navarre, Florida, strongly recommend getting several bids on every print job. Scott warns, however, "Don't necessarily always take the cheapest bid. Quality is important. We recently got quotes from about fifteen printers and took the third-lowest bid. It wasn't the lowest bid, but the quality and customer service were good and they responded quickly to the bid request." Of course, most home-based businesses are not printing as large of a quantity of material as the Gregorys, but the advice is sound. And the more you spend, the more important it is to comparison shop.

In order to compare apples to apples, you will need to send the same information about your project to every printer. To do that, Scott Gregory recommends sending a form called a request for quotation (RFQ). He recommends that your RFQ include the following:

➤ the title of your project

➤ author

➤ number of pages

➤ the dimensions of the project, also known as the trim size

➤ how you will be providing the information (i.e., on a disk in Quark 3.0)

➤ whether or not there are pictures and, if so, how many

➤ ink color

➤ the type of paper your want

➤ the type of binding you want (i.e., softcover)

➤ how the cover is provided (i.e., Photoshop 5.0)

➤ the number of colors on the cover

➤ whether or not to print the inside covers

➤ the type of paper you want for the cover

➤ what type of finish you want on the cover (i.e., film lamination)

➤ how the project should be packaged (i.e., shrink wrapped in cartons weighing less than fifty pounds each)

➤ where it needs to be shipped

➤ the terms of your agreement (i.e., half at the beginning and half upon delivery)

➤ how many copies you want

The Gregorys also ask about the cost of overruns, the cost of reprints, discounts, delivery charges, delivery time, and other miscellaneous charges. At the end of their RFQ, the Gregorys ask the printer to explain if there are any minor specification changes that will result in a lower price.

In looking for a printer, the Gregorys and other home-based book publishers we interviewed stressed that guerrillas should not be afraid to use out-of-town printers. If you are printing a pamphlet or book, get bids from national printers, not just local ones. Edith Flowers Kilgo, editor of *Creative Downscaling*, says that some people are reluctant to use out-of-state printers because they are afraid a shipment will be lost in transit. However, she says that in five years of business she has only had one lost shipment and, because it was shipped UPS, the printer was reimbursed by UPS and simply reprinted the order for her without charge. She adds that she builds in a two-week cushion on all of her deadlines to allow for shipping.

Publisher Coleen Sykora highly recommends joining the Small Publishers Co-Op, a paid membership service for small publishers of short print runs of 500 to 10,000 units that pools members' print jobs to lower costs. It costs $19 for a three-year membership, and you must sign an agreement to try to publish a minimum of 2,000 copies over the next year. The Co-Op prints on thirty-pound newsprint or white forty-five-pound bond paper only, glossy covers are optional. For more information, contact:

Small Publishers Co-Op
2579 Clematis Street • Sarasota, FL 34239
phone: (941) 922-0844 • fax: (941) 378-1583
web site: http://www.spco-op.com

For a list of national book printers and other helpful publishing information, read *Directory of Printers* by Marie Kiefer, *The Self-Publishing Manual*
by Dan Poynter, and *The Complete Guide to Self-Publishing* by Tom and
Marilyn Ross. You may also want to visit www.bookidea.com, an internet magazine site that has a full list of printers and articles on printing.

> *Barbara Brabec, a lecturer on self-employment and best-selling*
> *author of* **Homemade Money,** *from Naperville, Illinois, says,*
> *"One secret I learned: Printers always have lower prices when*
> *they are closer to the source of wood and paper. A printer in*
> *Chicago will cost you twice as much as one located closer to*
> *the printing supply."*

THE BASICS—PAPER, INK, AND DESIGN

First, determine what you need and will use before printing an assortment of materials. Start small, with just business cards, stationery, and
envelopes, perhaps. Or, just business cards. Ignore the temptation to
order personalized, matching postcards, memo pads, fax cover sheets,
and so on, unless you find a real need for them.

When you order printed materials, you will be faced with a myriad of
choices: Flat lettering? Blind embossed? Foil embossed? Embossed
means that the design is raised in a relief above the surface of the paper.
If the design is raised through the paper, but does not have any color or
foil on it, it is blind embossed. If the design is in gold or silver, it is foil
embossed.

Your best bet is to buy standard, white, twenty-pound watermarked
paper for stationery and eighty-pound paper for business cards. Avoid
raised lettering on stationery and envelopes because it usually costs more

and can jam laser and ink-jet printers. Black ink is professional-looking and costs about $10 less than colored ink. Black is also easier to read.

However, the cheapest and easiest way to add impact is with color so, if you want your materials to stand out more, you might want to consider one, two, or three ink colors. You can get various shades of a color by using screens. For instance, you can use a screen to get red and different shades of pink. This allows you to have more than one shade, while keeping it a one-color job. More than three colors or the use of color photographs requires a four-color process, which is much more expensive.

Another way to add color is to print your documents on colored paper. Editor Edith Flowers Kilgo says that orders for back issues increased dramatically when she began printing the offer on goldenrod paper. She says, "For all our forms, we experiment with different colors until we find the one that is best received. Color does matter." Lastly, Kilgo recommends going with standard sizes on all items printed. "Odd-sized business cards and envelopes cost more because of the waste."

If you don't take yourself and what you do seriously, nobody else will.

—Jaclyn Jeffrey, Allegiant Partners

ASK FOR ADVICE FROM YOUR PRINTER

If you find a need for more than just stationery, envelopes, and business cards, consider your needs and then ask your printer (or several) for advice on how to cut costs. For example, when Gary Dunn, publisher of *The Caretaker Gazette,* from Carefree, Arizona, started printing his newsletter, he printed it on the best paper available. It looked great. However, as the newsletter's popularity grew, he found it harder to afford the expensive paper. When Dunn met with the printer, he suggested Dunn use newsprint, the cheapest paper available. Dunn took a gamble and was surprised when, "nobody said anything! I realized my subscribers are after the content, and as long as it's readable, the paper doesn't matter. I didn't get one complaint and I saved at least 50 percent of my printing costs!" Cheaper paper is not always better but, in this case, it saved Dunn a lot of money. Ask your printer for advice and consider your customers' needs. You may even want to do tests with different paper stock and ask for feedback from your customers.

Marilyn Ross, co-author of *The Complete Guide to Self-Publishing* and home-based co-owner of About Books, Inc., a writing, publishing, and marketing consulting service in Buena Vista, Colorado, recommends timing your project to coincide with a printer's slow time to obtain the best price. For example, December is often a slow month for printers.

Neal Lubow, home-based owner of Ideas By-The-Hour, a marketing communications company in Portland, Oregon, says one way he keeps the cost of printing down is by buying high-quality, discounted paper at a paper distributor (look in the Yellow Pages) and taking it to the printer. "When you go into a copy shop or a quick print shop, one of their high markup items is paper," he says. "If you bring your own paper, you are only paying for the printing."

GANG RUNS

If you are not in a hurry for the material, Shel Horowitz, author of *Marketing Without Megabucks*, suggests asking the printer about taking advantage of gang runs, or piggybacking. According to *The Self-Publishing Manual* by Dan Poynter, *gang runs* are "putting numerous unrelated jobs together for printing by assembling them on a single print plate" in order to economize on setup charges.

For instance, if the printer already has another job that is using green ink, perhaps you can use green ink as well. Or, if the presses are already set for 5½" × 8½" for another job, and you originally wanted your document printed at 6" × 8½", you may be able to get a discount if you adjust the trim size by a half-inch.

Terry Morin, a home-based cartoonist at Terrapin Illustrations in Portland, Oregon, suggests asking your printer what size paper is being used on the run and if there will be any "wasted" space left on the paper after printing your document. If there is, you may be able to print postcards, bookmarks, thank-you cards, packing slips, or business cards for little or no additional cost. When Morin prints his four-color greeting cards, he also prints business cards for Ron Miller, home-based owner of Advantage Northwest. In exchange, Miller builds trade-show props for Morin.

The only drawback of using gang runs is that it may mean a delay in getting the job done, points out editor Edith Flowers Kilgo. For instance, if you have an order for blue ink, the printer might have to wait until he has sufficient additional orders to make a print run worthwhile. Kilgo says one way to get around this problem is to keep your printing simple: black ink on white paper.

John Kremer, author of 1001 Ways to Market Your Books, suggests being clear on everything you want the printer to do when you are gathering quotes. "If you aren't, you'll be surprised by the penny ante," he says. "If you forgot that you wanted it stapled or that there was a photo in it," you will end up paying a lot more later.

PROOFREAD

It is best to have at least three good spellers proofread your copy carefully before approving it. Why? If you find errors or omissions after a job has already gone to press, it is going to cost you dearly. The printer is not responsible if your address has a zero missing after you approve it.

Editor Edith Flowers Kilgo proofreads every piece of crucial information at least five times. She also recommends including an expiration date on all offers, and to say "Prices good to U.S. addresses only." She says, "I get tons of newsletters. I am shocked to see how many of them make it diffi-cult to discover who the editor is and what the annual cost is. Always put the price and address prominently on all items. People can't buy your goods if they can't figure out what they cost and where to get them!"

Also, be cautious when you examine the proof sheet at the printers. The last time Kathryn ordered business cards, the proof was printed on a half sheet with the ordering information beneath it. She was reprinting the same cards she always orders (i.e., the same font, size, and style) at the same store, so she assumed this was a miniaturized version of her card, and she was just supposed to use it to check the content. Wrong. A week later, the cards came back in eight-point type, barely readable. She finally got the manager to reprint them, but it could have saved a lot of grief if she had not assumed anything. When in doubt, ask. It is difficult to get a printer to redo a job under such circumstances because the printer has custom-made the item for you and cannot sell it to anyone else.

If you only need a few copies of a document, Jean MacDonald, home-based web designer at Well-Tempered Web Design in Portland, Oregon, recommends using photo paper in your color printer, instead of having it custom printed. "Anything looks better on good paper," she says, "and photo paper is the best because you can do a higher resolution, 1440 dpi. It's not cheap—it comes in a pack of twenty sheets for $15—but it's cheaper than having them printed at a printer" and they look fantastic.

MAIL-ORDER STATIONERY

The advantages of local stationers are that you can touch what you are ordering, and that there is a clerk to help you sort through the available choices. However, most local stationers ship your job out to be printed, which adds additional costs. Mail-order sources can be cheaper, but you need to be very careful in deciding what you are ordering. Take your time and read the fine print. If you do not know the difference between twenty-pound paper and twenty-four-pound paper, go to a local office supply store and compare, or ask the printer to send you samples. You do not want to discover that the paper you ordered feels like onionskin after you have custom-printed 1,000 sheets of letterhead.

Here are some mail-order stationery companies:

Quill Corporation
PO Box 94080 • Palatine, IL 60094-4080
phone: (800) 789-1331 • fax: (800) 789-8955
web site: http://www.quillcorp.com

Products: A comprehensive office products catalog, and several specialty catalogs, including one solely for desktop publishing supplies. You can also receive Quill's catalog on CD-ROM for free.

Shipping & Handling: Free on most orders over $45 in the contiguous forty-eight states. You have to pay shipping charges if you order equipment, such as a computer, or if you want rush next-day service. Quill charges a $2.50 small order processing charge for orders under $20.

Guarantee: Money back. Accepts returns for ninety days.

Hours: Monday–Friday 8 A.M.–9 P.M., Eastern time. Saturday 9 A.M.–3 P.M., Eastern time.

Comments: We received a coupon for 20 percent off our first order. Though the printed catalog is in color and has easy-to-understand pricing, it is very poorly organized. The table of contents is equally perplexing.

RapidForms
301 Grove Road • Thorofare, NJ 08086-9499
phone: (800) 257-8354 • fax: (800) 451-8113
web site: http://www.rapidforms.com

Products: Stationery, labels, printed postcards, desktop publishing supplies, imprinted promotional items (i.e., mugs and sweatshirts), and a limited amount of office supplies. The company has a good selection of stock logos from which to choose.

65

Shipping & Handling: Free if you prepay by check or money order (this discount does not apply to orders paid by credit cards).

Guarantee: Unconditional money back.

Hours: Monday–Friday 8 A.M.–8 P.M., Eastern time. Saturday 8 A.M.–12 P.M., Eastern time.

Comments: A color catalog with a mixture of photographs and drawings. Pricing charts are complex. Many of the charts contain the prices for several different items, such as ink-jet labels, laser labels, designer laser labels, and removable-adhesive laser labels, as well as the quantities and prices of each. There is an alphabetical index, but no table of contents.

The Stationery House
1000 Florida Ave. • Hagerstown, MD 21740
phone: (800) 638-3033 • fax: (800) 554-8779
web page: http://www.stationeryhouse.com

Products: The Stationery House has a wide selection of stationery, envelopes, forms, and business checks. They also carry certificates and custom-printed all-occasion cards.

Shipping & Handling: You pay.

Guarantee: Credit within thirty days of delivery. The company also guarantees to ship your order within five working days of receipt.

Hours: Monday–Friday, 7:30 A.M.–7:30 P.M., Eastern time.

Comments: The catalog is in color and has a table of contents, but no index. The catalog has a wide selection of papers, inks, and styles. The company gives free samples of products upon request and a 3 percent discount on prepaid orders.

In Chart 3-1, we compare three mail-order sources for business cards, letterhead, and envelopes. We wanted to order the simplest available: black ink on 1,000 twenty-pound bond envelopes and sheets of letterhead and 1,000 eighty-pound business cards.

In our research, we discovered dozens of companies that print business cards only, but few that print letterhead, envelopes, and business cards.

CHART 3-1 Mail-Order Stationery Comparison

ITEM	RAPIDFORMS	THE STATIONERY HOUSE	QUILL
Cards	$37.75	$41.50	**$30.96**
Letterhead	$82.75	$108.75	**$71.97**
Envelopes	$99.75	$146.95	**$68.98**
Subtotal	$220.25	$297.20	**$171.91**
Shipping	**Free**	$17.95	$13.61
Total	$220.25	$315.15	**$185.52**

The lowest price is in **bold.**

Most people want to order their whole package from the same company to ensure the font, paper, and ink-color matches. If you only need business cards or if you want an unusual design, such as a photograph on your card, you will have a wider selection of mail-order companies from which to choose.

> *Weigh materials before you have them printed to avoid excessive postage costs. Edith Flowers Kilgo, editor of* **Creative Downscaling** *newsletter, says, "Bear in mind that anything you mail may include other items in the envelope, such as an order blank or a business reply envelope. You don't want to exceed the 2-ounce postage rate. With our newsletter, we know that we can add one extra sheet of paper and not go over 33¢. That's why, when we want to include a business reply envelope, a coupon will be a one-third of a page insert."*

LARGE-QUANTITY PRINT ORDERS

When you order printed envelopes, stationery, mailing labels, business cards, brochures, or any other printed item, think big. Why? Because the costliest part of printing is the initial set-up fee. After the printer has prepared your job, it costs very little to run a few hundred more. Compare the unit price between 500 business cards and 1,000 at one mail-order

67

printer—$26.25 (or 5¢ each) versus $28.50 (or 3¢ each). You get twice as many for only $2.25 more! If the cost difference is minimal, order the maximum you can expect to use in a year.

However, John Kremer, author of *1001 Ways to Market Your Books*, warns against overprinting in the early days of your business, lest you change your focus or pertinent information. Also, you may want to talk to your phone company and post office before you place your order. Why? The post office occasionally changes zip codes and the telephone company changes area codes so rapidly that it is difficult to keep up. One way to avoid this predicament is to get a toll-free 800 or 888 telephone number. These numbers do not change when your area code changes, so you will not have to pay to reprint all of your stationery, brochures, and business cards.

Susan Lannis, a home-based professional organizer and owner of Organization Plus from Clackamas, Oregon, has avoided overprinting in another way. Lannis likes to use postcards for marketing. She prints 1,000 three-color postcards with her logo art on one side. Then, she stores them until she needs them. When she wants to send a mailing, she prints her current message on the blank side in black ink. For instance, if she wants to print fifty postcards to welcome new customers, she extracts fifty color postcards from her stash, takes them to her printer, and asks him to print the new message on the back in one color. Thus, she can get a bulk discount for a three-color postcard, but she pays for only a one-color job on the other side, and the postcards never get outdated.

Finally, regardless of the quantity, you should consider ordering several print jobs at once as some printers offer a discount. For example, when Kathryn ordered her business cards, envelopes, stationery, and mailing labels at the same time, the print shop gave her a multiorder 10 percent discount, which her saved about $20.

DO-IT-YOURSELF PRINTING

Instead of buying letterhead at the print shop, make it on the computer. Most computer word-processing software has a variety of fonts and

> *Edith Flowers Kilgo recommends asking the printer to save
> your plates, because additional orders are less expensive if the
> plates are already made.*

sizes; use one for your name and address and another for the body of
your letter. Barbara Winter, author of *Making a Living Without a Job* and
editor of the newsletter *Winning Ways,* from Minneapolis, Minnesota, has
run her business from her home since 1974. She has not had custom-
printed stationery for many years. When she needs letterhead, she just
makes it on her computer. Like Winter, more than half of the home-based
guerrillas we interviewed said they did not have preprinted stationery.

DESKTOP PUBLISHING SOFTWARE

Desktop publishing (DTP) software, available for $100 to $500, combined
with a computer and laser or ink-jet printer, can create professional-
looking stationery, brochures, business cards, labels, and newsletters
quickly and economically. It also gives you the flexibility to make
changes frequently or at the last minute. Another advantage of DTP over
print shops is that you can print documents as you need them, eliminating wasted paper.

Software programs, such as Adobe PageMaker, Corel Ventura, and
QuarkXPress, are expensive and mainly used by professional designers
and book publishers because they take more than a day's worth of training to use. Microsoft Publisher and Corel PrintOffice cost around $100,
and are geared to novices who occasionally make brochures, fliers, and
other documents. Before you buy a program, however, be sure it is com-
patible with your computer. Be sure to have the recommended amount
of memory, not the minimum, or else your software will run too slowly.

If you want to add graphics or unique fonts, you can buy add-on software for about $50 or download from the Internet, free. A good place to

find free stuff is at http://www.thefreesite.com. Here are a few Internet addresses to get you started:

Fonts:

http://www.microsoft.com/truetype/fontpack/default.htm

http://www.abcgiant.com/fonts/index.html

http://www.fontpool.com

Graphics:

http://www.freegraphics.com

http://www.freeimages.com

http://www.free-graphics.com

PREPRINTED PAPER

If you do not want to create your documents from scratch, you can buy a package of preprinted paper. Preprinted papers contain different border designs of one to four colors, and will work with or without DTP software. For example, an attractive business set of preprinted papers from Quill—fifty sheets of letterhead, fifty sheets of border paper, fifty envelopes, 100 business cards, fifty brochures, sixty postcards, and sixty labels—costs only $24.96.

Michele Foy, home-based owner of Dynamic Alternatives, a computer and general management consulting firm in Highland Park, Illinois, is a strong believer in preprinted papers. She likes the flexibility she has to change her brochures as her business grows. "We can keep current without wasting money."

These preprinted papers are so inexpensive and easy they have become common. Unfortunately, as a result, some people believe they broadcast your small-business status. The most problematic preprinted papers are the business cards, which may have an obvious perforated edge, and may be of light cardstock because they have to be fed through a printer. Despite this, Dave Wampler, home-based owner of The Simple Living Network, an online company in Trout Lake, Washington, that provides products and information on living a more conscious, simple, healthy, and restorative lifestyle, likes the preprinted business cards because of the flexibility he has to print twenty instead of 1,000.

Thus, preprinted materials are a viable alternative for guerrillas who move frequently or serve several different markets, because the information can be customized. A couple of good sources for preprinted papers are:

PaperDirect, Inc.
1025 East Woodmen Road • Colorado Springs, CO 80920
phone: (800) 272-7377 • fax: (800) 443-2973
web site: http://www.paperdirect.com

> *Products:* The catalog has a wide variety of letterhead, notecards, brochures, postcards, labels, business cards, newsletter paper, envelopes, and certificates.

> *Shipping & Handling:* You pay and it increases with the cost of your order.

> *Guarantee:* 100 percent, money back, no questions asked. Try five sheets in a box and if you do not like them, return them using the form included with your order. The company pays for return shipping.

> *Hours:* Monday–Friday, 8 A.M.–9 P.M., Eastern time. Saturday, 10 A.M.– 4 P.M., Eastern time.

> *Comments:* For a $5 shipping and handling charge, the company will send you a sample of any product and a $5 gift certificate toward any product order. The company offers template software for about $50, so you do not have to spend time measuring and laying out your information. The software contains templates for over 1,500 paper formats and designs that PaperDirect sells. The catalog is printed in color and is easy to read. It has a table of contents and a clever design/format index that tells you what formats your favorite design comes in. For instance, the golf design comes in brochures, business cards, paper, and postcards, and it tells on which pages in the catalog you can find them.

Paper Showcase

150 Kingswood Road • Mankato, MN 56001-8465

phone: (800) 287-8163 • fax: (800) 842-3371

web site: http://www.papershowcase.com

> *Products:* The catalog has a nice selection of colored paper, specialty paper, envelopes, formal invitations, announcement cards, postcards, brochures, business cards, newsletters, and certificates.
>
> *Shipping & Handling:* You pay, and it increases with the cost of your order.
>
> *Guarantee:* Money back, credit, or replacement order—your choice.
>
> *Hours:* Monday–Friday, 8 A.M.–11 P.M., Eastern time. Saturday, 9 A.M.– 8 P.M., Eastern time.
>
> *Comments:* The selection at Paper Showcase is not as large as that at PaperDirect, but it has some charming designs that you may not see elsewhere. Though it has a dozen or so business designs, overall, the designs in Paper Showcase appear to be focused on party events. For instance, the catalog includes announcements, wedding programs, formal invitations, and holiday papers. The catalog is clear and in color. It has a table of contents, but no index.

Even if you eventually take your camera-ready copy to a print shop, by using DTP software, you will save money on the design and set up while maintaining greater control over your document.

Design your materials with printing in mind. For instance, Edith Flowers Kilgo puts three renewal notices on a page and then cuts them as she needs them. Trout Lake, Washington home-based business owner Dave Wampler of The Simple Living Network, has just one 8½" × 11" flier brimming with information about his products.

CHAPTER 4
CUTTING COSTS FROM HERE TO THERE

Home-based guerrillas that regularly mail information or products to customers quickly realize that postage and shipping can be major expenses. They are inconspicuous expenses because you pay in small increments—33¢ here, $3.20 there—and you often do not realize how much a few sixteen-ounce packages are going to cost to mail until you are standing at the counter at the post office.

It is also an area in which it is difficult to pinch pennies, since the post office will not deliver your letter for less than the price of a stamp. Even so, do not short-change yourself. Be aware of your shipping options before you are rushed to meet a deadline.

PROPER POSTAGE

It may sound obvious, but the most important rule is to use proper postage. Some home-based businesspeople waste stamps because they are too busy to go to the post office—or the post office has closed already. To eliminate overstamping, keep a variety of stamp denominations on hand. Kathryn stocks 20¢, 22¢, 33¢, $1, and $3 stamps in her office.

If you regularly send the same products to customers, know how much each standard package weighs. For instance, if you sell personalized cross-stitched baby bibs, how much does one weigh? Two? The first ounce costs 33¢ and each subsequent ounce, up to eleven ounces, costs 22¢. For example, a seven-ounce envelope would cost $1.65 for first-class postage within the US. Keep a note of your calculations for future reference. Or look at the postage chart in Appendix C.

Another way to avoid overstamping is to weigh your packages at home. You do not have to lease a postage meter for $25 a month. In fact, the vast majority of the home-based guerrillas we interviewed felt that leasing a postal meter was an expensive waste. Instead, use a scale (Kathryn has a $3 food scale left over from her dieting days). If you do not own a suitable scale, it is worthwhile to invest in one. Coleen Sykora, home-based publisher of *Workers on Wheels* newsletter, says she bought one the size of a credit card at a post office for $5.

Lillian Bjorseth, home-based lecturer and author of *Breakthrough Networking: Building Relationships that Last,* says that her postage scale has paid for itself many times over. "We always pay exactly the amount, we never guess," she says. "That is one of the first things I suggest a home office get. If you just feel it, then you always put on the extra stamp. I can often take one piece of paper out of a mailing and save 22 cents if it's on the verge."

STAMPS BY MAIL AND ONLINE

Buying stamps by mail saves money in gas, and you will not lose valuable work time driving to and from the post office. Easy Stamp forms, available from your mail carrier, offer fourteen different postal items and promise that orders will arrive within three to five business days. We have often had ours come the next business day. Also, Uncle Sam pays the postage on the order form. If you live outside a metropolitan area, you can obtain Rural or Highway Contract Route Carrier Stamp Purchase Order forms from the nearest post office, which functions identically. Stamps are also available by phone (800) 782-6724, twenty-four hours a day, seven days a week, and online at http://www.usps.com; but a $1 service charge applies and the stamps do not arrive any faster.

In addition to buying stamps from the USPS, you can also buy postage online from Stamps.com and E-stamp. This service is convenient, especially if you mail a lot of packages, because you can print the postage immediately and do not have to wait for the stamps to be delivered. Also, it gives your letters the metered mail look without having to pay for a meter. However, the service is expensive.

E-stamp requires you to buy a starter kit that includes their software and electronic vault hardware for $49.99. It also comes with $25 worth of free postage and Avery labels, but this is still a hefty start-up cost. Then you need to pay for postage plus a 10 percent convenience fee (minimum $4.99, maximum $24.99). The main advantage to this system is that you do not need to connect to the Internet each time you need a stamp because the postage is stored in the electronic vault on your computer.

In contrast, Stamps.com has no start-up costs. You download the free software, register, and can start printing postage immediately. But, you must log onto the Internet every time you want to print postage. Stamps.com offers two payment plans, the business plan and the personal plan. The business plan charges a 10 percent convenience fee ($3.99 minimum, $19.99 maximum), while the personal plan charges a flat fee of $1.99 per month for up to $25 in postage (after $25 a 15 percent fee is charged on top of the $1.99 flat fee). If you spend more than $40 a month on postage, the business plan is a better deal. Both E-stamp and Stamps.com offer free address correction services. If you mail a lot of packages or rent a postage meter, you may save money by using one of these services. If not, the convenience is probably not worth the fees.

E-stamp
2855 Campus Drive, Suite 100 • San Mateo, CA 94403
phone: (888) 272-6526 • fax: (650) 554-8455
web site: http://e-stamp.com

Stamps.com
3420 Ocean Park Boulevard, Suite 1040 • Santa Monica, CA 90405-3035
phone: (310) 581-7200 • fax: none listed
web site: http://www.stamps.com

Lillian Bjorseth, home-based lecturer and author, recommends buying lightweight envelopes to reduce postage costs.

SELECT THE PROPER CLASS

Before you can make a frugal shipping choice, you need to be aware of the shipping options available. For example, you could ship an envelope first class, standard mail (A), registered mail, Priority Mail, or Express Mail. What's the difference?

➤ First class is the highest class of mail and is used for letters, postcards, checks, and money orders. The first ounce costs 33¢ and each additional ounce is 22¢. Postcards cost 20¢.

➤ Periodicals rate, also called second-class mail, is for use only by publishers of newspapers, magazines, and other periodicals sold on a subscription basis, who have been approved for second-class mailing privileges. The public may not use periodical rate. To use periodical rate, you must publish your periodical at least four times a year. There are other limits on advertising and methods of preparation. To gain approval to mail periodical rate, you must complete an application and pay a minimum of $305.00 for a permit. The cost of using periodical rate depends on the number of pieces, the weight, and mail preparation discounts.

➤ Standard mail (A), also known as third-class mail, is for advertising, catalogs, pamphlets, newsletters, direct mail, printed matter, and merchandise weighing less than one pound. To use standard mail (A), you must have 200 pieces or fifty pounds. The cost of using standard mail (A) depends on the size and weight of your mailing and mail preparation (i.e., delivery point bar-coding). For example, presorted letters going standard mail (A) cost between 20¢ and 23¢ each, automated letters cost 16¢ to 18¢ each, and presorted flats (large envelopes) going standard mail (A) cost 10¢ to 67¢ per piece. A $100 annual presort mailing fee is required.

➤ Standard mail (B), also known as fourth-class mail, is for parcels, books, circulars, catalogs, and other printed matter weighing one pound or more, but not more than seventy pounds. Standard mail (B) has several subclasses: parcel post, bound printed matter, special standard mail (no minimum weight), and library mail (no minimum weight). Parcel post is standard mail weighing one pound or more, that is not mailed in any of the other standard mail (B) categories. The cost depends on the weight and destination zone. Bound printed matter (BPM) is for catalogs, books, and other printed matter that weighs one to fifteen pounds. Rates are calculated based on weight and zone, beginning at $1.14 for 1.5 pounds for the local zone. Special standard mail, also called book rate, is for books of at least eight pages, printed music, printed objective test materials, sound recordings, video recordings, playscripts, manuscripts, educational reference charts, and medical information intended for distribution to hospital personnel. Library mail is for books, printed music, periodicals, sound recordings, museum materials, and scientific kits sent to, from, or between schools, colleges, universities, public libraries, museums, herbariums, and nonprofit organizations or associations. Library mail and special standard mail follow the same rate structure. The cost depends on the weight of the package. Steve Carlson, home-based publisher of Upper Access Books in Hinesburg, Vermont, noticed that depending on the package weight and destination, sometimes standard mail (B) bound printed matter was cheaper and other times standard mail (B) special standard mail was cheaper. He prepared a simple chart that showed the lowest rate for packages from one to ten pounds depending on the destination zone. Chart 4-1 illustrates which subclass of mail is cheaper—bound printed matter or special standard mail—for all eight zones. Zones are based on your location as it relates to the package's destination. Thus, to use this chart, you will need to obtain a "US Postal Service Official Zone Chart" from your local post office.

CHART 4-1 Bound Printed Matter vs. Special Standard Mail Rates

POUNDS	LOCAL	ZONES 1 & 2	ZONE 3	ZONE 4	ZONE 5	ZONE 6	ZONE 7	ZONE 8
1	$1.13	$1.13	$1.13	$1.13	$1.13	$1.13	$1.13	$1.13
1.5	$1.14	$1.54	$1.57	$1.58	$1.58	$1.58	$1.58	$1.58
2	$1.16	$1.57	$1.58	$1.58	$1.58	$1.58	$1.58	$1.58
2.5	$1.18	$1.60	$1.66	$1.76	$1.90	$2.03	$2.03	$2.03
3	$1.20	$1.63	$1.70	$1.82	$1.99	$2.03	$2.03	$2.03
3.5	$1.22	$1.66	$1.74	$1.88	$2.08	$2.30	$2.48	$2.48
4	$1.24	$1.70	$1.79	$1.94	$2.18	$2.42	$2.48	$2.48
4.5	$1.26	$1.73	$1.83	$2.01	$2.27	$2.55	$2.88	$2.93
5	$1.28	$1.76	$1.88	$2.07	$2.36	$2.67	$2.93	$2.93
6	$1.31	$1.82	$1.96	$2.20	$2.54	$2.92	$3.37	$3.38
7	$1.35	$1.89	$2.05	$2.32	$2.73	$3.16	$3.69	$3.83
8	$1.39	$1.95	$2.14	$2.45	$2.91	$3.41	$4.01	$4.11
9	$1.43	$2.02	$2.22	$2.57	$3.10	$3.65	$4.33	$4.39
10	$1.47	$2.08	$2.31	$2.70	$3.28	$3.90	$4.65	$4.67

Lightface: Bound Printed Matter
Bold: Special Standard Mail
Sources: Upper Access Books and the US Postal Service.

➤ Certified mail requires the signature of someone at the delivery address, and costs $1.40 in addition to required postage. You can request a return receipt, a card which is mailed back to you to show when your package arrived and who signed for it, which costs another $1.25. Delivery is usually within three to five days.

➤ Registered mail is documented at every post office it enters, and a receipt is returned to the sender. It is intended for tangible, valuable items such as appraised jewelry. Registered mail costs $6 in addition to postage without postal insurance. With postal insurance, the fee is on a sliding scale, starting at $6.20 for up to a declared value of $100 worth of merchandise.

➤ Priority Mail was mentioned by nearly every guerrilla we interviewed as a favorite way to save money on postage. Why? Priority Mail costs a flat rate of $3.20 for up to two pounds. It can even weigh over two pounds as long as it fits into the flat-rate Priority Mail envelope provided by the USPS! (Tracking costs an additional 35¢.) And since the post office provides free mailing envelopes and boxes, it is a fantastic deal. The only downsides to Priority Mail are, unlike its United Parcel Service (UPS) and FedEx counterparts, Priority Mail is not guaranteed to arrive within the advertised one to three days.

➤ Express Mail guarantees delivery overnight, but you pay dearly for the privilege: $11.75 for the first eight ounces and $15.75 for over eight ounces, up to two pounds.

UPS and FedEx also offer speedy delivery services. UPS, for instance, tracks every parcel and you can call to find out where it is, which eliminates the need for a return receipt. Or, you can track your package through their Internet site (http://www.ups.com). However, both charge based on distance from origin to destination, which means they usually charge more than the United States Postal Service (USPS) for overnight delivery: $10.25 to $20.50 for UPS and $11 to $20 for FedEx. And, unless you live near one of their collection centers or drop boxes, you probably will pay even more (about $3) because you will need to deal with a middleman like Kinko's or Mail Boxes, Etc. Moreover, both charge an additional fee for Saturday delivery (about $10). In addition, Toni Yount-Klein, home-based owner of TY West, a western lingerie designer and manufacturer, from Gillette, Wyoming, says she gets the money for deliveries sent COD from the USPS within a week, whereas UPS can take up to a month.

But if you want UPS's guaranteed delivery times or if you have a heavy package (UPS is more competitively priced with the USPS for larger items), author Lillian Bjorseth says she saves a little money by dropping packages off at the UPS warehouse rather than requesting pick-up services. And Laurie Dry, a home-based consultant who sells photographic supplies in Sonoma, California, says she saves money by shipping products to a business, rather than a residence, whenever possible. Why? UPS charges more to ship to a residential address because it says they are more difficult to find than businesses. (Home offices are considered residential addresses by UPS.) Thus, when it will not compromise profes-sionalism, Dry asks her customers if she can ship to their offices. Finally, shipping discounts from UPS, FedEx, and other delivery services are available for members in certain organizations or those with select credit cards. See Chapter 10, "Tightwad Transactions," Chapter 12, "The Frugal Fraternity," and Appendix A for more information.

What does all this mean for guerrillas? Do not procrastinate. Factor in mailing time when you calculate your deadline. Depending on the dis-tance your work needs to travel, mailing time can be anywhere from a day to a month (overseas). The longer you put off mailing it, the more expensive your options. Of course, damaging your reputation by not delivering the goods on time is the most expensive option, so do not mail your work first class and pray it arrives on the customer's desk tomor-row. Bite the bullet, pay for Express Mail, and vow never to leave an assignment to the last minute again.

PO BOXES

Some guerrillas may find it worth the $15 to $100 per year to rent a PO box. If, for instance, you move often and have to send change-of-address letters to all your customers every time, you will quickly accumulate enough in supplies, postage, and agony to justify a PO box.

However, do not get a PO box simply because you think it looks profes-sional. A PO box does not necessarily project a more positive image than a street address; in fact, some people are put off by PO boxes, thinking they suggest an unstable business. Another disadvantage is you will have to drive to the post office daily to collect your mail, which costs money in gas and lost work time.

On the other hand, home-based tax consultant Anthony Applebaum finds his PO box indispensable, because of the security it provides for the confidential documents he regularly receives. Mailboxes are available from other companies, such as Mail Boxes, Etc., which would give him a regular street address, mail forwarding, and the ability to receive packages from UPS, FedEx, and other carriers, but Applebaum found they cost a lot more (about $180 per year). Decide what type and how much mail you expect to receive. Many guerrillas can get by with the smallest box size available without any inconvenience.

> *Stamps damaged by moisture, unused postage, or prestamped stationery may be exchanged or refunded at full value, according to Postal Regulation 147.112. This means if you misaddress an envelope or do not use a self-addressed, stamped envelope, you can take it to the post office for a refund. Many postal clerks are unaware of this regulation and may be unwilling to help you. To avoid difficulties, obtain a copy of the* **Consumer's Guide to Postal Services & Products,** *Publication 201, and show them the section on refunds.*

DIRECT MAIL

Promotional materials mailed directly to potential customers, called *direct mail,* can be an effective sales technique, if it is used judiciously. Before you mail a ten-page press package, consider these hints:

➤ Avoid overkill. Press releases should be concise—one page is best. Do not pay extra for excess weight.

➤ Follow postal regulations. Mail that does not meet guidelines is returned to the sender. Proper dimensions for machinable, letter-sized mail are: 3½ inches to 6⅛ inches high, 5 inches to 11½ inches long, and up to ¼ inch thick. Mail smaller than the minimums, including post-cards, are not accepted. Proper dimensions for flat-sized mail (manila envelopes) are: 6⅛ inches to 12 inches high, 11½ inches to 15 inches long, and ¼ inch to ¾ inch thick.

➤ Use proper address format. Your mail will arrive more quickly, and you will have fewer pieces returned to you. The post office prefers addresses to be typewritten or machine-printed, have a uniform left margin, be in upper-case letters only, and have no punctuation except for the hyphen in the ZIP+4 code. For example:

JANE DOE EDITOR
THE NEW YORKER
20 WEST 43RD ST • NEW YORK NY 10036-7441
You can obtain more detailed information on proper designs and address format from the post office.

➤ Keep it small and light. The larger and heavier a piece of mail is, the more it will cost. Consider this when you are designing brochures and other sales materials.

➤ Avoid staples and paper clips, which add unnecessary weight and can get caught in postal machinery.

➤ Compile your own mailing list instead of relying on others. Home-based publisher Steve Carlson stopped renting mailing lists and now sends catalogs only to customers who request them or have bought from his company before. Though his catalog circulation is smaller, the percentage of customers who respond is higher.

➤ Clean up your mailing list. Every six months to a year, update your mailing records. Remove names of clients, editors, and public-relations representatives who have resigned or transferred. Change addresses or contact names. Correct or eliminate incomplete addresses, too, as those will be returned to you. The USPS offers a one-time complimentary "cleaning" of your mailing list on diskette in ASCII. This service, called ZIP+4 Diskette Coding, cross-checks your addresses with the USPS's national database, makes corrections, and adds the ZIP+4 code to each address. Ask for an application at a Postal Business Center.

➤ Print "Forwarding Service Requested" on the envelope. First-class mail is forwarded for the first year for no charge. After the first year, the mailpiece is returned with the new address attached for no charge. For standard mail (A), print "Forwarding Service Requested." For the first year, the piece will be forwarded without charge. After the first year, the mailpiece is returned with the new address attached. There is no charge for the address correction, but you will be charged return postage for the piece.

For more information on designing cost-effective direct-mail packages, check out the USPS's publication *The Small Business Guide to Advertising with Direct Mail*, available from Postal Business Centers. This free eighty-six-page guide contains a ton of information on how to develop a direct mail package, target your audience, print materials, and track responses.

BULK-MAIL DISCOUNTS

You can request bulk mail discounts if you have over 200 pieces of mail (or fifty pounds), all pieces are the same (i.e., letters or flat envelopes), and the pieces weigh less than sixteen ounces each. You will need to obtain a permit, and the mail must be sent from the post office from which the permit was obtained. A bulk mail permit costs $100 per year. Delivery time on bulk mail can range from two days to more than a week, depending on the distance and level of presorting.

A presorting discount is available if you arrange your mail so that pieces going to the same area are bundled together. This allows your mass mailing to bypass certain steps at the post office. The more levels of sorting you perform, the less you pay in postage. If you include a ZIP+4 code or a delivery-point bar code on your mail (some word-processing software has this capability, or you can buy special software), you can receive substantial postal discounts because it speeds processing and delivery. You might also qualify for a destination entry discount—destination bulk mail center (DBMC), destination sectional center facility (DSCF), or destination delivery unit (DDU)—if you deposit your mail at a post office close to where the mail is to be delivered. If you only want to target a specific geographical area, you may want to consider saturation mail. Saturation mail is the most inexpensive class of service, because it is delivered to every household and does not require sorting. Discounts vary by destination and class of mail.

Despite these discounts, many guerrillas we interviewed said they had poor experiences with bulk mail, and felt the postage savings was not worth the agony. Several guerrillas recounted tales of lost or mangled mail. Newsletter publishers, in particular, seemed to have difficulties with bulk mail, perhaps because their customers were upset if the mailing did not arrive promptly. For instance, Edith Flowers Kilgo says that when she used bulk mail, issues got lost and mangled, so she had to send replacements. And, worse, her subscription renewal rate nosedived.

However, Gary Dunn, home-based publisher of *The Caretaker Gazette*, says he saves a ton by shipping his newsletter via bulk mail. To avoid problems, he advises guerrillas to meet with a postal representative at a Postal Business Center. For example, a postal representative will teach you how to fold your mail so that the mail-sorting machinery grabs it from the folded side—not the open side—which will avoid problems. Dunn says by following the post office recommendations—using the delivery-point bar code and the ZIP+4 code, and sorting the newsletter in ZIP code order from lowest to highest—his subscribers often receive their newsletters within two days. That is first-class service at a bulk-mail price!

One thing is clear: preparing a bulk mailing is complicated, and you should get help from your local Postal Business Center. For more information, request Publication 95, *Quick Service Guide,* and Publication 49, *Preparing Standard Mail (A),* from your post office.

Laurie Dry, a consultant who sells photographic supplies, shares bulk mailings with another guerrilla so that they can both receive the discounted rate without having to reach the 200-piece minimum on their own.

BUSINESS REPLY MAIL

We have all seen the postage-paid cards that drop out of magazines, but many home-based entrepreneurs do not consider how business reply mail (BRM) might increase their sales. BRM allows you to entice customers with postage-paid offers, but requires you pay only on the mail returned. Newsletter editor Edith Flowers Kilgo says that her sales increased tremendously when she included a business-reply envelope with all potential customer inquiries.

A BRM permit, which costs $100 per year, is available for reply cards, envelopes, self-mailers, cartons, or labels. When you use your BRM permit, you guarantee payment of first-class mail postage plus a per-piece fee for pieces returned to you. Basic service costs 66¢ for letters and 50¢ for postcards (first-class postage + 30¢). The fees are paid through a postage-due account or COD. There are two other, more complex classes of BRM that cost less per piece (23¢ to 41¢ each), but they are recommended only if your return volume is over 1,000 pieces per year. When designing a BRM mailpiece or label, consult with your local Postal Business Center or post office to make sure that it conforms to specific layout guidelines. For more information, obtain Publication 353, *Designing Reply Mail,* from your local Postal Business Center.

POSTCARDS

It costs 13¢ less to mail a postcard than it does to mail a letter, so it benefits you to do so whenever it will not sacrifice professionalism. Postcards can also be effective direct-mail pieces because they are inexpensive and, unlike envelopes, the recipient is less likely to throw them away unread. Barbara Winter, a home-based lecturer on self-employment and author of *Making a Living Without a Job,* uses postcards to reply to letters and fan mail, as well as to remind readers to renew subscriptions to her newsletter, *Winning Ways.* She collects unique postcards while traveling, especially in her favorite city, London. As a result, Winter's London postcards have become a kind of trademark.

Marcia Yudkin, author of *6 Steps to Free Publicity,* from Boston, Massachusetts, has also used postcards. But in her case, it is the color—hot pink—that has become the recognizable feature. She says clients like them because they are easy to find in the incoming mail and later, on their desks. "I have a special first-class presort permit that allows me to send out postcards at around 18¢ each. The permit is $100 per year and you have to have special software that sorts the mailing list. But, I've worked it out, and I save money this way," says Yudkin.

Jim Amos, president and CEO of Mail Boxes, Etc. in San Diego, California, warns against overinsuring packages. For example, if an item is valued at $300, you may be tempted to insure it for $500, just to be "safe." However, if it were somehow damaged or lost, to collect the insurance, you would need to show a receipt. Thus, paying for $500 worth of insurance on a $300 item is a waste of money.

FAX, EMAIL, AND FACE-TO-FACE

The best way to save on postage is to avoid paying it altogether. Two ways to do this are by faxing and emailing. If you fax a document to a long-distance number, you will be charged for the telephone call. However, if your document is less than two pages, you may pay less in telephone charges than in postage, depending on how much you pay per minute for long distance. And, if the call is local, faxing the document is free!

If you already pay a flat rate for email and have a local Internet service provider connection number, using email is virtually free. And it is faster than the USPS. Kathryn regularly uses email to send articles to editors, to request information, and contact potential interviewees. Laurie Dry, a consultant, sends her quarterly newsletter to customers via email instead of U.S. Mail whenever possible.

Perhaps one of the best ways to avoid postage charges is by delivering documents personally. Though this can be time-consuming, it can pay off. Why? When you hand-deliver packages, clients are impressed by the personal attention, which often results in additional sales. Theresa Le, an independent consultant for a direct-selling cosmetics company in San Jose, California, says, "Since my business is a lot of face-to-face with customers, I try to give them brochures in person, rather than mailing them."

If you can, charge customers a shipping-and-handling fee that covers the cost of mailing your product.

POSTAL BUSINESS CENTERS

For more information on saving money on postage, you may want to visit a Postal Business Center. Currently, 121 Postal Business Centers nationwide offer free personalized assistance in designing mailpieces, preparing bulk mailings, obtaining postal meter permits, and answering questions. Postal representatives can teach you how to take advantage of first-class and standard and bulk-mail discounts. For more information, check out the post office's web site at http://www.usps.com.

CHAPTER 5 FRUGAL PHONING

The telephone bill is probably one of the largest expenses of any home-based business. Worse, telephone charges are among the most confusing expenses we face. Do you call during peak rate, off-peak rate, night rate, weekend rate, daytime rate, or blue-moon rate? You get the idea.

RESIDENTIAL VERSUS BUSINESS TELEPHONE LINES

As home-based businesspeople, we have the option of getting an additional residential line or a business line for our home offices. If you can, opt for the additional residential line, because residential telephone charges are much cheaper than business ones. Residential lines cost about $20 a month for basic service, whereas business lines cost about $70 a month. Unfortunately, many guerrillas are forced into obtaining business lines because they need to be listed in the *Yellow Pages* and, in most places, that means you must have a business line.

In that case, Jeff Berner, home-based author of *The Joy of Working from Home: Making a Life While Making a Living,* offers this suggestion: "Buy business service and list that number for incoming calls. But use a private, residential line for outgoing calls." This way you can pay the lower residential rates for your long-distance calls and still maintain a *Yellow Pages* listing.

You can also forego the second line altogether, and use your residential line as your business line. This is inexpensive, especially when you are just starting out. Some businesses find it relatively painless, because they conduct most of their business via mail or face-to-face. For example,

Diane Rosener, home-based editor of *A Penny Saved* newsletter from Omaha, Nebraska, does not have a separate line for home and business because she does not receive many phone calls.

However, this option can be problematic, depending on the amount of telephone calls you receive, and is not practical for every home-based business. So, before you decide to print your home telephone number as your business number on your business cards, consider: You will need to answer the telephone in a professional manner all the time and young children can not be permitted to answer the telephone. "My biggest mistake was that I didn't get a separate line for business phone. I have a separate line for fax. I never got a third line for business," says home-based freelance writer Marilyn Zelinsky and author of *Practical Home Office Solutions* from Fairfield, Connecticut. "I'm tired of picking up business calls at eleven o'clock at night because my home and business line are the same. Another line would be worth its weight in gold."

SECOND-RING SERVICE

If your business does not receive many telephone calls, another way to solve the home/business line dispute is to use second-ring service. This service allows you to have two telephone numbers ring on the same telephone line, thus eliminating the need for separate business and residential telephone lines. Like in the days when one telephone served several families, each number has a distinctive ring (i.e., the first number has one long ring and the second number has two short rings). This service costs a few dollars a month, but it is much cheaper than having a separate line which can cost $20 to $70 a month.

Second-ring service is also an option for those guerrillas who are undecided about whether to have one business line for voice and fax or two separate ones. Gerri Detweiler, a home-based financial consultant, speaker, and author of *The Ultimate Credit Handbook*, hooked her fax machine to her home telephone line and has a different ring for voice and electronic calls.

Do things right the first time.

—**Ron Miller,**
Advantage Northwest

CONNECTING A SECOND LINE

If you decide you want a second line, and you or someone you know is handy, you may be able to connect a new line inside the house for the cost of parts (under $10). The telephone company charges $100 or more for this service. (If you live in an apartment, this may be your only choice.) You will still need to pay the telephone company to connect the new line to the box outside your house. However, it is not overly difficult to connect a second line inside your house.

Most house telephone wiring has three color-coded lines (one which is being used for your residential service and two unused ones). Simply look at the telephone box outside of the house to find the new junction the phone company has installed. Then, strip the wires on one of the unused lines and screw it onto the junction backplate. Do the same thing to the wires at the jack in the room in which you want to install the second telephone line. Kathryn's home office has two lines (one for voice and one for fax) and her husband connected both of them. He simply bought a two-line outlet and wired it appropriately.

CALLING LONG DISTANCE DURING OFF-HOURS

If you have a long-distance calling plan that has cheaper off-peak hours (nights/weekends), try to make long-distance calls during those hours. One way to do this is to take advantage of time-zone differences. If you live on the east or west coasts, you can call cross-country during your off-peak hours, but during regular business hours for your clients. For instance, when Kathryn lived in California, she often called magazine editors before 8 A.M. pacific time—before 11 A.M. in New York—to take advantage of the cheaper rates.

Dave Wampler, home-based owner of the Simple Living Network, an online company in Trout Lake, Washington, has also altered his calling patterns to maximize long distance savings during nonpeak times. Sprint is his long-distance provider and, when the company offered a promotion where long-distance calls on Friday were free, Wampler saved his long-distance calling for that day.

Keep up to date on your carrier's current peak/off-peak rate structure and promotions so that you can adjust your calling patterns accordingly. Long-distance telephone rates are constantly fluctuating, and the only notification you may receive of a rate change is in tiny, four-point font on the back of your bill. Adds home-based publishers Scott and Shirley Gregory of Bookhome Publishing, "A lot of these companies will hit you with teaser rates. I recommend keeping an eye on your bill. According to federal law, they have to let you know, but the way they let you know is in very fine print buried in your bill on page 18. If rates go up, call them, question it, and threaten to leave."

Steve Carlson, home-based publisher of Upper Access Books, agrees: "We always watch our bills closely to make sure they're giving us the rates they promised. We've had to call back repeatedly to make sure they're not overcharging us on certain types of calls. They have so many different rates. You really have to watch out."

If you dial the wrong number or notice a billing mistake ("I do not know anyone in Guam!"), call your long distance telephone provider and have the charge erased from your bill. You are not required to pay for mistakes. Most long distance carriers have automated systems that will allow you to enter the number in question and will credit your account accordingly.

HOW TO FIND THE CHEAPEST LONG-DISTANCE PROVIDER

Over half the guerrillas we interviewed contracted with long-distance companies that were not household names (AT&T, MCI WorldCom, and Sprint). Many guerrillas proudly told us how much they were paying per minute for telephone service—the lowest was 5¢ per minute. However, many of the companies they contracted with were regional long-distance companies that may not serve your area. Also, since every business has different needs, it is difficult to endorse one particular carrier or plan. However, you should not be paying more than 12¢ a minute for long-distance service. Additionally, you want to keep an eye on your carrier's monthly fees and minimums. Many calling plans require a monthly fee to ensure a low per-minute rate.

For instance, the latest rage in long-distance service is the flat-rate calling plan, offering rates such as 10¢ a minute, twenty-four hours a day, seven days a week. This can be economical for individuals who find they must call customers during the expensive daytime hours. However, you should be aware that some of these plans also charge a monthly fee for participating (usually $5). Thus, low-volume users probably will not recoup the cost of the fee. Before you sign up, calculate whether the monthly fee will offset your savings or not (divide the fee by the difference between your current cost per minute and the flat-rate cost per minute to get the number of minutes you would need to talk to make the fee worthwhile). Occasionally, you can get this monthly fee waived by asking.

Whatever plan you choose, one thing is for sure: You need to periodically review your plan every six or twelve months to make sure you are still paying the lowest rate for what you need. The best way to find the cheapest plan is to send for *Tele-Tips*, a publication of the Telecommunications Research & Action Center (TRAC), a nonprofit organization that helps consumers make informed decisions about their telephone service. The organization publishes *TRAC's Residential Long Distance Chart* ($5) and *TRAC's Small Business Long Distance* ($7). Both publications require separate self-addressed, 55¢-stamped #10 envelopes. You can also join

TRAC for $25 per year (individual membership), which entitles you to all long-distance charts throughout the year, usually two business and two residential, as well as their other telephone-related reports. The long-distance charts list every major long distance carrier, including lesser-known ones such as LCI, Frontier, and Matrix, their rates, and their calling plans. TRAC's web site also has a formula that allows you to compare your phone bills, so you can find the best plan.

TRAC
PO Box 27279 • Washington, DC 20005
phone: (202) 408-1130 • fax: none listed
web site: http://www.trac.org

Though it is time intensive, you can also unearth this information yourself for free by calling all the long-distance providers in your area (on their toll-free numbers, of course). Regardless of how you obtain the information, it is worthwhile. June Langhoff, home-based author of *Telecom Made Easy: Money-Saving, Profit-Building Solutions for Home Businesses, Telecommuters, and Small Organizations*, from Pacifica, California, says, "People can save a ton of money if they analyze their phone bills and look at their long distance. The phone companies change their phone plans two or three times a year, so even though your plan made good sense a year ago, you may save a whole lot more if you switched. Some have only six months of a low rate and then it goes up and you may not even notice." Most people think that comparing phone bills is a lot of trouble and there is probably a better use of their time, but, she warns, "you better try it at least once." After Langhoff analyzed her bills, her phone costs decreased by 40 percent. Now she looks at her phone bills every four to six months.

In addition, publishers Scott and Shirley Gregory say guerrillas should not be afraid to switch from a major carrier to a lesser-known phone company. Says Scott, "I have never had a problem with lesser-known phone companies. I think that is just one of those things the big long-distance phone companies use to strike fear into you in their commercials." Publisher Steve Carlson also uses a lesser-known long-distance carrier and agrees, "We haven't had any problems with the telephone lines working."

The major long-distance companies offer special calling plans if you sign up on the Internet, and are automatically billed via your credit card or checking account. Your bills are delivered via email so it is environmentally friendly. Many of these plans are competitive—even more competitive than their traditional calling plans. For instance, AT&T One Rate costs 10¢ a minute, twenty-four hours a day, seven days a week, plus $4.95 a month. In contrast, AT&T One Rate Online costs only 9¢ a minute with no monthly fees! For more information about exclusive online long-distance offers, check out your long-distance carrier's web site.

SIX-SECOND BILLING

Most long-distance telephone companies bill in one minute increments. That means, if you make a long-distance call that lasts one minute and two seconds, you will be charged for two minutes. In contrast, six-second billing only rounds up to the next six seconds. Thus, in the previous example, you would be charged for one minute and six seconds. That may seem like quibbling but, if you calculate the number of calls you make per day and figure that you are probably being overcharged by at least 30 seconds per call, all those seconds—and pennies and nickels and dimes—add up. Therefore, when you select a long-distance telephone-service provider, ask if the company has six-second billing.

The best way to cut long-distance telephone costs is to cut telephone usage. Use email, fax, or U.S. mail instead. Kathryn regularly uses email to contact editors and potential interviewees. The voicemail of Todd Weaver, home-based owner of the Minstrel Music Network in Bremerton, Washington, states that callers can receive a faster reply via email than phone. Weaver says, "I avoid the phone at all costs. I prefer emailing. Our suppliers are slowly coming around. Initially, they would always call me and leave voicemail. I would just answer via email."

DIAL-AROUND (10-10-XXX) NUMBERS

Dial-around (10-10-XXX) numbers are seven-digit access codes, which you can dial to use a different long-distance carrier than the one you have chosen on your bill. Some dial-around (10-10-XXX) numbers offer very competitive rates, but many have expensive hidden fees. For instance, some charge a connection fee. Others charge for a minimum number of minutes, even if you hang up after thirty seconds, or a high per minute rate for short calls and a favorable per minute rate for calls over ten minutes.

Despite all these catches, if you know the rules, dial-around numbers can come in handy. For example, when Edith Flowers Kilgo's long-distance carrier tried to charge her a monthly minimum for long-distance calls, she balked. The *Creative Downscaling* newsletter editor did not make enough long-distance calls to meet the $5 monthly minimum, and resented being charged for something she did not use. She told her local phone company that she did not want a long-distance carrier, and now uses dial-around numbers whenever she needs to make a long-distance call. Another option is to find a carrier that does not have a minimum. Before you use a 10-10-XXX number, know the benefits and, more important, the draw-backs. For more information, TRAC publishes a helpful pamphlet titled *TRAC's Consumer Guide to Dial-Arounds (10-10-XXX Numbers)* for $1.

TRAC
PO Box 27279 • Washington, DC 20005
phone: (202) 408-1130 • fax: none listed
web site: http://www.trac.org

WORDS OF WISDOM

Don't be afraid to bargain. Almost everything is negotiable, especially bigger purchases.

—Ron Miller,
Advantage Northwest

HOW TO NEGOTIATE LOWER RATES

If you decide that you do not want to switch carriers, but would like a lower rate, you can also try to negotiate with your current carrier. We have all heard stories about individuals who have received $100 checks or 200 free minutes for switching or not switching. However, since they have become more publicized and consumers have learned how to use them to their advantage, those deals have become less frequent. And, although such deals are sweet perks, we do not recommend that you rely on them. Moreover, once you have reaped the benefits of the deal, such as using up the 100 free minutes, you may be paying a much higher rate for long-distance service, which quickly offsets any bargains.

Instead, contact your current carrier and ask if you are on the lowest plan available. Have your calling habit information handy to assist the operator, if necessary. In an informal survey published in *Consumer Reports* in September 1995, half the individuals who called their long-distance carriers found they could reduce their bills by 10 percent.

Another tactic is to call several competitors and ask what kind of deal they can offer you. Then, call your current carrier and ask them to match or beat the best offer. Say, "XYZ Company will offer me eight cents per minute with no monthly fees, can you match that?" Concentrate on bargaining for an overall reduced rate or waived fees, as opposed to incentive deals, such as free minutes, because the benefits will last longer and add up to more. Finally, if you decide to switch, be sure to ask your new carrier to pick up the $5 charge the local phone company will bill you to switch carriers.

It is worth constantly looking at the new long-distance promotions offered. As tiresome as that stuff gets, you can save hundreds of dollars by making sure you have the lowest priced service.

—Steve Carlson,
Upper Access Books

MEASURED-RATE AND LIMITED LOCAL CALLS

If the majority of your customers are located outside your calling area, you may want to consider changing your local calling option. Upon scrutinizing her bill, Kathryn realized that she made less than a dozen local telephone calls per month. She switched her local telephone service from unlimited local calling to a flat rate for fifty local calls per month. The change saved her $36 per year.

If you make even fewer calls, you may want to change to measured-rate service where you are charged 6¢ to 10¢ for each local call. For example, Neal Lubow, home-based owner of Ideas By-The-Hour, a marketing communications company in Portland, Oregon, got measured-rate service for his fax line because he sends few local faxes.

WORDS OF WISDOM

The lowest price is not always the best price if the company doesn't offer all of the things you need.

**—Scott and Shirley Gregory,
Bookhome Publishing**

LOCAL LONG-DISTANCE CALLS

If you live in a large metropolitan area, you may find that you are paying more to call a client twenty miles away than one who lives 2,000 miles away. That is because local telephone companies have begun to raise rates on what is known as *local long distance* or *local toll* calls. The tricky thing is that these calls may not require you to use another area code. For instance, major parts of San Diego and the surrounding area are served by the same area code (619) but, to call from north of the city to downtown will cost you quite a lot, perhaps more per minute than it would cost you to call Phoenix.

Kathryn discovered that to call around Detroit she was paying a whopping 25¢ per minute through her local carrier, as opposed to 9¢ per minute on her flat-rate long-distance calling plan. To avoid local long-distance charges, she now uses her carrier's 10-10-XXX number, so that the call appears on her long-distance bill instead of her local one. Ask your local carrier how much local long-distance calls cost per minute. If it is more than you are paying for traditional long-distance service, find out what your long-distance carrier's dial-around number is, and use it.

DIRECTORY ASSISTANCE

Directory assistance is one of the most expensive telephone services available—each call can cost as much as $1.40—so you want to avoid using it whenever possible. One way is to call toll-free directory assistance at (800) 555-1212. The toll-free directory will tell you if the party you want to reach has a toll-free telephone number. If they do, you not only saved the $1 you would have spent on directory assistance, you also save on the telephone call itself. Of course, toll-free telephone numbers are not free. The recipient must pay for your call, so consider that before you dial.

Another way to avoid using directory assistance is by using the Internet. If you already pay for Internet service, you can look up a telephone number in the online *Yellow Pages, White Pages,* or via search engines. Try http://www.555-1212.com, http://www.bigbook.com, or http://www.people.yahoo.com. In addition, if you happen to be heading to the library, you can look up telephone numbers in its collection of *White Pages.* Large libraries have massive collections of *White Pages* for cities nationwide.

If you find you must use directory assistance, be careful about the service you use. It used to be that 411 was local directory assistance and 1-(area code)-555-1212 was long-distance directory assistance. Not anymore. In many areas, those two services compete with one another, as well as with several long-distance companies, such as AT&T's 00 and the "10-10" numbers. A 1998 study by the Telecommunications Research and Action Center (TRAC), a nonprofit consumer organization, showed that Los Angeles consumers who made ten directory assistance calls using 411 would pay $1.25, while they would pay over $9 if they used AT&T 00 or

MCI WorldCom's 10-10-9000. One reason for the discrepancy might be that some local telephone companies allot you a certain number of free directory-assistance calls per month, then charge 99¢ per call if you go over that allotment. If you get some complimentary directory-assistance calls, you should use your local carrier first. Even if you do not get any free directory-assistance calls, check with your local carrier first, as it is usually cheaper than the other directory assistance services. Also, if you get a wrong number when calling directory assistance, be sure to call the company's business office and ask for a credit. Directory assistance is too expensive to not get what you paid for!

You can save a bundle by not signing up for call-waiting, call-forwarding, caller ID, and the other frills the telephone company advertises. Many of these services are unnecessary and can even be annoying. For example, when you have call waiting, a telemarketer can interrupt a call with a client.

FREE PHONE BOOKS FROM OTHER CITIES

If you live in a large metropolitan area, or often shop in a nearby city, it pays to have a *Yellow Pages* book from that area. Having a *Yellow Pages* reduces the need to call directory assistance. However, the telephone company usually charges $3 to $6 for *Yellow Pages* outside your local calling area. Instead, when the new books are issued, obtain the old books free from local recycling centers. The books will not be the most current, but much of the information will not change.

FRUGAL FAXING

Though facsimiles are becoming less common due to the increased popularity of email, they are still useful for sending documents that do not originate in your computer. If you have several faxes going to the same telephone number, save them and fax them in one batch, rather than individually. This saves money, because the first minute of a long-distance telephone call is usually higher than additional minutes. Thus, because you make only one call, you pay the lower rate for additional pages, instead of the high first-minute charge several times. This savings is even more important for international calls, where first minute charges can cost several dollars.

Many of the newer fax machines have a feature that will allow you to scan a document, then delay faxing it until late in the evening when some long-distance companies' telephone rates are cheaper. This is a handy feature but, if your fax machine does not have it, you can still duplicate it by popping into your office before bed or early in the morning to send a fax.

One caveat: Beware of faxing home-based guerrillas at odd hours. Some home-based guerrillas have their offices in spare bedrooms or their own bedrooms and faxing at odd hours may have the undesirable effect of waking them up. Therefore, save this tip for clients who have traditional offices.

Use simple fonts and avoid graphics when possible, because they often do not transmit well. If you do not, you may have to resend the fax, which results in being charged twice for the same document.

CALLING CARDS

Calling cards make it easy to place long-distance telephone calls—no more juggling quarters. However, they can also be expensive—often $1 per minute or more! As a result, you may want to consider using prepaid phone cards, instead of your credit card or telephone-company-issued calling card. Also, prepaid phone cards do not have a per call surcharge, as many calling cards do.

Kathryn switched to prepaid cards when she realized that local toll calls were costing her $1.20 for the first minute on her calling card. Now she buys prepaid phone cards when they go on sale at Target for 20¢ a minute or less. Examine how much your calling card is charging you. You may find it more economical to purchase a prepaid phone card.

CELLULAR PHONES

The best way to save on a cellular phone is not to have one. This may sound radical in this age of technological advancement, but many people do not need cellular phones. That is not to say that they are not convenient sometimes, such as when you are stuck in traffic, or downright life-saving, such as when your vehicle breaks down on a deserted highway in the middle of a blizzard. However, by working at home, you probably have greatly reduced the amount of time you spend in the car. And, since it is unsafe to talk on the phone while driving—it quadruples the risk of having a collision, according to a 1997 study in the *New England Journal of Medicine*—you need to determine at what other times you will use a cellular phone. The questions to ask yourself are: How often am I unable to find a telephone, and will my productivity increase enough to justify the cost of the phone and cellular service?

If you answer those questions and decide it is worthwhile to own a cellular phone, you should obtain a copy of TRAC's *A Consumer's Guide to Cellular Telephone Service* ($7.95 plus $1.50 postage).

TRAC
PO Box 27279 • Washington, DC 20005
phone: (202) 408-1130 • fax: none listed
web site: http://www.trac.org

In general, it is best to buy a plan that closely resembles the number of minutes you will talk, which is not necessarily the lowest minute plan (i.e., a 100-minute plan versus a fifteen-minute plan). That is because the cost per minute decreases as you purchase more minutes in your base plan. Also, additional minutes cost less on higher minute plans (i.e., 60¢

per additional minute on a fifteen-minute plan as opposed to 33¢ per additional minute on a 100-minute plan).

In addition, if your cellular phone provider charges you *roaming fees*, a per minute penalty of 50¢ to $1 or more for leaving the local area served by your provider, avoid roaming on the telephone. Instead, find a pay phone and use a calling card. Of course, even local calls placed on a cellular phone are much higher than those via a traditional phone with a phone card, so save your cellular phone for when you really cannot get to a traditional telephone.

Coleen Sykora, home-based editor of *Workers on Wheels* newsletter, owns a cellular phone because she often parks in RV resorts that do not offer phone service or in remote areas. "We have a real basic plan—$10 per month. We don't use it a lot, but it's there for a back up. If we're parked thirty miles out of town, it's worth the roaming fees to make the call on the cell phone rather than drive to a pay phone because on a good day, our vehicle only gets eight miles to the gallon."

For more information on cellular telephone service, visit http://www.wirelessdimension.com. The commercial site provides a comparison of different cellular plans in your area, as well as easy-to-understand answers to FAQs about cellular service.

I'm worried that more and more people are getting hooked on technology. They need to remember the things that give them joy in life: family, friends, relationships. Don't trade the beehive of a corporate office for the hamster cage of a home office. Take time to enjoy life. Don't work fifteen hours a day. Utilize the benefits, enjoy the freedom and flexibility. It is important to make a life while you make a living.

—John Knowlton,
Business @ Home

CHAPTER 6 SAVING IN CYBERSPACE

In only a few years, the Internet has become one of the most powerful communication tools in the world. If you do not have Internet access, you are missing out. Having access to the Internet means you have a virtual library in your own home, on which you can find information on any topic you can imagine. Having email means you can communicate with individuals halfway around the world for pennies a minute.

INTERNET ACCESS

Before you start absorbing the volumes of information and corresponding with colleagues worldwide, you will need to obtain Internet access. The type of access you obtain—and how much you pay for that access—depends mainly on your online needs. Do you intend to use the Internet for email? To download stock quotes? To transfer files to and from suppliers?

One guerrilla we interviewed made another good point: As a home-based entrepreneur, he was concerned with the Internet needs of his family, as well as his business. If your children will be using your Internet connection after hours, this may affect your choice of internet service provider (ISP). This home-based guerrilla decided on America Online (AOL) because his children planned to use the computer for schoolwork, and AOL offers several homework-help forums that you cannot access from other ISPs.

INTERNET ACCESS OPTIONS
· ·

You can access the Internet in more than a half-dozen ways. Knowing what is available for home-based guerrillas should help you make the best choice.

Dial-Up Lines. This Internet connection is where your computer's modem uses the telephone line to call your ISP's computer. Using your ISP's computer, you are able to access the Internet. This is the most common type of connection. It is satisfactory for most people, and costs about $20 a month for unlimited access. The drawbacks of dial-up lines are they can be slow to transfer information and if you try to call during a peak period, such as early evening, you may have trouble logging on due to busy signals.

ISDN Lines. ISDN, which stands for *Integrated Services Digital Network*, is virtually a direct link to the Internet. When you call your ISP, it is almost instantly connected. It is about five times faster than a regular dial-up line. In order to have ISDN, you must buy special equipment, called an *ISDN modem* (though it is not really a modem), that costs about $300, and pay for installation. ISDN service costs about $50 per month, including the telephone-company charges and ISP fees. It can accommodate 128K, and is ideal for guerrillas who must access the Internet quickly and constantly throughout the day, such as stock investors. One large advantage of an ISDN line is that it can be split into two 64K lines, if necessary. What this means is you can talk on the telephone and not lose your Internet connection, though your connection will be 50 percent slower.

DSL Lines. DSL lines, or *digital subscriber lines,* transform ordinary telephone lines into high-speed digital lines using a new modem technology. The most well-known type of DSL line is ADSL (asymmetrical DSL). The main advantages of ADSL are speed (256K), and that you can simultaneously talk on the telephone or send a fax while surfing the web, without sacrificing speed. In addition, your Internet access is constant: You are always connected. Currently, the service is available in Southern California and major cities and, since it uses copper telephone wires, it should become more widely available. Home-based web designer Jean MacDonald got ADSL service a few months ago and says, "Getting ADSL is very realistic for a home business. The speed difference is incredible. A file that used to take two hours to download now takes me ten minutes. And that definitely cuts down the time I spend at the computer." The equipment for ADSL costs $400 to $600. However, MacDonald says, in her case, "U.S. West offered the equipment for free. I did the installation myself (and I am no techno-geek), and the setup charge was $110." The monthly fee is about $30 to $40 plus ISP fees (about $25 a month). To find out if ADSL service is available in your area, visit the ADSL Forum web site at http://www.adsl.com.

T1 Lines.   The phrase *T1 line* refers to an Internet connection that has several different factions, categorized byte counts—128K T1, 256K T1, 512K T1, and 1024K T1. The advantage of having a T1 line means you do not need to pay a web-page hosting service, because you have the capability to host your own site. T1 lines also require the telephone company physically install a cable into your home. T1 lines are expensive: about $300 per month for the slowest, to over $1,000 per month for the fastest. T1 lines are for guerrillas who want to host their own web sites and anticipate large volumes of traffic. For instance, Todd Weaver, home-based owner of Minstrel Music Network, an online provider of compact discs from Bremerton, Washington, has a T1 line because of the large number of people who access his web site at any given time.

Cable.   There are two types of Internet access available via your cable TV connection: One is hooked to your PC using a cable modem, and the other is hooked to your television through a set-top box, a device that resembles a VCR. Guerrillas who opt for cable hooked to their PCs like it because it is fast (1.5 MB) and always connected.

Individuals who hook cable Internet access to their TVs do so because the system is easy to use and is less expensive than buying a computer (a set-top box costs about $400). For example, Barbara Brabec, speaker and author of the best-selling home-based business book *Homemade Money*, from Naperville, Illinois, chose WebTV for a couple of reasons. She did not have a modem or enough RAM to accommodate an Internet connection, but felt her computer equipment was sufficient for her other needs.

However, there are downsides to both types of cable connections: If you use your computer to fax, you will not be able to use a cable modem; you must use your cable company as your ISP; and, though cable is exceptionally fast, it is not available in every part of the country. Moreover, the speed of cable depends on the number of users on a line. Thus, as more users in a neighborhood get online at the same time, the speed decreases. A cable connection to the Internet costs about $100 to $200 for installation and $30 to $50 in monthly access fees.

Satellite.   You can also get Internet access via satellite. One of the more well-known satellite systems is called DirecPC. Downloading from the Internet via a satellite is fast (about 200K), but to upload or send email, you must use a dial-up line, thus, the satellite does not increase your speed in that direction. Another drawback: Availability is limited. The equipment costs $250 to $1,500, installation costs $250, and Internet access is about $30 a month.

FREE EMAIL AND INTERNET ACCESS

Several companies have emerged that offer free email in exchange for being allowed to place banner advertising on your messages. If you ignore the advertising, this can be a good deal, because it means you do not have to have Internet access in order to have an email address. You simply dial up the company's toll-free telephone number, download your messages, and send replies. The most popular free Internet email service is Juno at http://www.juno.com and (800) 654-JUNO. One drawback is that you are not able to send attachments to your email. However, even with ISP-based email, sometimes attachments arrive garbled or the recipient cannot open them. We prefer to send text-based documents in the body of the email message so that the recipient has no trouble accessing them.

Internet access is available at most major libraries, free. You may even be able to get free email that you can access from your home computer. Ask your librarian. Also, some community colleges provide free access. Laura

Martin-Buhler, editor of *The Gentle Survivalist* newsletter, in St. George, Utah, receives free Internet access at her local community college, even though she is not a student. She recommends visiting the computer labs after school or on weekends, when student demand is low.

HOW TO SELECT THE CHEAPEST INTERNET SERVICE PROVIDER

In the last few years, since the Internet has taken off, there has been an explosion of companies selling Internet access. Some things to consider when evaluating an Internet service provider (ISP) are:

➤ *The number of hours you get for the money.* ISPs charge by the hour (about $5), a flat rate for unlimited hours (about $20), or a flat rate for a certain number of hours, plus an hourly charge if you go over your allotment ($10 to 15 for twenty to thirty hours). If you intend to log on only occasionally to retrieve email and check a few bulletin boards, you can probably get by with a plan that charges by the hour or a flat-rate plan for forty hours a month or less. In contrast, if you plan to log on daily for several hours at a time, it is crucial that you have unlimited access, or you will rack up a fortune in hourly fees. By the way, if you have not had Internet access before, you may be surprised by how many hours you can "lose" by surfing the Net. Finally, by paying your flat fee in advance, as much as a year at a time, you can often earn a discounted rate.

➤ *The location of the dial-up telephone number.* A local or toll-free telephone number is vital, otherwise, you will have to pay long distance telephone charges on top of what you pay for Internet access. Ask potential ISPs for a list of the nearest dial-up numbers, and call the phone company to determine which ones are in your local calling area, if any. Also, if you travel regularly, you will want an ISP that has a toll-free number or a large network of nationwide local numbers, so you can access your email on the road without incurring a bunch of long-distance telephone charges.

➤ *Modem speed.* Like fraction problems in mathematics in which you must find the lowest common denominator, Internet transmissions can only go as fast as the slowest modem. Thus, you want to have a provider whose modems are as fast or faster than yours.

➤ *Service and reliability.* You may remember that, in 1997, many AOL customers could not log on due to busy signals. Some ISPs are plagued by mysterious lapses in service. If you are paying for a service you cannot use, it is a waste of money. An ISP should have immediate, pleasant customer service for troubleshooting, both voice and electronic. If you cannot log on, you need to have a telephone number you can call. Finally, you want a company that is going to be around for a long time, because your email address is linked to that company, which means if they quietly disappear, your email address does, too. Therefore, ask how long the company has been in business before you sign up.

Many of the guerrillas we interviewed had Internet access through Mindspring. Mindspring has several plans, including unlimited access for $19.95, twenty hours per month for $14.95 (additional hours $1/hour), and five hours per month for $6.95 (additional hours $2/hour).

Mindspring
1430 West Peachtree Street NW, Suite 400 • Atlanta, GA 30309
phone: (800) 719-4664 • fax: (404) 287-0883
web site: http://www.mindspring.net

When Diane Rosener, editor of A Penny Saved *newsletter, is in danger of exceeding her allotted Internet hours, she postpones less-crucial Internet research until the following month.*

WEB SITES

If you currently do not have a web site already, consider creating one. Marilyn Ross, home-based publisher of About Books, Inc. in Buena Vista, Colorado, says their business increased about 40 percent after posting their company's web page. And June Langhoff, home-based author of books *Telecom Made Easy* and *The Business Traveler's Survival Guide,* from Pacifica, California, says her web site has garnered her a lot of national publicity that she feels she would not have otherwise received.

A web site lends itself well to a national business that can deliver its products via technology or U.S. Mail. For instance, a home-based clothing manufacturer may do very well with a web site, whereas a local house-cleaning service may not realize enough benefit to make it worth the cost. Consider your market before you spend time and money creating and hosting a site.

If you like to do your own things, web page design is not rocket science. It depends on your level of motivation. If you're good at using software, understanding technical concepts, and structuring things, you can read a book that will take you from start to finish.

**—Jean MacDonald,
Well-Tempered Web Design**

DESIGN IT YOURSELF, OR NOT?

Three factors seemed to be the most important in deciding whether or not to design your own page:

➤ *Money.* Do you have the money to hire a web-page designer? Professional web page designers start at around $50 an hour, with a minimum of about five hours required to design a simple page.

➤ *Time.* Do you have the time required to learn how to design a site yourself? Designing your own site can take a few days or a few weeks.

➤ *Ability.* Do you have the inclination and talents required to learn how to design web sites? To create a site, you need to have strong graphic-design skills and the patience to learn computer commands.

Marc Eisenson, home-based publisher at Good Advice Press and co-author of *Invest in Yourself,* from Elizaville, New York, created his own page, as well as one for his brother and a colleague. "I have the time to do anything I want that is important. There are always changes to be made on the site, so it is handy to be able to do it myself," he says. Moreover, "HTML, hypertext mark-up language, is really very simple. There are great tutorials on the Internet. That is how I learned it. They show you step-by-step exactly how to do it. It takes time and it takes effort, but good web-site designers are expensive. Besides, I've always tried to develop skills that I might need someday." In addition to online tutorials, Eisenson recommends reading *HTML for the World Wide Web* by Elizabeth Castro. He says, "One of the most important ways I taught myself HTML was to focus on the sites that I liked. Then I would click on "View," then on "Document source." In an instant, I could see how others created what appealed to me. Seeing how others make something happen is truly the best way to learn."

Though Eisenson learned HTML, the computer language in which web pages are written, you can also design your site using web authoring computer software, also known as WYSIWYG (pronounced "wizzywig") software; the initials stand for What You See Is What You Get. For instance, Corel's Webmaster, Adobe's PageMill, or Microsoft's FrontPage cost between $100 and $300. If you want to design your own site, Jean MacDonald, home-based web designer at Well-Tempered Web Design, recommends reading *Creative HTML Design* by Lynda and William Weinman.

However, Coleen Sykora, editor of *Workers on Wheels* newsletter, initially tried to create her own site and eventually paid a professional designer. Why? "It didn't run as smoothly as I thought it was going to," she says. Also, "my web designer gives me suggestions of things that I didn't know were possible to do."

It seems as though just about anyone who can move a mouse purports to be a web-page designer. So, how can you find a good one and what should you look for? MacDonald recommends asking for referrals. If you do not know anyone who has had a web page professionally designed, she suggests looking at your local ISP's page for a list of local web-page professionals. You can also look for designers' signatures on pages you like. No matter how you find a professional, always request URLs that showcase their work. "There are people who technically know what they are doing, but the pages are horrible," says MacDonald. She recommends judging a page on overall looks, graphics, functionality, and loading speed.

If you cannot afford a designer, but lack the time and/or ability to design the site yourself, MacDonald recommends hiring a high school or college student. Many students are well-versed in web-page design. She suggests finding a school with a course in HTML, and asking the instructor about talented students. Even talented students are often eager to do web pages for half the rate of professional designers, because they want to add to their portfolios.

Diane Rosener, editor of *A Penny Saved* newsletter, worked with a local high-school teacher and one of the students to design her page. Laura Martin-Buhler's son, who was sixteen at the time, took a class in HTML at a local community college near their home in St. George, Utah, to create a web page for her newsletter, *The Gentle Survivalist.*

Regardless of who designs your site, you should develop an idea of what you want it to look like. To gather ideas, peruse a wide variety of pages. Write down what you like—and dislike. Things to consider: color schemes, types and numbers of graphics, overall structure, ease of use, number of frames, and so on. MacDonald recommends sketching a flow chart, or site map, of how you want the site to be organized.

One tip: Include a link to information on how to contact your company *on every page.* As a journalist, Kathryn contacts companies and individuals for interviews, and she often uses the Internet to obtain contact information. However, if a company's contact information is too difficult to locate on a site, she finds another interview source. Do not lose free media coverage or sales because journalists and customers cannot find your phone number or email address on your site!

Even if you get a professional to design your site, you may want to learn how to maintain, or update, it yourself. Ask your designer a lot of questions and take notes, as many designers will take a few hours showing you how to maintain the site immediately after posting it. Home-based web designer MacDonald says she always takes a few hours to show her clients around their web sites and instruct them on how to update them.

Finally, when your web site is complete, advertise it! A web page is useless if no one looks at it. Of course, you will want to include your URL on all your company's correspondence, but you will also want to register your site with as many search engines as possible. You can register your web site in two ways. First, you can pay a company to register your site with several hundred search engines for $30 to $40. Or, you can visit each search engine yourself, complete the necessary forms, and submit them free. Though visiting each search engine on your own seems time consuming, it is time well spent. Why? Search engines organize sites based on keywords and categories. If your site is inadvertently placed in the wrong category or if the description of your site does not include the keywords your customers use, you will not receive the hits you should. You are best suited to judge which search-engine categories and vocabulary will funnel the most potential customers to your site. Start with the large search engines, such as Yahoo! and WebCrawler, and work your way down to the smaller ones. Consider the time it takes to register as an investment.

The more things you can do for yourself, the more chance you have at succeeding at your business. If times change, you can switch gears if you need to.

—Marc Eisenson,
Good Advice Press

FREE HOSTING

Many home-based guerrillas we interviewed were lucky enough to know someone who was willing to host their site free, or in exchange for a link to another site. However, if you do not know any web wizards, you can still get free hosting.

First, check with your ISP to see if it offers free web pages to its email customers. Some ISPs will allow customers to have a web page. For instance, AOL allows members to have their own small web pages, and even has a directory for business pages. For example, Catherine Groves, home-based publisher of *The Christian*New Age Quarterly* newsletter, from Clifton, New Jersey, has her company's web page hosted by AOL at no cost. She says she finds it adequate because she simply lists one page of information about the periodical.

However, most ISP home pages do not offer any extras, such as multiple email addresses, and cannot accommodate large numbers of visitors. Other ISPs will only permit personal web pages, not business web pages. One way to circumvent this is to use your web page as a *presence*, not an active sales site. In other words, instead of soliciting new customers, you can use a noncommercial, free web site as a portfolio of your work. Then, you can refer potential customers to it for more information.

The other way to get a free site is through one of the many companies now offering them in exchange for allowing banner advertising on your site, similar to the free email companies like Juno.com, only your customers must suffer the ads, not you. To find a list of free web page services, visit http://www.thefreesite.com/freewebpages.htm. (By the way, The Free Site lists tons of good free stuff available on the Internet.) Our favorite free web page service is Angelfire at http://www.angelfire.com because the rules are straightforward, the frequently asked questions (FAQ) section is helpful, and you are permitted to advertise companies and products on your site.

However, free web-site hosting is not without drawbacks. First, the banner ads can be clunky and slow to download, which means that users get bored and leave. Second, you receive a very limited amount of web space (i.e., 5 megabytes), which can be a problem if you want to put a lot of graphics on your site. Third, your web site address could change or disappear.

However, a free web page is a good way to determine if your business will benefit from a web presence. Gary Dunn, publisher of *The Caretaker*

Gazette, has been happily surprised by his free web page. He has had his site hosted free on Angelfire with the same address for three-and-a-half years. Moreover, he asserts that his web site generates more business than any other marketing he does!

> You can't put up a web site and forget about it. It needs constant maintenance.
>
> —Marilyn Ross,
> About Books, Inc.

DOMAIN NAMES

A *domain name* is the Internet's version of a trademark. It is your address on the Internet: http://www.yourdomainname.com. The biggest advantage of a domain name is that you have a simple, easy-to-remember address that no one else can use. Another advantage to having a domain name is that, if you change your web-site hosting service, your address will not change. That means you can have your site hosted by a free web-page hosting service and, then, if you want to move it later, you can do so without sacrificing your Internet identity.

It cost $70 to register a domain name for two years and $119 to reserve one for possible future use. Since 1993, Network Solutions, Inc., also known as interNIC, has been the only provider of domain-name registration. In 1998, the government approved a change in its agreement with Network Solutions, Inc. that will allow more companies to provide domain-name registration. However, at press time, there were no other companies providing this service. For more information about domain-name registration, contact:

Network Solutions, Inc.
505 Huntmar Park Drive • Herndon, VA 20170
phone: (888) 771-3000 • fax: none listed
web site: http://www.networksolutions.com

HOW TO FIND AN INEXPENSIVE WEB-SITE HOSTING SERVICE

If you do not want your customers to be subjected to banner advertising on free web sites, you may want to pay a web page hosting service. Web page hosting service costs vary widely from under $20 per month to over $100 per month. Usually, it is cheaper if your URL is a subdirectory of your web-hosting service instead of a domain name. For instance, if your address is http://www.powertalk.com/yourbusinessname, as opposed to http://www.yourbusinessname.com. One word of caution: many subdirectory URLs have a tilde (~) at the end (http://www .powertalk.com/yourbusiness~). This can throws users off. It is disconcerting and may decrease traffic to your site. Also, the longer your URL, the less likely potential customers will remember the address. Web designer Jean MacDonald agrees: "It makes it difficult to give out your web address. I can't tell you how many people thought my address was 'earthlink.com/tildejeanmacd.' I was constantly saying 'tilde.' You know, that little squiggly in Spanish that's the upper-left shift on your keyboard."

One thing to consider while shopping for a web-page hosting service is how much technical service the company provides. Some will give advice or help you with problems on your web site, whereas others offer the space, period. Jean MacDonald says, "It depends on how much of a risk you are willing to take. You may see a web hosting service advertised on the Internet for $10 a month." But, for that price, "there has to be a drawback. Maybe it is so computerized that they don't even have to touch it. But, if something goes wrong, you're going to have a hard time getting help. You have to decide on what level of reliability you need for your site."

Two other criteria you may want to consider:

➤ The amount of storage space provided. If you want to include multimedia, such as video clips, on your site, you will need at least 5 megabytes (MB). If you are only including text, you may be able to get by with 2 MB.

➤ The amount of bandwidth provided. Bandwidth refers to the number of times your site gets hit over a certain period of time. Jonathan Miller, home-based owner of Reunited, Inc., a company that plans and executes high-school reunions in Fort Lauderdale, Florida, recommends looking for a company that does not charge additional fees for bandwidth over the allotted amount. If you must pay an additional charge, ask how much it costs and shop around. You should not have to pay more than 10¢ per additional gigabyte (GB).

Dozens of web-site hosting services are listed at ISPcheck.com (http://www.ispcheck.com) and The List (http://www.thelist.com). However, in our search for web-site hosting services, one name surfaced repeatedly: Mindspring. Mindspring charges $19.95 per month for its economy account and $49.95 for a standard account.

Mindspring
1430 West Peachtree Street NW, Suite 400 • Atlanta, GA 30309
phone: (800) 719-4664 • fax: (404) 287-0883
web site: http://www.mindspring.net

The web has a certain pressure to it, an immediacy. A web site can be a disadvantage if you don't keep it up. It can look like you're slouching. Customers don't expect you to redo your brochure every month, but they expect you to keep your web site up.

—Neal Lubow,
Ideas By-The-Hour

CHAPTER 7
SKINFLINT WAYS TO TRIM THE COST OF FURNITURE AND EQUIPMENT

Furniture is one of the easiest places for home-based guerrillas to save money. We rarely entertain clients in our offices, so we are free to use mismatched tables, old filing cabinets, and cinderblock bookcases. What we save on furniture, however, we often spend on equipment.

Unlike furniture which usually no one sees but you, equipment—or the results of it—is seen daily through your interactions with clients and colleagues. An ancient dot-matrix printer cannot compare to a laser printer. A computer blows a typewriter away. Home-based guerrillas' images are created through correspondence, so it is vital that every communiqué appears professional. That does not mean buying every top-of-the-line techno-gadget advertised. Instead, it means assessing your needs and finding a way to meet them without sacrificing quality or going broke.

FURNITURE

ALTERNATIVE FURNITURE

Some people get excited about decorating their new office space without giving any thought to function or finances. The most important thrifty rules to remember are: Less is better, and avoid paying retail. The only pieces of furniture you cannot do without are a desk and a chair though, eventually, you may want tables, bookcases, or filing cabinets. Before you dash out to the retail furniture store and plunk down $1,200 for an oak roll-top, consider what a desk really is: a flat surface on which to write, situated far enough off the ground for your legs to fit underneath comfortably. If you look at it that way, many objects fit the bill.

As Charles Long recommends in *How to Survive Without a Salary,* "Examine the need in terms of the objective, not the solution. Consumers say, 'We need a new car,' when they ought to be saying, 'We need a means of getting to work, getting out of town on weekends, to the in-laws at Christmas.' 'What will perform the function?' leads to more interesting, and cheaper, answers than 'What do I need to buy?' "

Think of the functions a desk must perform, instead of where to find a traditional desk, and you may come up with economical alternatives. Dig through your attic or basement to find:

➤ A door, countertop, or children's blackboard which can be laid across two sawhorses, stacks of milk crates, file cabinets, or piles of large books

➤ A sewing table

➤ A long hall table

➤ A card table

➤ A dining or kitchen table

➤ Lawn or garden furniture

Brainstorm on how to use what you already have. Long tables—the kind you see at church dinners—make great desks, because they give you a lot of space.

Susan Lannis, home-based professional organizer at Organization Plus, recommends, "Try to imagine what you want to have on your desk. What is in that drawer? How comfortable is it to reach this? How am I actually going to use it? How is it going to hold up? One of my clients made the mistake of buying some pieces that didn't physically fit in the space he allowed for them. They didn't hold what he wanted to put on them. Take measurements. How big is your phone, file-folder system, computer, and so on? Furniture is an investment. You want to be comfortable over the long haul."

Another option is to build your own desk. Maybe your father-in-law is handy with tools, and can make you a desk out of scavenged wood pallets. For instance, Neal Lubow, home-based owner of Ideas By-The-Hour, a marketing and communications company in Portland, Oregon, has two desks, both of them made from doors. One is mounted atop two filing cabinets, the other on an old drafting-table base. The second one cost him only $20 in materials.

If no one in your family can wield a hammer without ending up in the emergency room, or you just moved 2,500 miles with nothing more than a suitcase, you may be forced to consider other furniture sources.

NEW FURNITURE SOURCES

If you are partial to new furniture, warehouse membership clubs, such as Costco or Sam's Club, may be the solution. The simplest wood-veneer desk without drawers costs approximately $100. However, if you are not already a member of the warehouse club, you should also factor in membership dues (usually about $35 per year) when assessing a deal.

Another way to cut the cost of new furniture is to buy an unfinished piece of furniture and finish it yourself. For example, Kathryn bought an unfinished oak filing cabinet at a furniture store and saved herself several hundred dollars by staining the cabinet herself. It took a few hours, but she enjoyed the work, and was able to stain the cabinet so that it closely matched the other furniture in her home. This was important to her because the filing cabinet doubled as a bedside table in a guest bedroom.

USED FURNITURE OUTLETS AND THRIFT STORES

If you are not overly concerned about aesthetics, look at used furniture outlets that buy desks from companies that have gone out of business or remodeled. Such stores can be found in the *Yellow Pages* under "Office Furniture & Equipment—Used" or in classified advertisements. They sometimes keep odd hours, such as on Mondays, Wednesdays, and Fridays only, but the deals are worth the inconvenience. Expect to pay under $150 for a decent metal desk and $120 for a large swivel chair. Kathryn bought her current six-drawer metal desk at one of these stores for $90, and they delivered it free. The desk is not perfect; the drawers stick a little and one of them squeaks, but it is functional.

Thrift or consignment shops may also carry a limited amount of used furniture, though it sells quickly. Marilyn Zelinsky, home-based journalist and author of *Practical Home Office Solutions*, from Fairfield, Connecticut, bought a lateral two-drawer filing cabinet at a Salvation Army store for $22.

OTHER BUSINESSES

Eliminate the middleman by going directly to the source of used furniture. Look for companies that have moved, downsized, remodeled, or gone bankrupt. Chances are, the company wants to unload the old furniture and has no idea how much to charge. Such a climate is ripe for bargains. Call the company and ask to speak to the manager or owner. Always talk to the person who has the ability to negotiate a deal.

Ask at church, Kiwanis, or Rotary if anyone knows of a business that has extra furniture cluttering up the storage room. Kathryn's father picked up a swivel chair for $15, and several desks for $75 each, when he mentioned what he wanted to an acquaintance. The man knew of a trade association that had recently moved into a new building and wanted to get rid of some furniture. Her dad was thrilled with his bargain. He estimates the desks alone would have cost $500 each if they had been new. The trade association even offered to deliver them free!

Focus. Find something that you really love and can put your energy behind 100 percent. At times, the object of our affection requires 110 percent or even more, just to keep our heads above water and financially solvent. Without the will to go the extra mile, especially during periods of stress, the product quality will begin to suffer.

—Laura Martin-Buhler,
editor of *The Gentle Survivalist*

UNIVERSITY SURPLUS OFFICES

University surplus offices are little-known treasure houses. These offices collect old furniture, computers, and laboratory equipment from all over the campus, then sell them at rock-bottom prices to get rid of them. Do not be surprised if you see everything from computer monitors to incubators to Bunsen burners, but if you pick through the bizarre junk, you will find deals. For instance, Kathryn bought her last six-drawer metal desk at a university-surplus office for only $22! If she had not been so flabbergasted when the man quoted her the price, she may have haggled and spent even less.

The disadvantages to these bargain basements are that they are open extremely limited hours—usually one day a week or month for three or four hours—and have an unpredictable selection. However, if you are willing to scrounge around, it is definitely worth investigating. Look under the subheading "Surplus" under the nearest university's listing in the *White Pages*.

MILITARY SURPLUS AUCTIONS

The government buys large quantities of everything from office furniture to aircraft parts. However, the military is not able to use all of it, or only needs to use it for a short time. Afterward, the government must get rid of it. The Defense Reutilization and Marketing Service (DRMS) is the division in charge of reusing or reselling property that no longer meets the government's needs. Government property is often of better quality than similar civilian goods, so even used equipment can still be in good shape and serviceable.

The DRMS holds auctions year round at its Defense Reutilization and Marketing Offices (DRMOs) throughout the world. DRMOs are usually located near a military base, and the sales are open to the general public. Anyone over age eighteen can purchase goods at these auctions.

Each sale has an Invitation for Bid (IFB) catalog that gives the property listing and description; method of sale; Bid Opening Date (BOD), which lists the date and time that bids are opened; and the terms and conditions associated with the property and sale. To find out about a sale, you just need to get on the local DRMO's mailing list to receive a catalog. For more information, visit the DRMS's web site at http://www.drms.dla.mil.

> I'm not trying to impress anyone with my office. Most of my clients are multimillionaires. They are usually impressed that I'm not charging them an arm and a leg for luxuries.
>
> —Bruce Falkenhagen, environmental consultant

GARAGE SALES, ESTATE SALES, AND CLASSIFIED ADVERTISEMENTS

These secondhand markets can yield bargains, if you are willing to hunt and negotiate, since merchandise and prices vary widely. Look for multifamily or subdivision garage sales. Before visiting an estate auction, determine how much you are willing spend and do not get caught in a bidding war. Shel Horowitz, home-based author of *Marketing Without Megabucks*, bought most of his furniture at various yard sales and saved a bundle.

The prices of furniture in classified ads is usually higher than that of garage sales, simply because the people advertising are often trying to earn a little money instead of just clearing out space. And they need to cover the cost of the ad. Even so, Laurie Dry, a home-based photographic supply consultant, snagged a deal: a four-drawer, solid-oak filing cabinet for $50.

Also, some shopper publications and local newspapers have absolutely free classified sections. The advertisements are free and the things in them are free for the hauling. Such ads allow people to unload things cluttering up their homes. For example, one week in our local paper, the absolutely free section listed, among other things: an organ bench, two chairs, and a very large desk.

Ron Renner, home-based owner of Geppetto's Woodworks in Vancouver, Washington, says that older furniture is often of better quality than new. For one thing, it has withstood the test of time. Renner prefers desks made of solid stock, meaning one piece of solid wood, as opposed to veneer, which is high quality, thinly sliced wood laid on top of another piece. "The problem with the veneer is it's fragile," explains Renner. "It's easier to damage and harder to repair."

Since we're not a walk-in place, we set things up in ways that things are practical. We built our own desks with pieces of scrap wood. We just pick the cheapest way to be functional, rather than to look beautiful.

—Steve Carlson,
Upper Access Books

FRIENDS, FAMILY, ACQUAINTANCES, AND STRANGERS

The best price, of course, is free. How many times after you have bought a widget, has a friend said, "I wish you would have told me you were looking for one of those! I have an old one in the basement I would have given you for nothing." Before you buy, ask around. Offer to "take the furniture off of their hands" and free up space in their house. Or clean out an elderly family member's basement or attic in exchange for what you find. Judy Lawrence, owner of Common Cents Budget Consulting in Albuquerque, New Mexico, acquired her desk this way. Years ago, a neighbor asked Lawrence to haul an old desk to the dump in her truck. Instead, she stripped the solid oak desk and refinished it. It turned out beautifully.

Be sure to ask people who are moving or college students who have recently graduated. When Kathryn moved cross-country, she gave her heavy $22 desk to a friend who moved into his own apartment and started a Ph.D. program. The catch was he had to move it out of her second-story apartment. Each thought they had gotten the better end of the deal.

In many college towns, during the week that school starts in the fall and the week it ends in the spring, the streets are littered with furniture free for the taking. By the end of each week, all but the true junk has been claimed by bargain hunters. The same furniture probably has rotated throughout cities for generations.

CHAIRS

A chair is the most important piece of furniture in your office. Why? You may sit in it for eight, ten, twelve hours a day, six or seven days a week— an inferior chair will cause you back and neck problems. Stuart Watson, a home-based business writer from Portland, Oregon, says he bought a cheap chair and "it drove him nuts." He finally bought another, good quality chair. Like Watson, the vast majority of the home-based guerrillas we interviewed said they spent the bulk of their furniture budgets on high-quality chairs.

Furniture expert Ron Renner says a chair is the most abused piece of furniture in an office. Therefore, good, used chairs are rare. Moreover, they can be dangerous. Author Marilyn Zelinsky warns against buying chairs with four casters or feet. New chairs are built with five casters, but older chairs usually have only four, and they are prone to tipping over. One of Zelinsky's friends was seriously injured when, while reaching for the telephone, his four-caster chair tipped over on a concrete floor.

Randy Rabourn, CSP, CPE, project manager at the University of Michigan Center for Ergonomics in Ann Arbor recommends selecting a chair that can be easily adjusted up and down and has arm rests that do not interfere with job performance. No one chair will fit everyone, so you need to determine what type works best for you.

To buy a high-quality chair, Renner advises going to a chair manufacturer. Of course, that can be costly. Edith Flowers Kilgo, home-based editor of *Creative Downscaling*, paid $250 for a chair that was custom designed to her specifications, and that was an exceptional bargain, according to Renner and Zelinsky. They estimate that a good chair costs around $1,000. Zelinsky recommends looking for chair manufacturers and wholesale distributors in a business-to-business *Yellow* or *White Pages*, which you can find at the library. Or, look in your own local *Yellow Pages* under "Office Furniture & Equipment—Dealers" for authorized dealers of brand names, such as Herman Miller. "In just about every town, there is a dealership showroom that works with corporations like Steelcase, Haworth, and Herman Miller. They do not cater to the public. But some of them will sell to the public, if you ask," says Zelinsky. To get a deal, Zelinsky recommends asking if they have any old inventory they want to get rid of. " 'Old' to them is six months to a year," she says.

Regardless of where you obtain your furniture, Susan Lannis, a home-based professional organizer, offers this advice: "Whatever you're looking at, it is important to test it. Sit at that desk in that chair for as long as you can. If you can't sit on that chair for fifteen minutes without fidget-

> I've seen people spend $8,000 on a new computer sys-
> tem and $39.95 on a chair they'll be sitting in eight
> hours a day. They end up spending more on chiroprac-
> tic bills. The two most important pieces of office furni-
> ture are a door that closes and a good chair.
>
> —John Knowlton,
> editor of *Business @ Home*

ing, you'll be fidgeting all day. A desk and a chair are worth some inves-
tigation and time."

ALTERNATIVE OFFICES

Since we work at home and are free to use mismatched, but functional,
furniture, our offices are not always conducive to meeting with clients.
However, on occasion we may have the need to meet with customers
face to face. Instead of scrambling for a drastic, expensive solution, such
as buying new, matching office furniture, consider these inexpensive
alternatives:

➤ Go to the client's office or home. Clients will be impressed that you
  make house calls.

➤ Meet at a centrally located hotel, coffee shop, or restaurant. Choose
  one that is not too noisy, so that you will not have trouble hearing one
  another. Marcia Yudkin, speaker and author of *6 Steps to Free Publicity*,
  from Boston, Massachusetts, recommends Starbucks coffee shops. "It's
  good because you can sit there for two hours and they don't mind."

➤ Rent a conference room at a nearby office complex. Jaclyn Jeffrey, home-
  based owner of Allegiant Partners, a marketing information-gathering
  firm in Weston, Connecticut, says that she rents conference rooms for
  $30 to $40 an hour from a franchise office complex called American
  Executive Center. Jeffrey says the company does not advertise that they
  rent conference rooms to nontenants, so you'll need to ask.

EQUIPMENT

LEASING

Leasing equipment is rarely a good deal because, like car leases, you never stop paying. You use the equipment during its largest depreciation period, and do not reap the benefits of ownership later. However, in two cases, leasing may be the best option, at least temporarily.

One, you have very little capital to start your business. A business that needs a computer or other equipment immediately may not have enough money to buy a computer outright. In this case, it may be acceptable to lease equipment to keep the business running until you can afford to buy.

Or, two, your business is such that you need top-of-the-line equipment every two or three years. For example, Dave Wampler, home-based owner of the Simple Living Network, leases because he needs the latest computer equipment as his business is transacted almost entirely online. If you decide to lease, Wampler recommends insisting upon a two-year lease contract, as opposed to three or four, in order to reap the benefits of the latest technology.

> I've got dinosaur equipment. I know how it works. If it ain't broke, don't fix it.
>
> —Gary Dunn,
> publisher of *The Caretaker Gazette*

MAIL-ORDER COMPUTER COMPANIES

Some people prefer local computer companies, because they fear that if they have a problem with their equipment, they can take the machine back to the store and not have to deal with shipping. However, if you know what you want and are willing to sacrifice a little hand-holding, mail-order computer companies offer top-of-the-line equipment at very attractive prices. Moreover, with the Internet, it is much easier to locate computer information and mail-order companies.

Here are some mail-order computer companies:

Gateway
PO Box 2000 • 610 Gateway Drive • North Sioux City, SD 57049
phone: (800) 846-4208 • fax: (605) 232-2023
web site: http://www.gateway.com

PC Connection
Route 101A, 730 Milford Road • Merrimack, NH 03054-4631
phone: (888) 213-0259 • fax: (603) 423-5766
web site: http://pcconnection.com

Many home-based guerrillas, especially those in publishing and graphic design, prefer MacIntosh computers. However, if you have a MacIntosh computer, you have probably noticed the dismal selection of MacIntosh products at computer superstores. For you there is The Mac Zone and MacConnection. Both offer mail-order MacIntosh hardware, software, and accessories:

The Mac Zone
707 South Grady Way • Renton, WA 98055-3233
phone: (800) 248-0800 • fax: (425) 430-3500
web site: http://www.zones.com

MacConnection
Route 101A, 730 Milford Road • Merrimack, NH 03054-4631
phone: (888) 213-0259 • fax: (603) 423-5766
web site: http://macconnection.com

Michelle Foy, home-based owner of Dynamic Alternatives, a computer and general management consulting firm in Highland Park, Illinois, gets tremendous discounts on her equipment by buying discontinued models. For example, she got a handheld computer that was originally $450 for only $80!

Another way to cut the cost of equipment is to buy last year's model. Oftentimes, last year's printer, copier, or fax machine will accomplish all the tasks you need for a fraction of the price of this year's model.

ALTERNATIVE COMPUTER SOLUTIONS

If you still cannot find what you want at a reasonable price, there are a few other options. For example, to find the best bargains on the Internet, you can use a lowest-price search service, such as http://search.cnet.com, which solicits what you want to buy and what price you want to pay, then explores the web for a vendor.

Steve Carlson, home-based publisher of Upper Access Books, has discovered that local companies that can custom-make a computer for you charge much less than the name brands of similar quality. Home-based Gary Foreman, editor of *The Dollar Stretcher* newsletter, agrees: "You can find some local dealers that will assemble a PC to your specifications that will save you a lot of money." To find such companies, look in the *Yellow Pages* under "Computers & Computer Equipment Dealers—New" for advertisements of companies that custom-build computers.

Another alternative to buying new is to upgrade your existing system, especially if all you need is more memory. Why throw away a perfectly good keyboard or monitor? Home-based Gerri Detweiler, speaker and author of *The Ultimate Credit Handbook,* recently upgraded her computer for a fraction of what it would have cost her to buy a new one. Many of the local companies that custom-build computers are also happy to help you upgrade.

From paper clips to equipment, try to look for things that are still serviceable.

—Marc Eisenson,
Good Advice Press

THE HIDDEN COSTS
• •

Before buying any piece of equipment, Susan Lannis, a professional organizer at Organization Plus, recommends researching the cost of the consumables, such as ink cartridges. One model may appear cheaper than another but, if you factor in the cost of the consumables, the more expensive model may turn out to be a better value. For example, ABC printer costs $400 and XYZ printer costs $800. Initially, the $400 printer may seem like a better deal. However, ABC printer's ink cartridges cost $75 each, and need to be replaced monthly, while XYZ printer's ink cartridges cost $50 each, and need to be replaced every three months. One year of operating expenses will look like this:

$$ABC \ \$400 + (\$75 \times 12) = \$1{,}300$$

$$XYZ \ \$800 + (\$50 \times 4) = \$1{,}000$$

Therefore, in the long run, XYZ printer will cost less.

USED EQUIPMENT
• •

Used equipment is cheap, but, let the buyer beware. If you know a lot about computers or enjoy fixer-upper projects, you may be able to pick up some incredible bargains on used equipment from garage sales, classified ads, and such. For example, Marc Eisenson, home-based publisher of Good Advice Press in Elizaville, New York, is a self-proclaimed tinkerer. All of his office equipment is used, and he keeps every piece running.

However, if you are unfamiliar with how the machine works—as opposed to how to operate it—or are unwilling to spend the time required to learn, you may want to stick with new equipment or used equipment that comes from reliable sources. Friends, family, acquaintances, and strangers are great sources for reliable, used equipment. Ask around. Home-based tax consultant Anthony Applebaum, EA, from San Diego, California, got his fax machine from a cousin. "He had bought a plain paper fax and this thermal fax was just sitting on the shelf," says Applebaum. "I offered to pay him for it, but he said 'No, it is just gathering dust.'"

**Assess your needs. If you don't need high-end comput-
ing, you can get some real deals.**

—Michele Foy,
Dynamic Alternatives, Inc.

EDUCATIONAL DISCOUNTS

If you are eligible, you can receive enormous discounts on computers
and software from public-university bookstores. Check with your public-
university bookstore for eligibility requirements but, typically, all students and instructors are eligible and, occasionally, state employees and
parents of students. Editor Edith Flowers Kilgo bought all her computer
equipment and software from the state-university bookstore at 30 to 50
percent less than retail.

If you qualify, you can also mail order computer software from Campus
Technology. The company's catalog is small, but it lists all the major software manufacturers and popular programs. The company requires that
you mail a copy of your school-identification card and sign a purchase
agreement that states you are affiliated with a post-secondary school and
will not resell the product for two years. One caveat: Compare prices of
any software with a local retail establishment. We discovered that Campus Technology was much cheaper in some instances . . . and higher in
others. For example, OfficeMax charges $139.99 for Microsoft FrontPage
98, while Campus Technology charges only $71—almost 50 percent less!
On the other hand, OfficeMax charges $179.99 for Windows 98 and Cam-
pus Technology charges $205.00. Therefore, you can garner great savings,
but shop around first.

Campus Technology
751 Miller Drive, SE • Leesburg, VA 20175-8920
phone: (800) 543-8188 • fax: (703) 777-3871
web site: http://www.campustech.com

SHAREWARE AND FREEWARE

Shareware is software that is downloaded from the Internet on good faith, meaning that after the free trial period you are supposed to send the shareware developer a check. Most shareware programs are inexpensive: $10 to $20. If you do not send money, some shareware programs stop functioning after a thirty-day free trial period. Others just rely upon your conscience, occasionally reminding you with pop-up banners to "register" your software with the creator.

But make no mistake: Shareware is not shoddy. Often times, it is comparable or superior to store-bought software. Todd Weaver, home-based owner of Minstrel Music Network, an online company that sells compact discs from Bremerton, Washington, gets nearly all of his software from http://www.shareware.com. Another good source of shareware is http://www.passtheshareware.com. You can download all sorts of handy tools, such as calendars and database programs.

Even better than shareware is freeware. Freeware is free software available to download from the Internet. Again, there is a lot of high-quality software available free of charge. For example, http://thefreesite.com/software.htm lists twenty categories of freeware programs, including antivirus software and HTML utilities.

It is a good idea to spend money on some things that save money, such as virus protection software. If you get a virus, you might be out of work for two or three days fixing it.

—June Langhoff,
author of *Telecom Made Easy*

RECEIPTS AND WARRANTY INFORMATION

Hold onto your receipts and warranty information, in case your equipment fails you. Many computer companies offer replacement machines while yours is being fixed or replaced, but you must have your receipt to cash in on warranty work. Kathryn had owned her computer monitor for over two years when it died. Luckily, it came with a three-year warranty. Because she was able to dig up the receipt and warranty information, the company sent her a brand-new replacement.

Also, use technical support helplines. When Kathryn's fax machine started blinking "out of paper/paper jam" when it had paper and was not jammed, she randomly pushed buttons. She took the paper out, opened the case, replaced the cartridge, and so on. Occasionally, the fax would spring to life . . . only to die again after receiving a few pages. After living with it for a while, she called toll-free directory assistance and got the manufacturer's customer service telephone number. Within fifteen minutes, with the help of the support technician, Kathryn had fixed the problem. The fax has worked flawlessly ever since.

ALTERNATIVES TO OWNING

If you cannot afford to buy equipment, you do not have to do without. You can borrow or rent from lots of sources. For instance, you can use computers free at the library. University or large metropolitan libraries are your best bets. Laura Martin-Buhler, editor of *The Gentle Survivalist* newsletter in St. George, Utah, uses the computers at the local community college, even though she is not a student. She recommends visiting the computer labs after school or on weekends when the student demand is low. Printers are also available at the library, usually at a cost of 10¢ per printed page.

Another option: Register for an inexpensive continuing education class and borrow the school's equipment for a fraction of the cost of buying. For example, home-based editor of the newsletter *Workers on Wheels*, Coleen Sykora, says her husband Bob has taken low-cost woodworking project courses, which allow him to use the kind of equipment that he cannot haul in their trailer. Even if you have space to store equipment, you may want to take a cue from Bob. Buy only the tools that are essential. For fancy tools you rarely use, borrow or rent instead.

Also, you can rent computers and printers by the hour at copy shops like Kinko's ($10 to $12 per hour plus $1 to $2 per printed page). If you choose the rental route, write and revise your documents at home, then simply type them when you are on the clock. You do not want to spend money staring at the blinking cursor wondering what to say.

Clients often ask, "Can you fax it to me?" Your answer should be "Yes." But that does not mean you need to buy a fax machine. Copy centers, like Mail Boxes, Etc. and Kinko's, will send and receive faxes for you for about $2 per page. Keep their fax number by the telephone so you can rattle it off to clients as if it were in your office. "I rarely fax out, so we eliminated the fax bill. It is more cost-effective for me to use OfficeMax or Mailboxes, Etc. to fax, as I do this so rarely (once a month or less)," says editor Edith Flowers Kilgo. "I discovered a lot of people want to fax in to me, but most of what they want to send is junk (press releases, etc.), so by telling them I have no fax I eliminate a lot of unwanted paper coming into the office. If I had to receive a fax (this has not happened once in four years) I would ask that it be sent to Mailboxes, Etc."

Or, if you freelance part-time, you can ask your daytime employer if you can work out an arrangement that allows you to reimburse the company for any faxes you send (receiving costs only pennies for the paper and toner; sending can cost a lot in long distance telephone charges). Finally, you can make arrangements with friends, family, or other home-based guerrillas to share their equipment. Some businesses have little use for a fax machine, copier, or color printer, for example, and would do well to borrow rather than buy.

When you fantasize about fancy equipment, keep in mind a phrase we heard on an audiocassette by motivational speaker Dr. Bobbie Sommers: "Be. Do. Have." In other words, consider yourself an entrepreneur, sell your product or service, and then you will earn enough money to buy the things a home-based guerrilla supposedly needs, such as a photocopier, fax machine, voice-activated tape recorder, and so on. Do not buy things in an attempt to "be" an entrepreneur. You already are an entrepreneur, because you believe you are!

CHAPTER 8

INEXPENSIVE MARKETING AND ADVERTISING OPPORTUNITIES

Marketing is important for every business, but it is especially important for home-based businesses because home-based guerrillas cannot rely on traditional business avenues, such as foot traffic. No one will know your business exists unless you spend some time and money marketing it.

The best way to market your product or service without spending a fortune is through publicity, or getting the media to talk about your company. Publicity gives your business exposure, but it also gives you credibility, because your company is presented by an unbiased third party. In contrast, most advertising is expensive. "I have never spent money on paid advertising," says Barbara Brabec, author of the best-selling home-based business book, *Homemade Money*. Thus, plan to spend the bulk of your marketing dollars on publicity campaigns, followed by tightly focused niche advertising.

SHOULD YOU HIRE A PUBLIC-RELATIONS AGENT?

Most of the guerrillas we interviewed did all of their own marketing. However, the few who had hired PR agents were glad they did. Jeff Berner, home-based author of *The Joy of Working from Home: Making a Life While Making a Living,* says that until recently he did all of his own promotion. However, he found that he could not generate the amount of publicity he wanted on a regular basis. Since he hired a public relations agent a few months ago, he has had a radio interview almost every day. "Before publicity was intermittent, now it's consistent," says Berner. One of the main advantages to hiring a professional is that you gain media contacts. If you are not particularly media savvy, this can be a valuable benefit. The key questions in deciding whether or not to hire a professional are:

➤ *Can you afford one?* Most professional PR agents work on retainer and charge several hundred dollars per month ($800 and up). A few charge by the hour. In that case, the cost is around $75 to $125 per hour. One way to reduce the cost is to hire a PR agent by the hour for specific tasks, such as crafting a press release or arranging a book signing. Then, do the less-skilled labor yourself, such as preparing press-release packets for mailing. This strategy maximizes the PR agent's expertise.

➤ *Do you like marketing and want to spend your time on it?* Some guerrillas enjoy the challenge of crafting press releases, tracking down media contacts, and conducting interviews. Others would prefer to spend all their time working on their craft, be it woodworking, writing, or bookkeeping.

➤ *Do you have the stamina and persistence to do cold calls, letters, or email on a regular basis?* For marketing to be effective, consistency is key.

When you are starting out in business, a PR agent is probably well beyond your budget. However, once you become established, you may want to consider hiring a professional so that you can spend your time on your craft. Calculate the time you spend on marketing, and compare it to your hourly wage and the cost of hiring a PR agent. Would you be better off hiring a professional and concentrating on what you do best?

Or, perhaps you like the thrill of the marketing chase—tracking media contacts, pursuing leads, pouncing on interviews—in which case, you can keep your marketing budget lean.

WORD OF MOUTH

The majority of the guerrillas we interviewed said they attracted most of their customers through word of mouth. Word of mouth, or referrals from customers, is the best marketing you can get. Potential customers more readily believe the words of their friends and family than those of advertisers. Moreover, new clients who come via referrals are usually good clients; they are easy to work with and pay on time. As Nipomo, California environmental consultant Bruce Falkenhagen puts it, "I only work for someone who comes to me with references. For any work I do, I am extending them credit. If they don't pay, I've just lost money."

So, how can you generate more word of mouth referrals?

The first step is to overdeliver on your promises with smashing service and a terrific product. Melissa Giovagnoli, home-based lecturer and author of *Meganetworking* and *Make Your Connections Count* from Shaumburg, Illinois, likes to send new clients little gifts with clever sayings to keep in contact. For example, she buys a nice new pair of socks from Nordstrom's and wraps them up with a card that says, "In anticipation of knocking your socks off, here is a replacement pair."

The second step is to take your time with customers. Do not rush through your dealings with them. Give them personalized attention. If they need a little hand-holding, give it graciously. Kathy Dimond, a communications and public-policy strategist from Portland, Oregon, says, "Most of my marketing efforts come in personal time spent. I do a lot of face-to-face communication. I'm not buying advertising or printing. But it is not free, there is the cost of the hours I could bill out. But instead, I extend myself personally." Dan Cerveny, home-based musician, and owner of Czech Polka and Waltz Video Production Company from Omaha, Nebraska, agrees. Many of his customers are elderly and appreciate old-fashioned service. Some call him without a clear idea of what they want to order. Cerveny says that he just tries to be as patient and helpful as possible. "Take time with customers and they will become loyal."

The third step in generating word of mouth is to ask, ask, ask. Enlist current customers' help in getting the word out, but do not ask the tired, old question, "Do you know anyone who can use my services?" Instead, Giovagnoli suggests you narrow your request. "First of all, people don't like that phrase," says Giovagnoli. "Second, most people go into brain lock. They know lots of different people. If you're specific, the more it stands out in people's minds." For example, an accountant might say, "I am looking for a client who lives in Northville, has an employee payroll, and needs regular bookkeeping assistance in addition to tax-preparation services."

Author Jeff Berner says that he is no longer shy about asking for letters of recommendation. When clients say, "Jeff, that was a good job.' I say, 'Would you be willing to write me a testimonial that I can use on my web site?' They always say yes."

Doing a good job is the best thing you can do to get referrals.

—**Anthony Applebaum,
EA, tax consultant**

PRESS RELEASES

"I chase the media," admits Gary Dunn, home-based publisher of *The Caretaker Gazette* newsletter. Dunn sends sample copies, makes cold calls to radio talk-show hosts, and sends unsolicited email messages to select individuals. "Some of it is time intensive, but I've found it's worth it." It certainly is. As a result of his marketing efforts, *The Caretaker Gazette* has been mentioned in over 1,000 newspapers, and Gary was recently interviewed on a talk show on National Public Radio (NPR).

Publicity is like word of mouth in that it is praise from an unbiased third party. The difference is the reporter talking about your business is telling a few hundred or thousand potential customers, instead of a handful. So, how do you get the attention of the media? It is not as elusive as it may seem. Gaining publicity is just a matter of telling the right people about your business in a way that makes it newsworthy.

The key to doing this is to write and send a press release. There are dozens of books on how to craft a winning press release, but the main idea is to write a one-page news article that includes:

➤ a snappy title

➤ the words "For Immediate Release"

➤ media contact information: your name, address, telephone number, web site, email address, and so on, and the contact information of your public-relations agent, if you have one

➤ the reason that your product or service is newsworthy at this time, also known as the *hook*, such as a connection between your business and current events

➤ the basic facts: the who, what, where, when, and why

➤ a few quotations from you or one of your customers to spice it up

Once you have polished your press release, the next step is to figure out who to send it to. To create a mailing list you will need to decide which publications, radio shows, or talk shows are influential among your potential customers. To find associations and periodicals for particular industries, go to the library and look in the reference section for *Writer's Market, Bacon's Magazine Directory, Gale Directory of Publications and Broadcast Media,* and the *Encyclopedia of Associations.* Remember to include local media on your list.

Press releases are effective. For example, Barbara Winter, home-based author of *Making a Living Without a Job* and publisher of the newsletter Winning Ways, says, "I sent my first press release to the local paper. The next day a reporter called me up and did this huge story about me and my business. I hadn't even had my first customer yet! Then my phone started ringing."

One way to make your business newsworthy is create press releases that attach your product or service to national holidays. For instance, a greeting-card illustrator might craft a press release about Grandparents' Day, mentioning his new line of appropriate cards. Susan Lannis, home-based professional organizer and owner of Organization Plus, says she has had fantastic success using holidays as hooks. She uses *Chase's Calendar of Events*, a book that lists every national holiday, from the familiar Valentine's Day (February 14) to the obscure National Sleep Day (April 1). "I went through and wrote down any kind of holiday I could connect myself to," says Lannis. Then she took her list to the National Association of Professional Organizers and together they created new organization-related holidays to fill in the gaps between the holidays that were already in place. "We tried to spread them out." Then, Lannis compiled a twelve-month public-relations calendar. Lannis says this approach has garnered her several television interviews. "Once you become a good resource, they will come to you," she says.

Terry Morin, a home-based cartoonist at Terrapin Illustrations in Portland, Oregon, has found "new-product release" columns in magazines to be a great way to gain free publicity. Morin sells many of his cartoons to dental offices as appointment reminder cards and uses these columns to advertise his latest designs. He explains, "In some of the trade magazines, there are sections where companies can submit photographs or digital files to show what is new in the industry. They do a little write-up with the company information. Not all the magazines do it, but a number of them do. It's pretty effective." Morin adds that most magazines have a three- or four-month lead time, so keep that in mind if the product or service you want to advertise is seasonal.

Also, he says that some of the magazines add you to their reader service cards where every number on the cards inside the magazine corresponds with a product. If a reader circles your number and mails it back, the magazine passes the name and address along to you. "They even send me address labels to send out samples. And it's all free," he says. Morin anticipates that, eventually, the magazine will ask him to buy some advertising. But, until then, he plans to take advantage of the free publicity. Look in trade magazines serving your industry for "what's new" columns and then address press releases to the editors who write them. In this case, sending a photograph or a sample of your product can make a big difference in whether it is featured or not.

Pay attention to who your customers are and why they are buying. Be inside the experience of your customers. Give them more than they expect.

—Al Siebert,
Practical Psychology Press

MEDIA GIVEAWAYS

Another way to get the media's attention is to offer something free or inexpensive to their readers or viewers. Author Melissa Giovagnoli finds that she gets the best media response when she prints booklets that list tips related to her expertise, such as "101 Ways To Meganetwork." She creates a twenty-page booklet so that it fits inside a #10 envelope. Then she sends them to small- and medium-sized newspapers that are hungry for news copy. She gives the newspapers permission to reprint any of the tips, provided they include her name, address, and the statement that she will send a booklet to any reader who sends $5 and a self-addressed, stamped envelope (SASE). Giovagnoli says the booklets have been a phenomenal success. Though she did not print them as a moneymaker, she has made money on them. "The best part is I got the booklets printed for free," she says. How? "I asked." The printer used the booklets to showcase his talents and market to new clients as well.

Editor Edith Flowers Kilgo also gives away booklets in exchange for an SASE or $1 to cover postage. "This gives us an opportunity to send requesters our sales pitch along with the information they requested," she says. "If you send me an SASE, and I send you my materials, I get to market to you for free." One of Kilgo's most successful booklets is her *Simplicity/Frugality Resource Guide,* a twenty-page guide listing web sites, books, newsletters, magazines, videotapes, and products of interest to individuals looking to downscale. Guerrillas might consider creating a similar guide for their industries. For instance, a computer consultant might create a software-review guide or a favorite web-site list.

Send free samples of your product or gift certificates for your services to the disc jockeys at local radio stations. DJs have some discretion over what they say on the air and, if they like your product or service, they may plug your company on the radio, free.

LETTERS TO THE EDITOR

One way to get into print with minimal expense is to write a letter to editors of publications that your potential customers read. Read these periodicals with an eye on ways you can comment on a story they have printed. For instance, in response to an article in a woman's magazine on hosting a party, an event coordinator might write a letter elaborating on certain techniques or listing a few tips the author may have missed. Try to make your letter helpful, professional, and nonconfrontational. Newsletter editor Coleen Sykora writes a lot of letters to editors of RV magazines. At the end of her letter, she offers to send readers a free sample issue.

Newsletter editor Edith Flowers Kilgo also makes a habit of writing letters to editors of publications, especially large-circulation newspapers, commenting on stories they have printed. "Often they run my letter and it generates free publicity," she says. Recently, she responded to a letter she had seen in a column of "Dear Abby" and Abby Van Buren decided to print it. Kilgo was tickled. "I do this all the time and it frequently pays off." She says, "Publicity is everywhere. It just takes a lot of 'thinking outside the box.' Where is the inventiveness in just sending out press kits to the standard sources? I like the challenge of seeing if I can get into unexpected places."

WORDS OF WISDOM

Don't spend money on advertising, spend it on publicity. The exception is if you're a local business, get a *Yellow Pages* and a local newspaper ad. But be selective. I would put most of my money into getting publicity because that is much more credible than advertising. Getting publicity isn't as hard as people think it is. It's mainly a matter of persistence. In fact, they say in retail 'location, location, location.' In publicity, it is 'persistence, persistence, persistence.' Develop a relationship with the media.

—John Kremer,
author of *1001 Ways to Market Your Books*

AUTHOR'S BIOGRAPHIES

If you can write well, you can garner a lot of publicity for your business by writing articles in your area of expertise for magazines, newspapers, and newsletters. Most publications will allow you to write a blurb about your business in the author's biography at the end of the article. Many will even pay you! Even if the publication does not include a biography at the end of the article, it will use your byline, and you can still photocopy the article and use it for publicity purposes. Having published articles increases your credibility.

To locate magazines that accept freelance submissions, obtain a current copy of *Writer's Market*. Select a few magazines, read back issues at the library, and send for submission guidelines. You can also view some

writer's guidelines on the Internet at the periodical's web site or at
http://www.writersdigest.com.

Some commonly overlooked publications that may be eager for your
words include alumni newsletters, local weekly newspapers, and community education publications. For example, alumni newsletters often
print features on "what our graduates are doing now." If you are truly
committed, you may even be able to propose a weekly or monthly newspaper column to your local paper. Many small town papers are understaffed, and eager for original copy with a local slant. Be prepared to
submit several weeks' or months' worth of columns, and outlines for
more.

To learn how to pitch article ideas to editors, read *How to Write Irresistible
Query Letters* by Lisa Collier Cool, and *The Writer's Guide to Query Letters
and Cover Letters* by Gordon Burgett.

RADIO AND TV

Local radio and public-access television stations are always looking for
guests. If you can communicate your expertise clearly and concisely, you
may be a candidate for talk shows. Look for shows that cater to your customers. For instance, a landscaper would want to send a press kit to the
host and producer of a local gardening show.

Be sure to include potential questions the host can ask you. Many hosts
do not have the time to familiarize themselves with your product or service, so giving them the questions in advance makes both their job and
yours easier. Remember to keep your answers short and on the topic.
Your goal is to offer the listeners or viewers information that is relevant
and interesting, not to blatantly plug your business.

If something goes wrong, just keep talking. Professional organizer Susan
Lannis tells the story of her first radio interview done via telephone. She
and the radio talk show host established that the interview would be at
11 A.M. Unfortunately, the host, who was on the East Coast, thought Lan-

nis meant 11 A.M. Eastern time, so she called at 8 A.M. Pacific time. Lannis was in the shower. She scrambled to the phone and, instead of panicking, did the whole interview dripping wet. "I could have freaked. But instead, I had fun with it. I did my first national radio interview naked. In the end, it became a very funny story."

Be available to clients on short notice. Listen to what their needs are. If they need a quick press release at 11 o'clock at night, be there for them.

—Bonni K. Brodnick,
BKB Communications

LECTURES

Several home-based guerrillas we interviewed regularly give free lectures to community groups. If you are reasonably confident with public speaking, you should consider giving lectures on topics related to your expertise to civic organizations, such as Friends of the Public Library and Rotary International. Authors have used this technique to sell books for a long time, but other home-based entrepreneurs can benefit as well. Home-based photographic supply consultant Laurie Dry explains, "So many groups are dying for presentations: Lionesses, New Moms, Newcomers, senior centers, PTA groups, sororities, craft clubs, and so on." Dry gives free lectures on how to preserve photographs and create family scrapbooks, in hopes that some members of the audience will buy some of her products afterward. Even if it is not feasible to sell your product or service at the lecture itself (i.e., landscaping), giving lectures for free or for a nominal fee will build your name recognition. When members of the audience need the services you offer, they will remember you.

Develop a speech. Fifteen minutes is a good beginning length. Give it to your friends and family and incorporate their feedback. You may want to join Toastmasters International for additional guidance. Then, look on bulletin boards at the local library for groups that may sponsor a lecture. Ask for the name of the speaker coordinator and then send him a packet outlining your credentials, topic, and interest in lecturing.

After you have done a few free lectures, you may want to investigate the possibility of giving seminars at adult education centers, community colleges, or university extensions. Peruse the catalogs, and see if the school already offers classes in your area of expertise. If not, prepare a proposal. If accepted, you will not only be paid to teach, but your students may well become some of your best customers.

If you already have a large clientele and have space, you may even be able to teach in your own home. For instance, clients who came to view the work of home-based painter, Ruth Ann Weber, from Jackson, Michigan, often asked about painting classes. Now Weber teaches classes in her basement studio four nights a week. The classes constantly have waiting lists. Her furniture-painting business and her teaching fuel one another. When students come to classes, they see Weber's work and want to buy it. When clients buy her work, they want to learn to paint like she does.

You may be surprised by the power of public speaking. Something that originally started as a marketing strategy may turn out to be a major portion of your business income. For more information on how to use lectures to create publicity, read Marcia Yudkin's book, *6 Steps to Free Publicity.*

DONATIONS, FREE SAMPLES, AND COUPONS

Another way to gain exposure and name recognition in the community is to donate free products or services to civic organizations. For example, photo-supply consultant Laurie Dry contacts schools and churches and offers to donate photographic products or gift certificates for classes for their raffles or auctions. Dry donates a class for ten people at a value of $100, but she may get several new customers from it. Also, she contacts local hospitals and diaper services, and asks if she can enclose a coupon for a free class in their information packets given to new mothers. Why? Because new mothers are likely to be taking a lot of pictures of their new babies and, therefore, will be in need of photo albums. Dry determines who her market is and decides which organizations have access to potential customers. Then, she donates a certificate for a product or service to those organizations.

Newsletter editor Coleen Sykora markets her product in a similar way. She contacts the director of recreational vehicle conventions, such as Good Sam's state Samborees, and offers to give about 800 sample copies of the newsletter to include in the goodie bags they hand out at the door. The cost of printing extra copies of the newsletter is negligible compared to additional subscribers she acquires. "I'm really generous with samples," says Sykora. "It pays off."

Sykora circulates samples in another unique way. As she and her husband Bob travel around in their RV, she leaves sample copies at every trailer park they visit. "We leave them in the laundromat or by the phone and people pick them up. We always have an order blank in the newsletter and I code it, so I know where I left it. It's interesting to see where it came from," says Sykora.

If you do not want to give your product or service away absolutely free, you can discount it. Everyone likes to get a good deal and, when faced with two unknown vendors, customers will almost always choose the one for which they have a coupon. However, you must make the coupon worth the effort. It has to be tempting and not require a lot of additional investment on the customer's part. For instance, "buy four, get one free" is not a good coupon. How many potential customers are interested in buying four products they have not tried before? That is too much of a risk. Good coupons are those that give you something at a sizable discount, such as 25 percent off.

When home-based accountant Eva Webb, EA, opened The Income Tax Store in Sayetteville, Georgia, she printed flyers with $5-off coupons to advertise her new business. Then, she, her husband, and her children drove to nearby subdivisions and delivered the flyers on foot. With very little out-of-pocket expense, Webb built a large clientele.

Though samples and coupons may cost you a little money or time, they are well worth it. Most people will take something if it is free. And, once you are able to demonstrate your exceptional product or service to people, they are likely to buy from you in the future.

In their book Big Ideas for Small Service Businesses, *Marilyn and Tom Ross suggest incorporating "Bounce Back" merchandising into your marketing plan. That means if a customer buys something from you, include a flyer about other products or services with their shipment or bill. If they have bought from you before, they are likely to buy again.*

LOW-COST PARTICIPATION IN TRADE SHOWS AND EXPOSITIONS

Trade shows and expositions are other ways to showcase your product to potential customers. Since customers have made the effort to attend and sometimes even paid for the privilege, you know they are in the market for your products or services. Unfortunately, most trade shows are exorbitantly expensive. You must buy the space and props, then you must staff the booth yourself or pay someone else to staff it. So, how can you trim the costs?

Laurie Dry loves to exhibit her photographic supplies at craft and bridal expos, but she refuses to pay the $1,600 most charge exhibitors. Instead, she goes in a few days before the event and speaks to the director. "The worst thing for them to have is a vacant booth," says Dry. "I tell them if they have any cancellations at the last minute, they can call me. You can pick up the booth for half price or free because they want somebody to fill the space."

If you want to secure a spot, you can book ahead. But be aware that the booth fee may not be the final cost. Cartoonist Terry Morin regularly participates in trade shows, and has learned to ask what is included in the booth fee to determine what he will need to bring. "Sometimes it comes with carpet, sometimes not. Sometimes you have to bring your own draping. Then you need to be sure that the draping is fire retardant so when the fire marshall comes up you will not be ticketed." He also cautions that the booth price may not include electricity. At one show he attends, electricity costs $150 per day! If you need an outlet, request one beforehand, so there are no surprise fees. If you do not have all of the necessary accouterments, Morin recommends asking about packages for a completely outfitted booth. However, he warns that the quality of some of the components can be questionable, especially the tables, which tend to be rickety.

If you regularly participate in shows, can afford it, and are willing to transport the materials, you will probably receive better value from your money by buying and bringing your own. Moreover, "they have different workers to deal with for everything: the carpet, lighting, and so on. It can be a nightmare. If you have all of your stuff with you, you save a lot of time and money." Morin has trimmed the cost of his trade-show accessories by buying used props. "I go to a liquidator that purchases old retail store props," he says. "I bought a wooden card display rack that swivels for $60." Elsewhere, he has seen similar ones for several hundred dollars.

Understand that freelancing of any kind is: 20 percent doing the actual job, 50 percent marketing, 10 percent collections, and 20 percent maintenance (answering phone calls, accounting, taxes, etc.). Even if you are a genius in your field, a home-based business will not succeed unless you are able to accept the interruptions, unrelated chores, and occasional wasted days as part of the inevitable picture. Talent is not enough. You have to be a good businessperson to survive.

—Edith Flowers Kilgo,
editor of *Creative Downscaling*

BUSINESS CARDS

Most home-based guerrillas need business cards; but you can do more with them than just state your name, rank, and serial number. A business card can be a very effective marketing tool. For instance, Ron Renner, home-based owner of Geppetto's Woodworks in Vancouver, Washington, has his information printed in gold leaf on a piece of high-quality wood. The card smells like cedar. You can bet that recipients remember it. Another sidenote: Renner says that the name of his business—Geppetto's Woodworks, from the childhood story Pinocchio—earns him more attention than anything else. "It brings up a good connotation: being tucked into bed and their parents reading to them," says Renner. "People stop me on the freeway for nothing more than the sign on my truck. They want to talk about furniture, all based on the name of my business. A unique business name, to some degree, has a bearing on how well you are received."

INTERNET OPPORTUNITIES

The Internet is a fantastic tool for frugal marketers, mainly because—aside from Internet connection and web-hosting fees—it is free. You do not need to pay for printing or postage. There are several ways to market on the Internet. Some of them pertain to all home-based guerrillas and others only to those with web sites.

One way to gain exposure is to post questions and answers on a bulletin board, chat group, newsgroup, or mailing list. Look for a handful of groups in which you would like to participate. Once you find some you like, and that seem pertinent to your business, remain a passive observer for a while to get the feel of the group and to avoid raising topics that have been recently discussed. In the meantime, read what others have written. Then, if someone asks a question or presents an issue about a topic you know well, answer. You can introduce your business subtly over time, or you can write a line or two about it at the bottom of your correspondence.

Even if you do not post to list groups, it is a good idea to develop a business-related signature that appears at the bottom of every email message you write. For instance, editor Edith Flowers Kilgo's email signature is: her name, business name (*Creative Downscaling*), address, telephone number, and the descriptive phrase " 'Upscale, simplified living on a downsized budget' Published bimonthly. Subscription rate: $16/year.' " If you have a web page, you should also include your web page address. To create a link to your page within your message, type the complete address, including the prefix http://.

A more aggressive marketing technique is to search out web sites with free classified advertising space. Many sites offer free classifieds of approximately fifty words. The ads are purged regularly, though, so you must keep posting. To find sites with free classifieds, enter keywords related to your business into a search engine and then browse the sites that appear.

Home-based guerrillas with web sites have even more opportunities for free marketing. It is important that you register your site with as many search engines as possible. For more information on registering your web site, see Chapter 6, "Saving in Cyberspace." Next, look for noncompeting, related web sites with whom you can trade links. Nearly all the home-based guerrillas we interviewed that had web sites spoke of exchanging links with other home-based guerrillas as a way of publicizing their businesses. Exchanging links is free and increases the traffic of your web site because it increases the routes along which potential customers can find you.

Once customers reach your site, get as much information from them as they are willing to give. Do not seem pushy, or they may be dissuaded from ordering from you. However, if you can get an email or home address, you can create a personalized mailing list for future marketing campaigns. Also, make it easy for visitors to contact you. Include your address, phone, and fax numbers on your site, as well as your email address. Do not hide from potential customers or the media! Plaster your contact information all over your site.

Take care of existing clients because that's where repeat business comes from. It cuts down on the time necessary to generate new clients. Nobody pays you to make cold calls. It's much better if you nurture the relationships you already have.

—Stuart Watson,
freelance business writer

SELECTIVE DIRECT-MAIL MARKETING

Aside from publicity, selective direct-mail marketing gains the greatest results with the lowest cost. Of course, the key is to determine who your customers are. This usually requires a good deal of research and brain-storming time, but careful planning pays off.

For instance, when Jane Bluestein, Ph.D., home-based owner of Instructional Support Services, Inc. and ISS Publications in Albuquerque, New Mexico, started publishing teacher's education materials in 1983, she had more time than money. So, instead of buying a mailing list, she went to the library and researched all the colleges that had teacher's education programs. Then she sent each education department a direct mail flyer about her new book, *Being a Successful Teacher.* She received a 13 percent response rate—well above the national 3 percent average!

Tax consultant Eva Webb also targets her niche very closely. In addition to referrals, she generates new business through a very select direct-mail campaign. She buys an inexpensive mailing list of all the new homeowners in her county each year and sends them letters telling about her services. "This is low-cost advertising with good results and I get a high caliber of clients this way," says Webb.

Buying a mailing list is more expensive than compiling your own, but it may be worthwhile if the desired information is obscure. Mailing lists usually cost about $45 to $110 per 1,000 names, with a 5,000-name minimum. Before you do a mass-mailing using a rented list, do a pilot test of

1,000 names or so. Even though you will pay for all 5,000 names and use only 1,000, the largest cost in a direct-mail campaign is in the postage, and you do not want to send 5,000 64¢ mailers to discover the list is not the right one for you. See if the percentage of return is worth the cost of sending the package to the whole list. If so, you can always send to the rest of the list. If not, you can continue your search until you find a successful list. To find companies that sell lists, look in the *Standard Rate & Data Service* publications in the library. For more information on direct-mail marketing and other marketing techniques, read *Guerrilla Marketing for the Home-Based Business* by Jay Levinson and Seth Godin.

ADVERTISING

Though advertising can be expensive, it may work if you can narrow your target market enough. And, unlike publicity, you can predict when it will appear, where it will appear, and what it will say when it does. To save money on advertising, consider the following tips.

Participate in Cooperative Advertising with Other Guerrillas.   Home-based publishers Scott and Shirley Gregory have done cooperative direct mailings with other publishers to share the costs. For this strategy to be effective, your partners must be targeting the same market, but not have a product that competes with yours. For instance, a book publisher who sells psychology books might cooperate with a spiritual-book publisher. Though the target market is similar, the books would not compete.

Establish Your Own "Advertising Agency."   Steve Carlson, home-based publisher of Upper Access Books, explains this technique: "Ad agencies get 15 percent discounts on most of the ads in a publication as a commission. So, you can automatically save 15 percent by calling yourself an ad agency." However, he cautions that you must "submit the ad typeset and in finished condition."

Buy Remnant Advertising Space.   Remnant advertising space is the space left over in a periodical after they have sold the majority of their advertising space. For example, the way in which a newspaper is constructed is that each page is really four pages, because one page is printed on both sides and folded in the middle. Therefore, it must add pages in increments of four. Say a newspaper has four pages. It has stories on the front page and one inside page. If it sells an ad on the back page to a major department store, the paper has three pages filled. The fourth page is called remnant—leftover—space. In order to fill it, which it must do, the newspaper discounts the cost of the remaining advertising space. Catherine Groves, home-based publisher of the *Christian*New Age Quarterly*, trades remnant classified advertising space with another newsletter publisher. Many years ago, when Kathryn worked at a local weekly newspaper, the paper had an agreement with an insurance agent to run his ads in remnant space. The ads varied in shape and size based on the leftover space but, invariably, the agent received at least one ad in the newspaper and often three or four, at a discounted price.

Volunteer in Exchange for Advertising Space.   Community events are always understaffed. You may be able to garner advertising space in a local theater program by volunteering to usher. Or, ask about staffing a state-fair booth in exchange for advertising on the maps.

Establish a PO Arrangement with a Magazine, Radio Station, or TV Station.   In a *PO* (per order) *arrangement,* a magazine, radio station, or TV station runs your advertisement for free and, in exchange, it keeps a percentage of the profits from the sales generated from the ad. PO arrangements are not usually publicized, so you will have to ask at the advertising department of the medium in which you are interested. For more information on PO arrangements and other marketing techniques, read *Guerrilla Marketing* by Jay Levinson and Seth Godin.

Remember Small, Niche Publications.   Advertising space in smaller publications is usually cheaper than in large ones, and it may be a better value because smaller publications have very targeted readerships. Consider advertising in church bulletins, and college and high-school newspapers. Look for periodicals that serve your potential customers in *Gale Directory of Publications and Broadcast Media.*

Whatever advertising route you take, remember to be consistent. A large advertisement run once will probably not pull in as much business as a small one run for many months or years. Moreover, do not feel that you need to constantly change your marketing strategy. This is expensive and unnecessary. Change your strategy only when the current one stops working.

BE CREATIVE

For the most part, to get your customers' attention, you just need to be creative. One of the advantages of being a home-based guerrilla—as opposed to an employee at a large corporation—is that you do not have to ask anyone for permission to do things a little differently. This entrepreneurial freedom can be used to your advantage to make customers feel special, and to demonstrate your commitment to personalized attention.

For example, to ensure that his correspondence stands out from the deluge, author Jeff Berner uses antique postage stamps. Berner buys the 1930s stamps at face value from dealers who only want to keep the collectible ones and are eager to sell the rest. Berner says that his clients have come to expect the stamps and, when they spot his trademark, unique postage, eagerly pick his letters out of the stacks of mail they receive daily. "They give the stamps to their kids or friends," says Berner. "It's value-added. You are paying attention to your clients. And it's fun."

This is just one simple example of how you can make an ordinary transaction memorable, and it exemplifies the heart of any guerrilla-marketing strategy: Be creative, be personal, and know your market.

CHAPTER 9

THRIFTY WAYS TO IMPROVE YOUR SKILLS

Some home-based guerrillas, such as accountants, require continuing education credits to keep their licenses current. However, all home-based guerrillas should spend some time and effort keeping their skills up to date, as well as learning new ones. That does not mean that you must spend a lot of money. Books, periodicals, audiotapes, seminars, conferences, and business counseling can be acquired for free or next to nothing.

BOOKS

Books are among the best bargains for instruction. Imagine, for under $30 you can bring the world's most renowned experts—living and dead—into your home to entertain, educate, and inspire you. And you can bring them to life again and again just by opening the cover. If you forget how to make a French knot or write a business proposal, you can simply look it up. The majority of home-based guerrillas we interviewed relied on books as their primary source of continuing education. It is not surprising since books are probably the most convenient, least expensive way to learn.

However, before you buy new books, weed out your old ones and sell them at a garage sale or used bookstore. Do you own books that no longer reflect your current tastes or goals? Sell them, or donate them to a library and take a tax deduction. Look for a pattern among those books you have discarded. Many people read this year's bestsellers once, then leave them on a shelf to gather dust. Perceive your library as a living resource instead of an inanimate collection, and you may alter your buying habits.

Once you have purged your library of old books you no longer use, and have a plan to replace them with ones you will use, where should you shop?

Warehouse Membership Clubs.   Though you must consider the membership fee, if you already belong or if you buy a lot of books, a warehouse club may be a good source for new books. Warehouse clubs sell bestsellers, children's books, cookbooks, and computer software manuals for 25 to 50 percent off cover prices. However, the selections are usually small and inconsistent. If you see something you want at a warehouse store, buy it immediately, as it may not be available in a few weeks.

Book Clubs.   Ten books for a penny? Can it be true? Yes and no. Book clubs can be bargains, but you have to understand the fine print. Usually, by joining you commit to buying one or more books at the club's regular prices, which could be outrageous when you include shipping and handling. Also, joining a book club can be a costly inconvenience because you have to return forms saying you do not want this month's selection; if you do not mail your reply on time, you may have to pay the shipping to return an unwanted book.

If the featured books really appeal to you, calculate the cost of the commitment, shipping and handling, and postage for replying to their offers. If it is less than the cost of the free books—and you would have bought the books anyway—join.

Online Bookstores.   Books are one of the most popular items to buy on the Internet. And why not? You do not need to touch the fabric to know that it will not wrinkle or try it on to make sure it fits. Online bookstores do not need to cover the overhead of a store, so books are usually cheaper than in traditional bookstores. There are several large online bookstores that are fairly competitive. But, since the Internet makes it easy to comparison shop, check prices first. All of the following online bookstores charge the same for standard shipping ($3 for the first book and 95¢ for each additional book):

Amazon.com • http://www.amazon.com
Barnesandnoble.com • http://barnesandnoble.com
Borders.com • http://borders.com

Kathryn orders all her new books online. It saves her the time of travelling to the bookstore, and most of the books are cheaper, even with the shipping and handling fees. Because of the tiered shipping structure, Kathryn tries to wait until she has a list of several books she wants in order to minimize the shipping charges.

Used Bookstores, Garage Sales, and Library Sales.   The good thing about books is they do not get used up. A book read 150 times contains the same amount of interest and usefulness as a new volume. Thus, why not buy a used book for half the price of the same one new?

Before you buy, scour your bookshelf for books you could trade. Used bookstores vary in their selection and trade-in policies, so shop around. Some will pay cash, others only credit. Visit several stores over a few months before trading in any books; you want to make sure the store will still be around when you want to use your credit. Used bookstores can provide other perks as well. A used bookstore Kathryn frequents holds a "free book day" once a month. If you buy a book on that day, you receive a second one of equal or lesser value free.

Garage sales have less reliable selections than used bookstores, but usually have lower prices (between 5¢ and $2). Garage sales near universities will have more textbooks and classics, while suburban neighborhood yard sales will probably feature more cookbooks, children's books, and bestsellers.

The best places to pick up next-to-new books for next to nothing (usually $1 for hardbacks and 50¢ for paperbacks) are library book sales. That is because some patrons buy the latest hardbacks, read them once, then donate them. This is also the librarian's opportunity to purge her shelves to make room for new books. Another advantage to library sales is that the books are usually in good condition because people who donate to the library usually care about books. For the widest selection, get to the sale when it opens on the first day and bring a bag or box for your finds. For the best bargains, visit during the last few hours of the sale when the remaining books go for "a buck a bag." At a recent sale Kathryn attended, she bought a like-new recent bestseller for $1. It still had the $12.83 price tag on it.

Don't assume you know everything you need to know. Read the books you need to read to learn your business.

—John Kremer,
author of *1001 Ways to Market Your Books*

PERIODICALS

If you read a magazine regularly, consider subscribing. A subscription is cheaper per issue than buying off the rack every month—and you do not need to drive to the newsstand. First-time subscribers usually can get the best deals—often times, 50 percent or more off of the cover price.

When it comes time to renew, wait. Most magazines start sending renewal notices months before your subscription runs out, and will continue sending notices regularly until your subscription expires. With one magazine, Kathryn discovered that the longer she waited to renew, the lower the price became. So, she just waited until her subscription was about to expire and took the last deal they sent. It cost several dollars less than the first notice.

Another place to get discounted magazine subscriptions is from Delta Publishing Group, which sell magazines for waiting rooms, such as doctors' offices. Some of the publications available through Delta Publishing Group require that a business name be included in your address, or that you include a business card or a sheet of company letterhead with your subscription. However, the fantastic bargains are well worth this minor inconvenience. For example, a one-year subscription to *Home Office Computing* costs $16.97 if you order it using the business-reply card in the magazine, but costs only $9.95 through Delta Publishing Group! Also, you can renew subscriptions originally ordered elsewhere.

How can the company offer such low prices? Delta Publishing Group lists several reasons: It makes money through volume sales, it requires prepayment of all orders so it does not lose money on individuals who order a subscription and then cancel after one issue, and the majority of its customers order more than one title, so it can service them one renewal notice. Diane Rosener, home-based editor of *A Penny Saved* newsletter, buys all of her magazines through Delta Publishing Group. For a catalog, contact:

Delta Publishing Group, Ltd.
1243 48th Street • Brooklyn, NY 11219
phone: (800) SAVE-SAVE • fax: (718) 972-4695
web site: none listed

In addition, you may also be able to get magazines free from the airlines. Some airlines will trade frequent-flyer miles for magazine subscriptions. For example, Kathryn recently got *Home Office Computing* and *Utne Reader* for 1,800 miles from TWA. Obviously, if you plan to redeem the miles for a free flight, this is not a deal. However, Kathryn did not have enough miles for a ticket, and did not foresee earning any more in the near future. If you have old frequent-flyer miles, it may be worthwhile to contact the airline to ask if you can cash them in for free magazine subscriptions you can use.

Another way to get free magazines is to ask. Ron Miller, home-based owner of Advantage Northwest, a custom machining and fabrication company in Hillsboro, Oregon, says that he gets a half-dozen magazines a month, free! He went to the library and researched all of the publications in his field. He noted the circulation numbers of each and then wrote letters to those with low circulation asking about their subscription policies. Many sent him subscriptions free. Why? Miller explains: "They are paid for by advertising. The more subscribers they have, the more they can charge for advertising."

Finally, if you have Internet access, you can often read excerpts from many magazines and newspapers on their web pages for free. For example, *USA Today* has a good site at http://www.usatoday.com and *Home Office Computing* has a terrific site at http://www.smalloffice.com. For a list of periodicals' web sites, visit http://www.mediainfo.com/emedia. You will not be able to read whole publications online, but you can get a good introduction to new periodicals, or you can visit a few favorites whose print versions exceed your budget.

Home-based publisher Marc Eisenson of Good Advice Press and co-author of Invest in Yourself: Six Secrets to a Rich Life, *from Elizaville, New York, reads dozens of magazines a week that he has plucked from the local recycling center—sometimes before the magazines hit the newsstands!*

AUDIOTAPES

In the last decade, audiotapes have become more popular, especially for travelers who use transportation time to learn new skills. However, audiotapes are expensive if you are going to listen to them just once. And, since it is more difficult to skip around on a tape than in a book, you are less likely to refer back to important passages. Thus, with the exception of foreign language audiotapes, avoid buying tapes. Borrow or rent them instead. Scour used bookstores, which are starting to delve into audiotape rentals. Or, rent from your local video store.

If you travel regularly and audiotapes are your primary learning method, you may enjoy a subscription to:

Tape Rental Library, Inc.
One Cassette Center • PO Box 107 • Covesville, VA 22931
phone: (804) 293-3705 or (804) 263-5875 • fax: (804) 263-5543
web site: none listed

The subscription is not cheap: $132 per year plus postage ($63 on average). But it is cheaper than buying dozens of cassettes at retail prices ($10 to $80 each). A subscription to the Tape Rental Library, Inc. allows you to rent as many cassette tapes as you want during the year, two at a time, from their vast inventory, including tapes on selling, marketing, success, telephone skills, and self-development. For example, the "Entrepreneurship" category contains titles such as, "Growing a Business," "How to Start and Succeed in Your Own Business," "Secrets of Successful Self-Employment," and "Entrepreneurial Thinking."

You may exchange the tapes as often as you'd like or keep them as long as you wish. The cassettes are sent via first-class mail and take about three to five days to arrive. The catalog reports that most subscribers exchange once per week, which means you could listen to 104 tapes at a cost of about $1.25 per tape plus postage ($1.50 per cassette), for a total of $2.75 per tape or $288 per year. Consider how much traveling time you have, and calculate how much you spend annually on cassettes to determine whether this is economical for you.

You have to be self-driven and be well-read. Without that, you aren't going to make it.

—Toni Yount-Klein,
Ty West

REDISCOVER THE LIBRARY

Many people forget the best place to find a book, audio-, or videotape is at the library. No matter how cheaply you buy a resource, you still cannot beat free. If your town's library is tiny, you can always order books through interlibrary loan, a service that allows your library to borrow a book (and sometimes other resources) from virtually any library in the country for up to three weeks. It usually takes one to four weeks for the item to arrive.

Kathryn saves money on books and, by taking notes while she is reading, is able to refer to information years later. She files the notes under the appropriate topic. If she needs to quote from a book, she knows the exact page number and, many times, the exact quotation. This whole system may sound tedious, but Kathryn has found it to be worthwhile, particularly for feature-article writing. Think about when you were in school. You learned more when you took notes, right? What is the point in reading something if you do not remember the information when you need it? Notes also take up less room than the books themselves. If you find the whole book is rich with information, you may want to own it. But, do you really want to buy, store, and dust a book for one chapter or a half-dozen ideas?

Many libraries also stock large circulation magazines, such as *Entrepreneur* and *Consumer Reports.* Current issues must remain in the library, but previous months' issues circulate for one week at a time. Having a time limit also forces you to read the magazine quickly, which means you can put any advice into practice. How often have you received this month's issue of a magazine and still have not finished reading last month's? If you discover an article you will want to refer to later, you can photocopy it and still save money over buying the magazine.

Libraries also stock a wealth of information on audio- and videotape. If you want to learn how to lay bathroom tile, market to a niche group, or get motivated about selling, you can probably find a how-to audio- or videotape. Rediscover the library. You may be surprised at what is available free.

ONLINE INSTRUCTION

Distance learning options—formal and informal—abound on the Internet. You can get an MBA degree from a university and never even set foot on the campus! Also, online instruction can be extremely cost effective, because you do not need to drive to the school or pay for parking. You may even be able to eliminate child-care costs, depending on the ages of your children and the demands of the class.

Informal online learning options include bulletin-board newsgroups, in which individuals can post questions and answers; mailing-list servers, which are like newsgroups only the messages are distributed via email; and chat groups, which are like being in a room with several other people and talking (typing) in real time.

Catherine Groves, home-based editor of the *Christian*New Age Quarterly*, says she has learned a lot from online chat rooms. When she needed help with the design of her web site, she logged onto a user group. An individual corresponded with her via email and offered suggestions on improving her site. Jean MacDonald, home-based owner of Well-Tempered Web Design, agrees, "Mailing-list servers are the best things about the Internet. I have learned more from the people on the list servers than I've ever learned from books." To find a user group, you can look at http://www.dejanews.com, or simply do a keyword search through one of the online search engines.

Formal online courses are becoming increasingly popular. Some are free or inexpensive, while others cost as much as it would to physically attend the school. Many major universities around the country offer online classes. For instance, University of California, Los Angeles Extension, advertises a wide variety of online classes, such as the Principles of Accounting and Writing for Public Relations at their web site http://www.onlinelearning.net. Unfortunately, the fees are quite steep: $450 to $575 per class. However, online learning is still cheaper than physically traveling to the class, because transportation and child-care costs are eliminated. For more information, visit The National Universities Degree Consortium at http://www.sc.edu/deis/nudc, California Virtual University at http://www.california.edu, New Jersey Virtual University http://www.njvu.org, and Western Governors University at http://www.wgu.edu.

Free and inexpensive online classes are available; it just takes a little more research to find them. For instance, the American Express Home Business Exchange has an online tutorial that teaches you how to write a business plan at http://www.americanexpress.com/smallbusiness. Like the American Express site, many web sites post information that is top-notch. For a list of our favorite business-related sites, see Appendix B.

Judy Lawrence, a financial counselor and author of **The Budget Kit,** *from Albuquerque, New Mexico, got a $360 two-day computer software class free through a promotional offer. The computer instruction company offered a free class in hopes that attendees would sign up for additional classes.*

COURSES OR SEMINARS

Business courses and seminars are available at almost every university, community college, and adult-education center. Community groups and private companies may also offer inexpensive classes. For instance, The Learning Annex in San Diego advertises a class on How to Open a Bed & Breakfast Inn and another on How To Create Killer Advertising, for under $40 each.

How do you find a bargain? Shop around. Adult-education centers usually have the cheapest courses, followed by community colleges, universities, and, lastly, private companies. For example, Coleen Sykora and her husband, Bob, register for free or inexpensive adult-education classes whenever they park their trailer for a while.

Another place to look for inexpensive courses: the city, county, state, and federal government. Many government agencies, such as the county extension office, offer continuing-education courses free of charge. For example, the post office offers fantastic free classes on mailing. Home-based tax preparer Eva Webb, EA, needs continuing-education credits to keep her enrolled agent designation with the IRS, but she never pays for courses. Instead, she goes to all the free tax seminars the IRS and Georgia Department of Revenue hold throughout the year.

Price should not be your only criterion, though. How else can you evaluate a prospective course? Classes can be superb or pointless, depending almost entirely on the instructor. The content of the course is irrelevant, if the instructor does not fulfill the catalog's promises. An informed, enthusiastic speaker will engage your interest and teach you a great deal. In contrast, an unprepared, unqualified, monotonous, passionless speaker will waste your time and money.

Before you register, do a little research. Ask yourself these questions:

➤ *Is this a new course or has it been advertised in previous catalogs?* In order for a course to last more than one semester, it has to attract sufficient enrollment to pay the school, instructor, and overhead expenses. Though some good courses die for unknown reasons, a good class usually appears in the catalog regularly.

➤ *Do you know anyone who has taken the course?* Ask around. What did she think of it? Would she recommend it? If you do not know any previous attendees, look in the catalog or brochure for excerpts from student evaluations. When Kathryn attended the University of California, San Diego, she used *Course and Professor Evaluation* books, a compilation of students' evaluations, to plan her schedule. Look for similar guides at the campus bookstore.

➤ *What credentials does the instructor have?* How long has she been in the field? Has she published any books or articles? Are her publication credits recent? If the instructor has written a book or two, check them out of the library and note the copyright dates. Kathryn once took a course on character development taught by a woman who had published a children's book—thirty years ago! As far as Kathryn could tell, she had not done anything since. Her materials were reproduced on a mimeograph, and the information was just as ancient. Had Kathryn taken twenty minutes to find the woman's book in the library, she might have realized the instructor was out of touch and would have saved herself $50 and a sunny Saturday afternoon.

In addition, if you have a knack for teaching, you may be able to save on tuition by becoming an instructor yourself. Many community colleges and universities offer free tuition to their instructors as a benefit. If you teach one class, you may be able to take several others free or for the cost of materials (in addition to getting paid for teaching your class!). Lawrenceville, Georgia—based Gerald Sweitzer, a home-based consultant and owner of Ruralburbia, a company that helps people relocate to small towns, is able to take classes for free or next to nothing at his local college by teaching a course on how to relocate.

Last, before you register for a course, see if you can find the same information elsewhere for less. Has the lecturer written a book or produced an audiotape series on the same topic? At the beginning of her writing career, Kathryn paid $50 for a writing seminar and then discovered the exact same material in the lecturer's book for $12.95. If she had found the book at the library, she could have gotten the same information free.

Attend the first class before you buy any of the books. You may discover the books are optional. If you buy the books, and do not want to keep them after the class is over, sell them back. Most university bookstores hold a used-book buyback at the end of every term. You can recoup about 50 percent of what you paid.

SMALL BUSINESS DEVELOPMENT CENTERS

The Small Business Development Center (SBDC) program was created through the U.S. Small Business Administration to provide low-cost and free assistance to budding entrepreneurs. There are 900 centers around the country, usually located at community colleges or public universities. SBDCs provide advocacy, training programs, one-on-one counseling, and customized research prepared on behalf of small businesses.

Editor Edith Flowers Kilgo says that the instruction at her local SBDC is first rate: "The best advice I ever got came from the SBDC: 'Imagine you are on the fifth floor of an elevator. An acquaintance you have not seen for a long time gets on. He asks what you do. If you cannot explain what you do before the elevator gets to the ground floor, you need to refine and focus.' "

Susan Lannis, home-based professional organizer, also attends her local SBDC and raves about it. "I get one-and-a-half hours of private, one-on-one counseling for my business. My counselor is a $2,000-a-day business consultant. I pay about $6 an hour." To find a SBDC near you, look on the association of SBDCs' web site at http://www.asbdc-us.org.

WORDS OF WISDOM

I love to take classes. It keeps you fresh. It gives you an opportunity to learn about other people and how they do things.

—Ruth Ann Weber,
It's Something Special

SERVICE CORPS OF RETIRED EXECUTIVES

The Service Corps of Retired Executives (SCORE) is a national, nonprofit association with 12,400 volunteer members and 389 chapters in the U.S. Like the SBDC program, SCORE is a resource partner with the U.S. Small Business Administration. Working and retired executives and business owners donate their time and expertise to counsel fledgling entrepreneurs. Counseling is free and confidential. SCORE chapters also provide workshops and seminars for modest fees. Seminars cover such topics as "Starting Your Home-Based Business" and "Developing a Business Plan." You can get free advice via email at SCORE's web site. For more information, contact:

SCORE Association
409 3rd Street SW, 6th Floor • Washington, DC 20024
phone: (800) 634-0245 • fax: none listed
web site: http://www.score.org

HIGH-SCHOOL AND COLLEGE STUDENTS

High-school and college students are resources that should not be overlooked. You can hold contests to get new ideas, enlist a high-school class for help on a specific project, or employ a work-study student. Toni Yount-Klein, home-based owner of Ty West, a designer and manufacturer of western lingerie, says she has learned a lot from local high-school and university students.

Yount-Klein employs students on work-study exchanges. She introduces students who are interested in clothing design to the field. In exchange, they give her "free help in computers and design," says Yount-Klein. One student taught Yount-Klein how to streamline her patterns using a computer. She says, "They need projects to do and it's better for them to have real, hands-on projects than to dream them up. And it's satisfying to know you had an impact on a young kid's life."

CONFERENCES AND CONVENTIONS

You could save money by not attending conferences and conventions, but that may be costlier in the long run. Conferences and conventions give you opportunities to network with colleagues and potential clients. The contacts you make may result in new assignments, or you may glean several nuggets of information that increase your sales. The only problem with these benefits, as with most things in life, is that they are not guaranteed. What if you pay all of that money, and do not rub elbows with any leaders in the field, earn any new assignments, or learn anything? Those are the risks you take.

You *can* minimize the possibility of such misfortunes occurring. How? Choose a conference or convention carefully. Which conference you choose greatly determines whether you spend your money wisely or foolishly. Take your time and examine several brochures. To rank events, ask yourself the following questions:

➤ *What do you want to gain?* Decide what you want to learn, then choose a conference or convention that meets your needs, not the other way around.

➤ *Who will be speaking at the conference or convention?* Are you interested in spending time with these speakers? Read the participants' biographies carefully. A strong event has a well-rounded mixture of experts.

➤ *How many people will be speaking?* If there will be thousands of attendees and only a dozen speakers, you probably will not have an opportunity to converse with any speakers on a one-on-one basis.

➤ *What topics will be covered?* Do these topics interest you? Are they aimed at your experience level? If the speaker tells you what you already know or speaks over your head, you are wasting your time and money. If you are a novice in an area, look for broad topics words like *overview* and *basic* in the descriptions. Such sessions will teach you the fundamentals. On the other hand, if you are more knowledgeable in an area, concentrate on niche sessions.

➤ *How long is it?* Divide the total cost by the number of hours to find the hourly rate. The lower the hourly rate, the better value it is. Also, can you really afford to be out of the office for the duration of the event? If you cannot attend all of it, you may waste your money.

➤ *Where is it held?* If you must travel more than 200 miles to attend, you will have to add lodging, transportation, and food to the admission price. Travel expenses can more than double the cost. Unless the event is spectacular, a local conference may be a better value.

Once you have found a conference and plan to attend, what can you do to ensure that you get maximum value for your money?

Participate! The best instructors in the world cannot teach you anything if you do not want to be taught . . . or if you do not show up. Assume a positive, openminded attitude, and take advantage of every aspect of the conference. Be involved. If you cower in the corner the whole day, we guarantee you will waste your money. Take notes, ask questions, offer suggestions, smile. Attend all the free social events associated with the conference. That includes breaks, as well as complimentary coffee hours. Do not use that time to collect voicemail messages. Strike up a conversation while waiting in line. Hang around. Breaks are some of the best opportunities to talk to the speakers individually. No matter how intimidated you may be to speak to someone, keep reminding yourself this is your only chance. Take it.

Register Early.   The earlier you register, the more likely you will receive your first choices in workshops and lectures.

Come Prepared.   You thought you could just show up and absorb knowledge like a sponge? Not if you want to get your money's worth. Bring several portfolios of your work and dozens of business cards. Also, as the maxim goes, "dress for success." At a recent writer's conference Kathryn attended, she was flabbergasted to see attendees wearing T-shirts, sports jerseys, jeans, and tennis shoes. You are meeting colleagues and clients for the first time. Remember, first impressions count. Dress accordingly.

Arrive Early.   Being early gives you the freedom to find a (free) parking space, locate the conference, select the best seat, and have coffee and doughnuts with the speakers or other attendees. Remember, you may learn as much from the other participants as you do from the speakers.

Audit.   Some conference workshops allow you to audit for 25 to 30 percent less than it would cost to participate in the discussion. You can still take notes and learn.

Pay to Attend only a Portion of the Conference.   Conferences are usually structured in several parts: individual workshops, group workshops, small group lectures, whole-conference lectures, and panel discussions. You do not need to pay to attend the whole affair. Which parts interest you most and best match your budget? When Kathryn started writing, she could not afford to attend the five-day Santa Barbara Writer's Conference, but she desperately wanted to go. So, she attended the public lectures held nightly for $5. She got a glimpse of the conference, learned something, got inspired, and had enough money left over for stamps.

Consider Brown-bagging It.   If you can attend the keynote speaker's lecture without buying the $12 catered lunch, you may want to do so, but be aware that you may miss out on some networking opportunities. For instance, one year, Kathryn attended a writer's conference where the catered meal was a box lunch. Attendees who had brought their sack lunches mingled with those who had paid for the $6 box lunch. The next year, however, the catered meal was a sit-down banquet. Those who had brought brown-bag lunches were not permitted to enter the dining room until after the banquet was over and, when they did, they had to sit in rows of chairs away from the other attendees.

Avoid Buying Any Conference Paraphernalia.   Book bags, T-shirts, pens, and pencils proudly advertising your attendance at the conference are a waste of money. Imagine yourself on the cover of *Entrepreneur*. Would you be caught dead wearing or using any of your conference souvenirs? If not, do not throw money away now.

Seek Out Financial Aid.   Many major conferences, such as the Santa Barbara Writer's Conference, sponsor contests. First prize is paid tuition to the conference. You can also apply for a scholarship. Full and partial scholarships are often available for those who qualify (usually students or novices). Call the conference for more information, and be prepared to submit a portfolio of your work with your application.

Volunteer Your Time in Exchange for Admittance to the Conference. Volunteers are always needed to register attendees, staff sales tables, and assist speakers. You may even get uninterrupted time with one of the lecturers as you shuttle him to and from the airport.

Think Twice before Buying Books and Cassettes.   Can you get a paperback version of a hardback book elsewhere? Would you get a 10 percent or more discount if you bought it at the local bookstore or online, instead? If a book or audiotape is unique and would be difficult to find elsewhere, go ahead. Or, if you would like an autographed copy, whip out your wallet. However, if the book or audiotape is widely available and you cannot obtain an autograph, you may want to look elsewhere.

Home-based publishers Scott and Shirley Gregory recommend that if you are not able to attend a conference, look into buying audio- or videotapes of the program. Cassette tapes are much cheaper than traveling to a conference, where you must pay for transportation, lodging, and food for three or four days. When the Gregorys are not able to attend the BookExpo America, a major annual publishing convention, they buy audiotapes of the seminars. An additional benefit: They have no trouble hearing the speaker and can listen to the seminar as many times as they wish.

Be a Speaker.   Though home-based publisher Dan Poynter of ParaPublishing in Santa Barbara, California, attends a lot of conferences, he cannot remember the last time he paid for one. That is because he attends as a speaker. And, he says, this option is open to anyone with applicable experience, not only to entrepreneurs who have been in business a long time. "Just because you're new at your home-based business, doesn't mean you don't know something. Get last year's program and put together a proposal. Say you just came into publishing, but you were in office equipment for fifteen years, tell them how to save on office equipment; that will get you in free." He adds, "It gets you a lot of other perks, too. You might get paid for speaking or get free hotel accommodations. You certainly get into the cocktail parties," where a lot of networking takes place.

When home-based photographic supply consultant Laurie Dry goes to a conference, she always looks for a friend to share a hotel room and split the cost.

CHAPTER 10
TIGHTWAD TRANSACTIONS: MONEY-MANAGEMENT TIPS

Now that you have worked so hard to save your hard-earned cash, it is important to manage it wisely, which means you should avoid going into debt. Debt can sink a business faster than anything else. When you buy a bunch of things on credit, you gain a false sense of security. When you work and live within your means, you may have to do without some niceties, but you also stay solvent.

Another money-management pitfall is high bank fees. Banks look upon fees as sources of revenue, and they seem to find new ways to charge you all the time. Want to use a live teller? That will cost you. Want to write checks? That will cost you. It may take some time to find a financial institution that meets your needs without charging a fortune, but it is a worthwhile investment.

USING CREDIT CARDS

Credit cards can be valuable money-management tools when used wisely. You can borrow a lot of money with no questions asked, and typically have twenty-five days to pay. However, at the end of the twenty- or twenty-five-day grace period, you should pay. To allow a balance to carry over from month to month is expensive, as many credit cards have two-digit interest rates. If you need a long-term loan, financial planner Gerri Detweiler recommends finding a card with a fixed low interest rate, "The average personal-loan rate is around 13 percent. You can get a fixed-rate credit card lower than that, but you must shop around."

What should you look for in a credit card? No annual fee. If you must carry a balance, consider the interest rate and grace period. If you do not carry a balance, look at the perks the company offers. You probably receive dozens of personal credit-card offers in the mail every week, but you may not be aware of the different types of business credit cards available. Thus, we have included a couple of business credit cards that do not charge annual fees:

American Express Optima Platinum Card
PO Box 31549 • Salt Lake City, UT 84131-9953
phone: (800) 782-2377 • fax: (801) 965-2885
web site: http://www.americanexpress.com/smallbusiness

Fee: None

Interest Rate: Prime + 6 percent

Perks: 15 percent off Hertz car rentals, 10 to 15 percent off Hilton Hotels, and 10 to 20 percent off UPS delivery. Free travel-accident insurance, rental-car damage insurance, baggage insurance, purchase protection insurance against theft or damage of items purchased with the card, and the buyer's assurance plan, which extends the terms of the manufacturer's warranty on items you purchase with the card.

AT&T Universal Business Card (Mastercard)
PO Box 84004 • Columbus, GA 31908-9915
phone: (800) 682-7759 • fax: none listed
web site: http://www.att.com

Fee: None

Interest Rate: Prime + 9.4 percent

Perks: 10 percent discount on calling-card calls

Jonathan and Beth Miller, home-based owners of Reunited, Inc., a company that plans high-school reunions in southern Florida, pay many of their bills with their American Express credit card in order to rack up reward points. They are able to redeem the points for free hotel accommodations. Every year they go on a ski vacation that is virtually paid for with reward points.

> *Laurie Dry asked her credit card to change her billing cycle so that it ends the day before she needs to place orders to her supplier. She then has the full twenty-five days before it appears on her statement and another thirty days before she is required to pay—in effect, a free fifty-five-day loan!*

ACCEPTING CREDIT-CARD TRANSACTIONS

People use credit cards for almost everything now. If you sell products or services to the general public, it is truly a detriment to your business if you cannot accept credit card transactions. Home-based guerrilla Laurie Dry says that she has noticed a significant increase in her sales since she started accepting credit cards, which more than offsets the cost of offering the service.

To accept credit-card transactions, you will have to obtain what is called *merchant status.* In the past, some home-based businesspeople have found it difficult to obtain merchant status through their banks, because the banks were suspicious of businesspeople who did not have a storefront. However, that seems to be changing.

Dan Poynter, home-based owner of Para Publishing and author of *The Self-Publishing Manual* from Santa Barbara, California, suggests visiting five or so banks and asking for their merchant packets. "Don't tell them anything about yourself," he cautions, as some tellers will not give the packet to home-based entrepreneurs because many merchant accounts exclude home-based businesspeople. Poynter recommends taking the packets home and reading them carefully, looking for the exceptions to the rules. For instance, some banks will not allow entrepreneurs who work from their home to have a merchant account . . . unless they own the property. Or, you cannot have a merchant account if you accept telephone transactions . . . unless you have been in business for one year. Then, complete the application and send it in. "Some people don't even try their banks because of the horror stories they have heard. I would encourage people to apply at their own bank first," recommends Marcia Yudkin, home-based author of *6 Steps to Free Publicity*, from Boston, Massachusetts.

If you have trouble obtaining merchant status through your bank, you can also use an Independent Selling Organization (ISO), which is a middleman between banks and merchants. However, it can be more expensive than working with your own bank. Also, some businesspeople have had trouble with fraudulent ISOs, so be careful. Dry uses Discover-NOVUS at (800) 347-6673 to process her credit cards, and is very pleased with the service. The nation's largest ISO is Cardservice International. For more information, call them at (800) 948-6457.

One of the easiest ways to obtain merchant status is by belonging to a professional organization that offers card services as a benefit of membership. See Appendix A for a list of home-based business and professional associations. You may also be able to apply for merchant status from American Express at (800) 528-5200, which is easier for home-businesses to obtain, according to the home-business guerrillas we interviewed. Once you have an American Express account, it becomes easier to get Visa, Mastercard, and Discover merchant accounts.

A few words of caution, though: Obtaining merchant status and processing credit card transactions is not cheap. The initial application fee ranges from $100 to $400. Then, you need to process the transactions, somehow, usually through a point-of-sale (POS) terminal, which you must rent ($20 to 100 per month) or purchase ($250 to $1700). On top of all that, you must pay service fees of 2 to 7 percent of all transactions. Some companies also charge other fees, such as monthly statement fees, per transaction fees, or minimum monthly fees.

If you sell to the general public, you will probably more than recoup all of these fees in additional sales. However, if you deal mainly with other businesses, accepting credit-card transactions may be more trouble than it is worth. For example, Al Siebert, home-based publisher of Practical Psychology Press in Portland, Oregon, does not accept credit cards because he deals mainly with college bookstores, and does not believe the monthly merchant fees would be worthwhile. On the rare occasion that a reader calls him directly to order a book, he gives her the toll-free · telephone number of his book distributor, who can handle credit card transactions.

PROCESSING CREDIT-CARD TRANSACTIONS

Once you have achieved merchant status, you will need to find a way to process credit card sales. The most common way is to obtain an electric point-of-sale (POS) terminal, which allows you to swipe the credit card or input the numbers on a keypad. These are easy and usually flash step-by-step instructions on the screen. However, they are also expensive. As we mentioned in the previous section, renting costs about $20 to $100 per month, and buying costs upward of $250.

However, there are other alternatives to the POS terminal. For example, Publisher Dan Poynter uses computer software, his computer, and modem instead of a terminal. You can obtain PC Authorize or MacAuthorize computer software from the Internet. Says Poynter, "It's cheaper and much faster than any terminal. You hit the button, it goes out and back. You get authorization very quickly."

Another low-tech option is to use a manual credit-card terminal and carbon paper. Author Marcia Yudkin still uses "a manual swiper. I deposit the receipts directly into my bank account and get credited immediately," she says. "I've never had to buy that electronic machine or software. Any amount above $50, I call to verify the card and get an authorization number. I have investigated the price of going to an electronic system, but for the volume I have that goes on credit cards every year, it is not worth the switch. As long as my bank allows me to use this manual system, I'm going to continue." Another advantage to the manual machine is that Yudkin can accept credit cards anywhere; she has no need for a telephone jack or electric outlet, which makes it easy to sell books at her lectures.

> Get to know the decision-makers at your bank. Develop a relationship. At my bank, I know the president. When I want a loan, I go see him.
>
> —John Kremer,
> Open Horizons Publishing

SELECTING A BANK ACCOUNT

It is a good idea to open a separate bank account for your business transactions, so as to keep your business and personal finances more organized. Also, it helps avoid hassles with the IRS, should you ever get audited. There are two types of accounts you can open: personal and merchant. If you are operating the business under your own name, we recommend using that name on the account to avoid merchant fees. If you use a fictitious business name, many banks will require that you have a merchant account.

It is ridiculous to pay monthly fees to the bank for the privilege of storing (and lending) your money. You should not pay any monthly maintenance fees on your bank accounts. None. If you are, look for another account or financial institution. Kathryn does not pay monthly maintenance fees on any of her personal or business bank accounts.

There are many ways to circumvent maintenance fees; it is just a matter of sitting down with the bank's brochures and figuring out how to avoid the monthly charges. Do not just ask the teller or the new-accounts manager how to avoid fees. Sometimes, they do not know of all of the tricks available. Read the small print, looking for the exceptions in the footnotes.

Many banks waive fees if you keep a minimum balance. Sometimes that minimum is calculated as the sum of all of your accounts. Do you conduct all of your personal banking at that institution as well? Your business account may not need to maintain a high balance. Home-based editor Coleen Sykora's account has a $500 minimum-balance requirement. Originally, she had an account with a credit union, but when she wanted to accept credit cards she needed to get a merchant account at a commercial bank. She says, "If you shop for banks and are persistent, you will find ones that will give you a commercial account with no service fees and no per-check charges or charges for each check you deposit."

Or, you may be able to obtain a free checking account by agreeing to write fewer than ten checks a month. Use your credit card for most purchases, then use one check to pay the credit-card company. The point is, you should not have to pay to have a checking account at a financial institution. Invest some time and determine how you can avoid paying monthly fees.

> *Dave Wampler, home-based owner of the Simple Living Network in Trout Lake, Washington, does virtually all of his banking by mail, which saves him time and gas. Most banks also allow you to conduct transactions via phone and online.*

CREDIT UNIONS

Your bank may have seemed like a good choice when you first opened your account. Maybe they offered you 500 free checks, or required no minimum balance for one year. Now the year is over, however, you are almost out of checks, and the bank is charging you $7 a month because your account regularly falls below the outrageous minimum balance. Join a credit union. Of the home-based guerrillas we interviewed, more than half said they did their business banking through a credit union.

There are more than 12,000 federal and state-chartered credit unions operating in the United States. Credit unions have recently become more popular, because of looser eligibility requirements and increased services. Credit unions are financial associations, formed among individuals with a common bond called a *Field of Membership*. "There are three types of credit unions: single common bond, such as occupation-based or association-based; multiple common bond, such as a group of small businesses banding together; and community-based," explains Cherie Umbel, spokesperson for the National Credit Union Administration (NCUA). For instance, Kathryn belongs to the Community Federal Credit Union in Michigan, which is a community-based credit union open to anyone who lives or works in the cities of Novi, Northville, Canton, or Plymouth, or Ostego, or Montmorency Counties.

Credit-union members pool their savings, then make low-interest loans to one another. Unlike banks, credit unions are nonprofit and tax exempt. As a result, they have lower operating costs, which are passed on to members through lower fees and higher savings interest rates.

From the outside, a credit union looks much like a regular bank with tellers and transactions but, if you look closely, you will notice a few differences. The biggest difference is members cooperatively own shares of the credit union. At some credit unions, this ownership is reflected in the names of the accounts: savings accounts are often called *share accounts*, checking accounts are *share draft accounts,* and certificates of deposit are *share certificates.* But, not to worry, all of these accounts function in traditional ways.

Another difference is that credit unions may charge new members a nominal, one-time entry fee (usually $5). After depositing a minimum amount (usually $5 to $200), an individual becomes a member with voting rights. Each member has one vote, regardless of the number of shares he owns, to elect an unpaid board of directors to oversee the credit union, and make decisions on interest rates, finance charges, and loan limits.

Like accounts in Federal Deposit Insurance Corporation (FDIC) banks, federal credit-union members' accounts are fully insured, up to $100,000 per individual per account, by the NCUA, which supervises and periodically examines all federal credit unions. However, not all credit unions are federally insured; some are *cooperatively insured,* which means the credit unions form their own insurance companies. "The vast majority of credit unions in the United States—97 percent—are federally insured," says Umbel. Is this an important criterion in evaluating a credit union? Yes. Another advantage of federal credit unions: They must operate in compliance with all federal consumer protection laws, including the Equal Credit Opportunity Act.

What are the advantages of joining?

High-interest Savings.   Credit unions' interest rates on share savings, money markets, and certificate accounts are usually 0.25 percent to 1 percent higher than those offered by banks.

Low-interest Loans.   Credit unions usually charge 0.25 percent to 1 percent less than banks.

Fewer Fees.   Many credit unions believe that charging fees contradicts the original credit-union philosophy. Thus, when credit unions charge fees, they do it to cover the costs of providing services, or to penalize members who mismanage their accounts, such as for insufficient funds and overdrafts. Banks, on the other hand, view fees as a way of increasing income. For example, 70 percent of credit unions offer some form of free checking, compared to only 13 percent of banks, according to the Credit Union National Association, Inc.

Even when credit unions do charge fees, their fees are significantly lower than banks. The average cost of an interest-bearing checking account at a credit union that does charge is only $5.01 per month, as opposed to $7.65 at a bank. Chart 10-1 illustrates the difference between bank and credit union fees.

CHART 10-1 Credit Union vs. Bank Fee Comparison

% Charging Fee			Average Fee Among Those That Charge	
	CREDIT UNION	BANK	CREDIT UNION	BANK
Economy Checking				
Monthly Fee	15%	81%	$3.50/month	$3.38/month
Per Check Fee	5%	95%	31 free checks, then 20¢/check	13 free checks, then 40¢/check
Overdraft	70%	90%	$9.48	$16.10
Stop-Payment	97%	100%	$9.64	$14.19
Cashier's Check	50%	100%	$2.19	$3.13
Annual Credit Card	13%	35%	$12.30	$15.92
Owned ATMs	19%	11%	88¢/transaction (92% allow some free, average 5.9/month)	74¢/withdrawal
Other ATMs	76%	71%	93¢/transaction (61% allow some free, average 5.1/month)	$1.07/withdrawal

Note: All percentages are limited to financial institutions that offer the service.

Sources: *Credit Union Executive's 1999 Credit Union Fees Survey Report* and Sheshunoff Information Services, Inc., *Pricing Financial Services 1998.*

Low Minimum Balances. Minimum balances at credit unions can be as low as $50. Even if you fall below the minimum balance, you may not be charged as you would be at a bank. Instead, your account might simply stop accruing interest until it is replenished.

Typical credit union benefits include:

➤ *Discounted American Automobile Association (AAA) memberships.*

➤ *Car-buying locator programs.* This free service saves you time and, ideally, money. A representative scours local automobile dealerships for the exact make and model you want, then helps you negotiate the best price.

➤ *Discounted movie tickets.* At some credit unions, members can buy movie tickets at 50 percent off regular admission prices.

➤ *Warehouse club membership day passes.* Being a member of a credit union may make you eligible to join a warehouse club, such as Sam's Club.

➤ *Discount coupons* for local attractions, such as zoos and amusement parks.

➤ *Financial education courses.* Credit unions hold classes on car buying, how to secure a mortgage, how to budget, etc.

Friendly, Personalized Service.   When you belong to a credit union, you are more than customer number 100,029. You are a member with a name. "I've been with a credit union for over ten years and I would never go back to a commercial bank," says home-based tax consultant, Anthony Applebaum, EA. "If there's a problem with my account, they call me. You never get that kind of service from a bank."

If you are anxious to transfer all your accounts to a credit union, be cautious. There are drawbacks. First, consider which financial services are important to you. Though credit unions have fantastic values, they may not meet all of your banking needs. A case in point: A recent survey showed 66 percent of members do not consider their credit union to be their primary financial institution. Why?

Inconvenient Locations.   Credit unions usually have only one or two locations in a city. Occasionally, these locations are housed inside another building, making a quick stop next to impossible. For example, the only La Jolla, California branch of the San Diego Medical Federal Credit Union is located inside the Veteran's Administration Hospital. If you visit the VA Hospital regularly, this is extremely convenient. If you do not, it is bothersome.

Some credit unions, like the San Diego Medical Federal Credit Union, solve this problem by providing a mobile service. A credit-union representative travels around town in an RV, spending one day a week at different scheduled locations. Before joining, ask for a list of the credit union's locations to verify that one will be convenient for you.

Limited ATM Access.   Many credit unions are too small to operate a string of automatic-teller machines, so they contract through other financial institutions or form cooperatives with other credit unions. Sometimes these ATMs are convenient, sometimes not. Also, credit unions may charge a $1 to $2 fee for each transaction, though many allow several free transactions per month before charging. If you are accustomed to banking by ATM, you may have to change your habits or you will pay a small fortune in charges.

Shorter Hours.   Some credit unions operate during typical banking hours, but many close earlier than banks and are closed, or open for only a few hours, on Saturdays. A few even close for lunch! Credit unions may also close one day a month or quarter for "maintenance." However, many offer electronic forms of banking, so this is becoming less of an issue. For instance, several credit unions have sites on the Internet on which members can learn about promotions, apply for loans, transfer funds, verify deposits, and check balances. Other credit unions offer free twenty-four-hour telephone banking services, through which members can do many of the same things.

To become a credit-union member, you must be eligible under the credit union's "common bond" provision. The good news is it is fairly easy to be eligible. So easy, in fact, that many banks have cried foul. Outraged banks have been lobbying Congress to more strictly limit credit-union membership, but, luckily for consumers, they have not succeeded. Some typical eligibility requirements include:

➤ You live in an area served by a community credit union. Check the *Yellow Pages,* or call the Credit Union National Association at (800) 358-5710 or visit their web site at http://www.cuna.org for the number of your state credit-union league, which will help you find an institution.

➤ You are a student, faculty, or staff member at a university with a credit union. Call student information, the registrar's office, or look in the campus telephone directory.

➤ You belong to an association with its own credit union.

➤ You are related to a credit-union member. Most credit unions invite spouses and children to join. Some also allow extended family to become members—grandparents, siblings, even cousins!

➤ You live in the same household as a credit-union member.

Summarizes Steve Carlson, home-based publisher of Upper Access Books in Hinesburg, Vermont, "We have a lot of small transactions. We write lots of checks for $20, $30, $50 and get a lot of checks in those amounts. The commercial bank we were dealing with started to charge us 11¢ for each check we deposited or wrote. For a small business, that was turning into several hundred dollars a month. We are members of the Teachers' Credit Union and, it turned out, we could have a business account with no bank fees at all. A lot of people are qualified, and it doesn't occur to them that they can set up their business account through the credit union as long as they are still members."

Before you start a home-based business, get your own personal financial house in order.

—Dave Wampler,
Simple Living Network

CHECKS BY MAIL

If you are buying checks from the bank, stop. You do not need to buy checks from the bank in order for the bank to process them. It costs twice as much to purchase them through the bank as it does to buy them from a mail-order company.

A box of 150 duplicate checks from the bank costs around $15, the same checks from a mail-order company cost about $10 ($7 plus $3 shipping and handling). To mail-order your checks, send the company a voided check from your existing supply, and they will print up a new set with your name, address, and account number. Using standard shipping, an order takes approximately fourteen days to arrive, so plan ahead. To save even more, buy large quantities of single checks with the simplest design and font available.

Here are several mail-order firms:

Checks In the Mail, Inc.
2435 Goodwin Lane • New Braunfels, TX 78135-0001
phone: (877) 397-1541 • fax: (800) 822-0005
web site: http://www.checksinthemail.com

Current
Check Products Division • PO Box 19000
Colorado Springs, CO 80935-9000
phone: (800) 204-2244 • fax: (800) 993-3232
web site: http://www.currentchecks.com

Image Checks
PO Box 548 • Little Rock, AR 72203
phone: (800) 562-8768 • fax: (501) 455-4896
web site: http://imagechecks.com

Start small and slowly. It violates the American notion that instantaneous is the way to go, but it gives you a much better chance at succeeding.

—Marc Eisenson,
Good Advice Press

CHAPTER 11

UNCLE SAM TAKES HIS SHARE: TAX-RELATED SAVINGS

"We pay our taxes and think people should. Time spent in prison is not very productive," jokes Marc Eisenson, home-based publisher of Good Advice Press. Seriously, though, it is tough to save on taxes since you have to pay what you owe. But the trick is not to pay *more* than you owe—in other words, you want to take every deduction for which you are eligible. When you are self-employed, the name of the game is reduce taxable income. In addition, you do not want to spend more money than necessary in preparing your income-tax return.

Tax laws change faster than the weather. So, although we have made every effort to make sure that the recommendations here are accurate, the regulations may have changed since we went to print, so investigate specific tax codes prior to filing.

RECORD-KEEPING

The most important part of saving on your taxes is to keep impeccable records. Keep receipts for *everything* related to your business, and keep them organized. For items for which you have no receipts, such as mileage, maintain a log. Keep the log as you go along. Do not try to reconstruct your mileage months later. ("Was it October or November that I drove to New Jersey?")

Coleen Sykora, home-based publisher, says she and her husband, Bob, keep track of every penny they spend in order to maximize their tax deductions and monitor their spending in general. "If Bob bought a can of pop or a newspaper, he writes it down. Having to be accountable for it, you're aware of those little things. It's so easy to have a $20 bill and then it's gone and you have nothing to show for it," she says. "I categorize expenses. What are we spending on what? Is that worthwhile to us? Do we want to be spending that much? Just keeping track of it to that extent really makes a difference."

It takes commitment to keep such detailed records, but it can add up when you complete the deduction portion of your income taxes. You may not be willing to keep such detailed records in every area of your life, but you should when it comes to business expenses. If you do not, you are over-paying Uncle Sam. You may find it easier to keep detailed records by using a computer-software bookkeeping program. Many of the guerrillas we interviewed recommended Intuit's QuickBooks. For more information on how detailed record-keeping can help you control your expenses, read *Your Money or Your Life: Transforming Your Relationship with Money and Achieving Financial Independence* by Joe Dominguez and Vicki Robin.

WORDS OF WISDOM

Pay taxes on time. Penalties can kill a small business.

—**Edith Flowers Kilgo,**
editor of *Creative Downscaling*

THE HOME-OFFICE DEDUCTION

Many home-based guerrillas are reluctant to claim the home-office deduction, because they have heard that it is a red flag to the Internal Revenue Service (IRS). If you do not feel comfortable with it because you fear you may be audited as a result, do not claim it. However, most home-based guerrillas we interviewed took the deduction and summarized it this way: "I keep great records. Everything is legitimate. I'm entitled to it. I'm claiming it."

If you can legitimately claim it, the home-office deduction will definitely save you a ton of money in taxes. You can write off part of your mortgage based on the size of your office. For example, if your house is 1,500 square feet and your office is 300 square feet, you can deduct 20 percent of your mortgage, after subtracting the value of the land. If you are a renter, you can deduct 20 percent of your rent. Moreover, you can deduct a portion of your property taxes, homeowner's insurance, and utilities. However, the deduction cannot be greater than the profit generated by your home-based business. (If it is, you can carry over the remaining portion to the following year.)

In 1999, claiming the home-office deduction became easier for those people who conducted most of their business outside their office, such as house painters. In the past, those people could not deduct their home offices because they did not conduct their primary moneymaking functions there. Now, the home office is deductible if you use it exclusively for administrative and managerial tasks, such as billing clients, and you have no other fixed location where you conduct these activities.

To claim a home-office deduction, your home office must meet three tests: It must be your principle place of business; a separately identifiable space in your home, such as a converted garage or spare bedroom; and regularly and exclusively used for business, meaning you cannot use the space for anything else. Thus, your home office must be devoid of any furniture that is not used for business—no beds, dressers, or Nintendo Game Systems. The one exception is if you are deducting a portion of your home for the storage of inventory or product samples. In that case, the exclusive-use test does not apply.

However, even if your office qualifies, you still may not want to claim the home depreciation portion of the deduction, if you plan on selling your house in the next two years, says Anthony Applebaum, EA, a tax consultant from San Diego, California. If you take the home-office depreciation portion of the deduction and then you sell your home, you may have to pay capital-gains tax, depending on how large your office is in relationship to your home and how much it has appreciated in value since you bought it. Applebaum explains: "Let's say you claim 10 percent of your home as your home office. That means that if you sell your home at a gain, you have to take 10 percent of that gain and include it in your income. Let's say you made a $100,000 profit. Normally, you wouldn't have to pay any taxes but, if you used 10 percent as a home office and you did not disqualify your office for the last two years, you would have to pay capital-gains tax on $10,000. You have to look at what your tax savings for the next two years for the home office are versus what you would have to pay in liability if you were to sell the house." He says that this is particularly important in places where real estate appreciates quickly, and it is not uncommon to make $200,000 in profit when selling a home. "For some people, like those who live in two-bedroom condos, 50 percent of their space is home office. If you had to pay income taxes on 50 percent of the profit of the sale of your home, it wouldn't be a good idea to claim the home office" deduction.

However, Eva Webb, EA, home-based owner of The Income Tax Store in Sayetteville, Georgia, says that if you do not take the home-depreciation portion of the deduction, you do not need to pay any capital gains. "I always advise my clients not to take depreciation and take all the rest of the expenses (a percentage of mortgage interest, taxes, insurance, utilities, etc.). Then there is no problem if the house is sold," she says.

If you decide your home office qualifies and you want to claim the deduction, you will need to complete IRS Form 8829, which requires the separation of all your home-related business expenses into two categories: direct (those related to the area of your home that is used as an office, such as tract lighting installed above your desk) and indirect (all other costs, such as electric bills, repairs, and homeowner's insurance). Indirect expenses are partially deductible, based on the percentage of your home that your office occupies. For more information, see IRS Publication 587, *Business Use of Your Home*.

Remember, you do not need to claim a home-office deduction in order to claim other expenses related to your home-based business!

WORDS OF WISDOM

If you ever get audited, hire a professional to represent you. People get into audits and they already have their guard up. The auditor picks up on that and immediately you start off on a bad foot. A professional is better able to deal with the auditor. Most people will go into an audit and end up paying a lot of taxes they may not have to pay. Tax professionals deal with the IRS on a weekly basis. They know the system. They know how to best make your case. You wouldn't represent yourself in court. Don't represent yourself in front of the IRS.

—Anthony Applebaum,
EA, tax consultant

COMMONLY OVERLOOKED DEDUCTIONS

Most people know to deduct expenses for office supplies, furniture, and equipment, but overlook other legitimate deductions. "A lot of people miss deductions because they don't think they're deductible," says Applebaum. "Most people just look at the standard set of categories on the Schedule C. They need to look at things outside of those categories. On page two of the Schedule C there is a whole list of blank lines for other business expenses. A lot of people don't even think about that."

Section 162 of the Internal Revenue Code states that deductions are "all the ordinary and necessary expenses paid or incurred during the taxable year in carrying on any trade or business." Therefore, you can claim any business expense that you incur, with the exception of donations, fines, and state and federal income taxes. For instance, did you know that subscriptions to professional periodicals are deductible? Other commonly overlooked deductions you may be entitled to include (some are only partially deductible, others are 100 percent deductible):

- Professional association dues

- Advertising

- Auto expenses, including tolls and parking

- Bank service charges

- Books, magazines, and newspapers related to the business (remember to save the receipt for this book!)

- Business gifts

- Holiday cards for business associates

- Internet-access charges

- Legal and professional fees, such as accountant fees

- Postage

- Printing and copying charges

- Professional-development expenses, such as conferences, seminar tuition, or college tuition as it relates to your business

- Product displays or sample cases

- Business travel expenses, including transportation, accommodations, and meals

"A lot of people don't realize that when you're traveling you're allowed to take a standard meal allowance, a fixed amount based on the city you're traveling in. Did you eat meals? You don't need receipts. You're allowed X dollars a day depending on where you're traveling. That's a deduction that people miss," says Applebaum. The standard meal allowance rate for travel in 1998 was $30 a day for most areas in the U.S. However, other locations in the U.S. are designated high-cost areas, and qualify for higher standard meal allowances of $34, $38, or $42 per day. Obviously, this system favors those who eat cheaply. If you can eat for less than the standard meal allowance (and you should be able to), you benefit.

If you want to thank clients, consider sending gifts instead of taking them out to eat. Meals are only 50 percent deductible. A gift worth $25 or less is 100 percent deductible. However, a $100 meal would be better than a $100 gift ($50 deduction vs. $25).

DEDUCTIBLE DOES NOT EQUAL FREE

Some people think that if something is deductible, it does not cost them anything. For example, they think if you buy a laser printer for $1,000, they will save $1,000 on their taxes. Not true. For every dollar spent, most people will save 20 to 40 percent, based on their income level. Using the previous example, you will save $200 to $400 of the cost of the $1,000 laser printer. That means, it still costs you $600 to $800 to buy the laser printer. Thus, do not spend money extravagantly just because the expense is deductible. Do not use it as a rationale for buying things you do not need. Spend only the money you would spend were it not deductible.

Edith Flowers Kilgo, home-based publisher, recommends timing purchases for the best tax advantage. For instance, by reviewing her tax liability regularly, she can see if it is expedient to purchase computer equipment in the last quarter of the year. Or, she can buy postage in large quantity in December if she needs the extra deduction.

HIRE FAMILY
· ·

Home-based businesses are often family affairs. Everyone pitches in. For instance, Kathryn's husband reads all her writing and has become a constructive (and strict) editor. Publisher Gary Dunn's wife also edits his newsletter, *The Caretaker Gazette*.

If your spouse and children work in your business, you may want to put them on the payroll. Why? Employees' salaries are 100 percent tax deductible. Children under eighteen make the best employees; they are not subject to Social Security or Medicare taxes, and they do not need to pay income taxes on the first $3,000 of earned income. There is no minimum age limit for child employees. If they can do the work, you can hire them. That means you can hire your nine-year-old to file, fill orders, or stuff envelopes. She earns spending money and you save on taxes—everyone wins!

If you buy your own health insurance or have a self-employed retirement plan, then you should also consider hiring your spouse. As of 1998, self-employed persons are allowed to claim a 45 percent deduction of their health insurance premiums, but can claim 100 percent if they have employees. So, by hiring your spouse, you can deduct 100 percent of your health insurance, as well as all of the medical, dental, and vision expenses not covered by insurance.

If you hire your spouse and have a self-employment retirement plan, then your spouse is entitled to be covered under your retirement plan, which means that as a couple you can defer more taxes through retirement savings because your maximum allowable contribution limits are increased. (For more information, see the next section.) However, unlike minors, a spouse's wages are subject to income tax withholding, Social Security, and Medicare taxes. Thus, for it to be worthwhile to hire your spouse, you must buy your own health insurance and/or include your spouse in your retirement plan.

To take advantage of the health-insurance premium deduction, you will need to create a Medical Reimbursement Plan under Section 105 of the

Internal Revenue Code. The easiest way to do this is to buy a ready-made plan, AgriPlan/BizPlan from Total Administrative Services Corporation, a third-party administrative service. It provides all of the documentation necessary to comply with the IRS. Total Administrative Services Corporation estimates that its participants save an average of $2,450 per year. For more information, contact:

Total Administrative Services Corporation
2302 International Lane • Madison, WI 53704
phone: (800) 422-4661 • fax: (608) 241-4584
web site: http://www.plan105.com

Finally, it is a good idea to keep timecards for all employees, and to pay family members the same wage you would pay nonfamily members for the same work. For more information on hiring children and spouses, read IRS publication 15, Circular E, *Employer's Tax Guide*.

RETIREMENT PLANS

Another way to reduce your taxable income is to defer your taxes through a retirement plan. According to a 1997 survey by Fidelity Investments, 38 percent of home-based business owners rated saving for retirement as their top financial goal. However, only two in five were confident that they would have enough saved for retirement, and the majority said they had saved less than $50,000.

One reason home-based entrepreneurs are not saving enough may be because many are unfamiliar with the retirement plans available to them, especially the Self-Employed Pension-Individual Retirement Accounts (SEP-IRA). Of those polled, 45 percent had an IRA, but only 17 percent had a SEP-IRA, which allows many home-based guerrillas to save significantly more than a traditional IRA. There are five basic plans available for self-employed individuals: traditional Individual Retirement Accounts (IRA), Roth IRAs, Keogh plans, Saving Incentive Match Plans (SIMPLE), and SEP-IRAs.

Most people are familiar with traditional IRAs. They are great vehicles for deferring taxes, and are easily established at any financial institution with a minimum amount of paperwork and as little as $50. However, your contributions are limited to $2,000 per year ($4,000 per year per couple, $2,000 in each spouse's name).

In 1998, the new Roth IRA was introduced. The main difference between it and a traditional IRA is that investment earnings are tax-free if you have held the Roth for at least five years and the withdrawal is made after you reach age fifty-nine-and-a-half, because of severe disability, or to buy a first house for you or family members. For this reason, many young guerrillas are opting for Roth IRAs. If your business is just starting out, a Roth IRA may be a good choice. Like a traditional IRA, your contributions are limited to $2,000 per year.

The three basic retirement plans that you may not be familiar with are those that are exclusively for self-employed individuals: Keogh plans, SIMPLE plans, and SEP-IRAs. The advantages of a Keogh plan—there are two types: profit-sharing plan and money purchase pension plan—are that your contributions are tax-deferred and you can contribute more to it than to any other tax-favored retirement savings plan. Depending on the type of Keogh you choose, you can contribute up to 15 to 25 percent of net income or $24,000 to $30,000, whichever is less. However, if you have a Keogh plan and you have employees, you are required to make contributions on their behalf. Moreover, Keogh plans are complex and, due to the amount of paperwork and regulations involved, probably require the assistance of a financial planner.

On the other hand, SIMPLE plans are relatively easy to establish and require minimal record-keeping. There are two types of SIMPLE plans: the SIMPLE IRA or the SIMPLE 401(k). Most entrepreneurs prefer the SIMPLE IRA because it is easier to establish and more cost-effective. One major difference between SIMPLE IRAs and regular IRAs is that the penalty for early withdrawal is quite a bit higher—as much as 25 percent! Another potential drawback: If you have employees, you must contribute to their accounts with dollar-for-dollar matching up to 3 percent of their salaries, or by contributing 2 percent of their salaries (up to $3,000), regardless of whether they contribute to the plan. Moreover, all employees are immediately 100 percent vested, which means businesses with high turnover may want to shy away from SIMPLE plans. The maximum amount you can put away in a SIMPLE IRA is $12,000 ($6,000 maximum contribution plus $6,000 in matching).

A SEP-IRA is also easy to establish, and it can have higher maximum contribution levels than a SIMPLE IRA, depending on your income. The main advantage of a SEP-IRA is that you are able to contribute up to 15 percent of your net income or $24,000, whichever is less. Therefore, you can defer taxes on as much as $24,000! And, you can still have a SEP-IRA, even if you have a 401(k) plan at your day job. The only potential drawback is that if you have employees who have worked for you at least three out of the last five years, you must make contributions on their behalf as well. For more information on Keoghs, SIMPLE IRAs, and SEP-IRAs, see IRS Publication 560, *Retirement Plans for Small Business.*

QUARTERLY ESTIMATED INCOME TAX PAYMENTS

Even if your business is modest, you will probably have to make quarterly estimated income tax payments on Form 1040-ES. Though it is difficult to estimate your profit until the year is over, you must make your best effort. If you do not make estimated tax payments four times a year—April 15, June 15, September 15, and January 15, the IRS will charge you an "underpayment of estimated taxes" penalty, which is currently about 5 percent annually. Use last year's tax liability as a guide, and aim to pay 100 percent of it in four equal installments. This way you can avoid the penalty even if you have no idea how much you will owe. There is no penalty if your total unpaid tax liability for the year is less than $1,000.

WORDS OF WISDOM

New business owners shy away from paying for expert advice. But if you don't spend money on certain things you're going to be sorry later. Any time you find yourself thinking, 'I really should do X, Y, and Z, but it costs too much money,' think about what are the potential consequences of not spending money. Sometimes you just need to spend the money.

—Marcia Yudkin,
author of *6 Steps to Free Publicity*

PREPARE YOURSELF OR NOT?

Like most things, doing your own taxes is cheaper than hiring a professional. And new computer tax-preparation software programs, which cost under $75, have made preparing your own taxes easier than ever. Programs such as TurboTax and MacInTax, which cost between $10 and $70 depending on the program's features, walk you through Schedule C and explain it in plain English. Scott and Shirley Gregory, home-based publishers, like the tax-preparation software because it recommends deductions and other points to consider, things a professional would do, but at a much lower price.

If you are really ambitious, you can just sit down with the forms, a calculator, pencil, and paper, like Catherine Groves, home-based publisher of the *Christian*New Age Quarterly*. She has been doing her own taxes since she started the periodical eleven years ago. One of the advantages of doing your own taxes is that you know your business. You know what you do and where you keep things, so you do not need to spend a lot of time explaining it to someone else.

However, some home-based guerrillas have found hiring a professional to be valuable, especially if they have employees, which makes the taxes infinitely more complicated. For instance, Dave Wampler, home-based owner of the Simple Living Network, can do his own taxes and does not have a regular accountant, but he prefers to have a professional look it over at the end of the year, as a system of checks and balances. The Washington state resident also feels the professional advice is worth the money. For example, accountants can offer suggestions for reducing your taxable income, alternatives that the computer tax-preparation software may overlook. For instance, publisher Gary Dunn's accountant recommended he incorporate the business. Most home businesses start out as sole proprietorships or partnerships, because they are easy to establish. However, if your business brings in taxable income of over $100,000 per year, you may want to incorporate, as it may offer you significant tax advantages.

If you decide you want professional help, who should you hire? There are three types of accounting professionals: certified public accountants (CPAs), enrolled agents (EAs), and tax preparers. CPAs have the most training, have passed exams from the American Institute of Certified Public Accountants, and must be licensed by a state agency. EAs are licensed by the IRS after passing examinations, and must complete a minimum number of credit hours each year of continuing education. Many EAs are former IRS employees who are qualified because they have had a minimum number of years of experience. In contrast, tax preparers do not have to pass any exams or be licensed. If you have an extremely complicated return, hiring a CPA is probably best. However, if you have a fairly simple return, an EA will cost less and offer comparable services. For more information on selecting a CPA, contact the American Institute of Certified Public Accountants at (888) 777-7077. To locate an EA in your area, call the National Association of Enrolled Agents referral line at (800) 424-4339.

Concentrate on what you do best. Pay a professional lawyer, accountant, or public relations agent to do what they do best. If taxes and accounting were easy, there wouldn't be tax preparers and accountants. There are only so many hours in a day.

**—Anthony Applebaum,
EA, tax consultant**

FREE TAX INFORMATION AND ADVICE

Incredible as it might sound, the best place to get tax information and advice is from the IRS. They have many useful publications, such as IRS Publication 334, *Tax Guide for Small Business,* and you can count on their accuracy. You can obtain copies of publications by calling (800) 829-3676 or visiting the IRS's web site at http://www.irs.gov. Also, you can visit the reference section of a large public library, which will probably have a set of IRS publications. For recorded tax information on over 140 topics, you can call the IRS at (800) 829-4477, or to receive help from a person, you can call (800) 829-1040.

A lot of people don't know that when you get your audit report back, that's not the final word. If you don't agree with the examiner, you can ask for an informal appeal. Then, if you still don't agree, you can do a formal appeal, then you can go to tax court. Of course, it gets expensive, but a lot of people see the audit report and they think that's it. I've seen so many get changed in appeals. Most small business-people don't know about this stuff. It's important that you do. If you appeal and you get your taxes cut in half, you just saved yourself half.

—Anthony Applebaum,
EA, tax consultant

CHAPTER 12

THE FRUGAL FRATERNITY: ASSOCIATIONS

Associations are great places to meet other home-based business professionals to network and trade ideas. However, association dues can become expensive, and meetings are time consuming, so guerrillas need to be selective in their membership. In Appendix A, we list dozens of associations in which you may be interested but, in this chapter, we will discuss the advantages and disadvantages of joining, what to look for in an association, and how to reduce the costs of membership.

THE ADVANTAGES

The greatest advantage of association membership is networking. Lillian Bjorseth, home-based speaker, trainer, and author of *Breakthrough Networking: Building Relationships that Last,* from Lisle, Illinois, believes it is imperative for home-based guerrillas to belong to associations in order to maintain contacts and to develop professionally. She likes associations because of the opportunities she has to meet with peers and potential customers. She views her memberships as sources of advice, support, and information.

Bjorseth brings up another advantage of associations: camaraderie. People who work in a traditional office have co-workers with whom they can exchange ideas, celebrate victories, and commiserate over defeats. Working at home can get extremely lonely, especially if you are a people person. The right association can provide a work-related support system.

Vicki Nelson, home-based owner of Work Group Resources, a computer sales, service, and consulting firm in Novi, Michigan, belongs to several associations, and says that new businesses can benefit greatly from membership because it helps increase word-of-mouth. Some associations give members free advertisements in their publications. Associations also often offer cooperative marketing programs.

When you are new to a field, associations can also help you increase your skills. For instance, Gerri Detweiler, a home-based financial consultant, speaker, and author, says she learned a great deal about public speaking by belonging to Toastmasters and the National Speakers Association. "At Toastmasters, I improved my speaking skills every week," she says. Ruth Ann Weber, home-based painter, teacher, and owner of a hand-painted furniture painting business, says she likes belonging to organizations because she gets on mailing lists to receive notices about seminars.

The best benefits, however, may be the discounts you get as a member of some organizations. For instance, Steve Carlson, home-based publisher, receives a 62 percent discount on shipping through his membership in Merchant Shippers. Members of the National Association for the Self Employed (NASE) pay $72 in dues and receive lots of discounts, including savings on overnight shipping with Airborne Express; vehicle rental discounts from Alamo, National, and Hertz; and a $10,000 Common Carrier Accidental Death Benefit insurance.

Many associations provide discounted health-insurance rates for members. If your family does not have insurance through another source, it pays to investigate the health-insurance coverage provided to members. The coverage often costs much less than that which you can get on your own. Many home-based guerrillas we interviewed get their health insurance coverage through an association. "It pays to belong to organizations," says Carlson. "We belong to several organizations that may cost $75 to $90 a year in dues, but the benefits we get quickly pay us back and more, in addition to any educational benefits we receive through the newsletters."

You should join only those organizations where you can really develop relationships, which would mean only joining one at a time.

—Melissa Giovagnoli,
author of *Meganetworking*

THE DISADVANTAGES

More than half the home-based guerrillas we interviewed said they did not belong to any associations. Of those, most cited expense as the main reason. Annual dues can cost anywhere from $30 to $500. If you do not utilize all the available benefits, the cost-to-benefit ratio is extremely poor. Barbara J. Winter, home-based author of *Making a Living Without a Job,* has found that to be true. She travels a lot and cannot attend meetings regularly, so she does not think she receives sufficient value for her money.

Belonging to associations can also be time consuming. Michelle Foy, home-based owner of Dynamic Alternatives, warns that association meetings can be tremendous wastes of time. She questions the effectiveness of networking in which "coiffed women sweep into a room and present their business cards like magicians."

The time when you have the most influence with an organization is when you are joining. Call ahead, ask for the person in charge of new members, and express interest in exploring joining. Request to go to a meeting. Explain your market and the people you would like to meet. Ask to be introduced to a couple of people and sit with someone. That can really help you move into the inner circle on the front end.

—Melissa Giovagnoli,
author of *Meganetworking*

WHAT TO LOOK FOR IN AN ASSOCIATION

➤ *Who belongs.* If you want to join an association in order to network with colleagues or clients, it is important to know if any of your colleagues or potential customers already belong. Ask current customers to which associations they belong. If you know others working in the field, request their opinions on specific associations. Also, many home-based businesspeople we interviewed felt that some industry-specific organizations do not cater to the needs of home-based guerrillas. Thus, before you join, ask how many members have home-based businesses.

➤ *Location.* Some associations are national but, if you do not live near the headquarters or a branch chapter, you will probably miss out on the major networking benefits. Also, consider who your potential customers are. If you are a local business, such as a house-cleaning service, you will gain more benefits from belonging to the local chamber of commerce than if you are a national business, such as a online CD retailer.

➤ *Meeting frequency.* If an organization meets more than a couple of times a month, you may find you are spending more time networking than working.

➤ *Cost.* Guerrillas know to examine how much dues will cost. However, it is also important to consider other hidden costs. For instance, some organizations pressure members to contribute to favored charities or political campaigns. Also, as Henry David Thoreau said, "We should distrust any enterprise that requires new clothes." One of the advantages of being a home-based guerrilla is you can wear anything you'd like to work. As a result, for most of us, our professional wardrobe is more limited than those who go to a traditional office. If you go to a professional luncheon every week, it is unlikely you will want to wear the same blue suit again and again. So, how many new outfits will you need, and how much will they cost?

➤ *Benefits that you will use.* The key words here are *you will use.* Some associations offer a lot of benefits but, if you do not use them, the dues are a waste of money. Calculate the approximate monetary value of the benefits and weigh them against membership costs. For example, does association membership provide any discounts for products or services you use? Will you receive any publications containing information you cannot find anywhere else?

Associations with web sites often post useful information to entice new members. Some parts of the site may have restricted access, requiring a membership number to enter. However, other parts are free and open to anyone.

HOW TO GET MAXIMUM VALUE FOR MINIMUM DOLLARS

One businessman we interviewed recommended running for president of the association you decide to join. Why? First, as president, you always know what is going on in the group and the industry. Second, and more important, whenever reporters need to contact an association, they usually want to speak to the president. This exposure results in tons of free publicity for the association, but also for you and your business. Of course, holding an association office can also be time consuming, so research the requirements of the job and ask the incumbent for an estimate of the time commitment involved before you start your election campaign.

Even if you decide not to run for office, be an active member. Attend the meetings. Participate in events. Talk to people. Use available discounts. In other words, *get your money's worth.*

Anthony Applebaum, EA, does not belong to any associations, but he has found ways to garner some of the benefits of membership without paying high membership fees. He keeps an eye out for events hosted by organizations in which he is interested. Oftentimes, he can attend the event by paying a nonmember's fee. For example, once a month, he attends a dinner hosted by the Inland Society of Tax Consultants, an accounting association in his area. For $20, he gets dinner, a program by a keynote speaker, and two hours of continuing-education credits, which he needs to keep his license current. Of course, the evening costs only $15 if you are a member, but to become a member costs $105 per year. Ask what is available to nonmembers for a fee.

Most associations provide members with free subscriptions to their periodicals or significant discounts. However, some allow nonmembers to purchase publications separately. For example, *HR Magazine* is free to members of the Society for Human Resource Management with their $160 annual dues, but it is available for $70 per year to nonmembers. If you are mainly interested in the industry information available through the association, ask if you can purchase publications separately.

Attendance at annual conferences is also usually open to nonmembers, though admission costs quite a bit more than for members. A great deal of networking occurs at these conferences. You may get more networking for your money by paying the nonmember conference admission than the annual dues.

Barbara Brabec, home-based speaker and author of *Homemade Money,* reminds home-based guerrillas not to overlook free associations or organizations. When she was a computer novice, she joined a computer group at the library. About 100 computer users met once a month to exchange ideas and solve problems. Brabec says she learned more from the group than she had from books, and she never had to hire a computer consultant to get answers to her questions.

Catherine Groves, home-based editor of the *Christian*New Age Quarterly*, has had similar experience with free, informal groups. She meets weekly with a well-known Bible scholar and a handful of others to discuss religious issues. She says, "It's a better education than I could find in a formal setting."

Finally, if your business is mainly local, consider volunteering at charitable organizations instead of paying to join associations. Jonathan and Beth Miller, home-based owners of Reunited, Inc., a company that plans high school reunions in Florida, get most of their customers through word-of-mouth advertising among Florida residents. Thus, the Millers find they gain greater exposure by being involved in community organizations than in professional ones. They are active in their children's PTA, the local branch of the University of Florida alumni club, and an organization that raises money to feed the homeless. They not only help their business, but also the social organizations with which they are involved.

Just because you have email, fax, and phone doesn't mean you're supposed to cocoon at home. Don't withdraw. Get involved with people and the community. Get to know your neighbors, do volunteer work. You may be wired, but are you connected?

—Jeff Berner,
author of *The Joy of Working from Home*

BARTER ASSOCIATIONS

We have listed barter associations separately, because they offer different advantages and disadvantages than traditional industry associations. A barter association, or a trade exchange, is a group of 300 to 3,000 businesses that trade goods and services. There are approximately 400 such groups around the U.S. The company that operates the trade exchange usually charges an annual fee of $100 to $800 and may collect an additional fee on all transactions. Trade dollars, also known as *scrip*, are reported to the IRS as earnings, so you must pay income tax on any exchanges.

Joining a barter association can have several benefits:

➤ You may attract new customers that you would not have reached otherwise.

➤ You can conserve cash and still get what you need or want.

➤ You can make good use of your off-peak periods or sluggish inventory.

Shel Horowitz, home-based author of *Marketing Without Megabucks*, belongs to a couple of trade exchanges and has been very pleased with them. He has bartered his public-relations and writing talents for: a Persian rug, massage therapy, and professional-organizer services. In the future, he plans to exchange trade dollars for a vacation and a copy machine.

However, there are potential disadvantages to barter associations. If you sell a niche product or service, you may not be able to attract enough trade dollars to recoup your membership fee. For instance, a ballet teacher may have a lesser demand for her services than a hair stylist. Another potential pitfall is not being able to spend your accumulated credit. An exchange may have several hundred members, but if you do not want the products or services of any other members, you are stuck with a lot of unusable trade dollars.

Says Horowitz: "To some degree you're captive to it. When you get the credit, you look at what you need or would like, and then look for a vendor that accepts trade dollars. In the case of my Persian rug, I can have this thing of great beauty and craftsmanship that would be totally out of the question if I were paying cash."

If you are interested in joining a trade exchange, you may want to read *Barter: How to Get Almost Anything Without Money* by Constance Stapleton (it is currently out of print, but you might be able to find it at the library or in a used book store). Also, you can contact:

National Association of Trade Exchanges
27801 Euclid Avenue, Suite 610 • Cleveland, OH 44132
phone: (216) 732-7171 • fax: (216) 732-7172
web site: http://www.nate.org

CREATIVE ALLIANCES

Though most of the home-based guerrillas we interviewed did not belong to a formal trade exchange, over half said they swapped informally with friends, family, and acquaintances. Or, as one home-based businessperson called it, formed "creative alliances." Striking up a friendship, or creative alliance, with a colleague whom you can help and who can help you, may save you both a lot of money.

For instance, Terry Morin, a home-based cartoonist with Terrapin Illustrations in Portland, Oregon, has a friend who is a photographer. Morin occasionally does graphic design and printing favors for him. In return, Morin calls his friend when he needs photography. Morin has other friends who host his web site, lend him their fax machine, and prepare his income-tax return. He says the services he receives from his friends save him a lot of money and have been crucial to his success. Morin is representative of many of the home-based guerrillas we interviewed. The most commonly traded service? Web site design and hosting.

Neal Lubow, home-based owner of Ideas By-The-Hour, is a strong proponent of informal alliances. "If you're good to people and treat them well and fairly, you develop relationships. There are opportunities within that," says Lubow. "The gentleman who installs my computer equipment is a friend, and any time he has a need for marketing design or promotion, I'm there."

Lubow prefers informal one-on-one arrangements to formal barter exchanges. For him, trade exchanges present "too many unknowns. I wouldn't know who I was dealing with. I thought I might have a problem getting what I wanted. This is personal, informal, and low-key." Lubow concludes, informal strategic alliances are more than just "getting something at a bargain. You get something you really can't pay for. It has real value in human equity."

APPENDIX A PROFESSIONAL ORGANIZATIONS

Associations are great places to meet other home-based business professionals like yourself to network and trade ideas. However, association dues can become expensive and meetings are time consuming, so guerrillas need to be selective in their membership. We have compiled two association lists: one for home-based businesspeople and another for individuals in specific fields, in order to save you the time and money of finding these associations for yourself. This way, you can concentrate on evaluating which ones may be of use to you.

Some listings are more detailed than others, because those organizations provided more specific information. We have listed only the major benefits of membership or those benefits which we feel guerrillas can only receive through membership.

HOME-BASED BUSINESS ASSOCIATIONS

American Association of Home-Based Businesses
PO Box 10023 • Rockville, MD 20849
phone: (800) 447-9710 • fax: (301) 963-7042
web site: http://www.aahbb.org

> *History/Mission Statement:* A nonprofit organization formed in 1991 in the Washington, DC metropolitan area to support, educate, and advocate for businesses in the home.
>
> *Number of Members:* 850
>
> *Eligibility:* Any part- or full-time home-based business owner.
>
> *Dues:* $30 per year for home-based business membership (add $15 for international memberships).

Meetings: None.

Publications: Newsletter, *The Connector,* (included with membership). Fourteen free pamphlets ($1.50 for shipping) on topics pertinent to home-based business professionals, such as "Making the Most of Time in Your Business: Ten Ways to Make the Most of Your Home-Based Business Hours" and "Working at Home with an Infant—Can It Work?"

Benefits: Access to merchant services, discounted long-distance telephone rates, travel services, prepaid legal services, and discounts on books.

American Business Women's Association
9100 Ward Parkway • Kansas City, MO 64114-0728
phone: (800) 361-6621 • fax: (816) 361-4991
web site: http://www.abwahq.org

History/Mission Statement: An organization that brings together women of diverse occupations in order for them to grow personally and professionally.

Number of Members: 80,000

Eligibility: Students, businesswomen, and retired businesswomen.

Dues: $30 to $100 per year depending on membership designation

Meetings: Optional monthly and bimonthly meetings.

Publications: Women in Business magazine (included with membership). For Company Connection members only: "Nationwide Business Owner's Directory" and "A Quick Guide to Starting Your Own Business."

Benefits: Eligibility to apply for ABWA educational scholarships; 10 to 30 percent discount on training products and services from Career-Track; a discounted service that allows you to incorporate your business; 20 percent discount on business-training workshops from National Seminars Group; discounted rates on select hotels; a free Accidental Death and Dismemberment insurance policy; health and auto insurance discounts; a 7 percent discount on IBM home computers; a credit card with no annual fee; 15 percent discount on TWA airfares; and car-rental discounts from Alamo, Avis, and Hertz.

American Home Business Association
4505 South Wasatch Boulevard, #140 • Salt Lake City, UT 84124
phone: (800) 644-2422 • fax: (801) 273-2399
web site: http://www.homebusiness.com and
http://www.homebusinessworks.com

History/Mission Statement: Founded in 1994, the organization strives to link entrepreneurs with resources to help them move their businesses home.

Number of Members: 20,000

Eligibility: Anyone interested in small offices/home offices.

Dues: $29.95 per quarter.

Meetings: None

Publications: Home Business News (a quarterly magazine) and *Hotline* (a newsletter published eight times per year) are both included in membership. The organization also sends members audiotapes on specific topics, such as tax relief.

Benefits: Merchant status, discounted long-distance telephone service, discounted toll-free telephone service, group coverage insurance, discount-travel club, discounted office products, and discounted UPS service.

Home-Based Working Moms
PO Box 500164 • Austin, TX 78750-0164
phone: (512) 266-0900 • fax: (512) 266-0879
web site: http://www.hbwm.com

History/Mission Statement: Founded in 1995 to support parents who work at home, or want to work at home to spend more time with their children.

Number of Members: 600

Eligibility: Anyone working at home or wanting to do so. The focus is on parents who work at home, but there are some childless members.

Dues: $39 per year.

Meetings: None.

Publications: Eight-page monthly newsletter (included with membership). The organization also has several pamphlets, "Over 200 Home

Business Ideas and Opportunities" ($5), "How to Promote Your Home Business" ($4), and "Tips for Selecting and Starting a Home Business" ($2).

Benefits: Discounts on car rentals, office supplies, and computer furniture; free listing on association's web page; and two free classified advertisements in the association's newsletter.

Mothers' Home Business Network

PO Box 423 • East Meadow, NY 11554
phone: (516) 997-7394 • fax: (516) 997-0839
web site: http://www.homeworkingmom.com

History/Mission Statement: Established in 1984, the association provides ideas, information, and inspiration for start up and growth.

Number of Members: 6,000

Eligibility: Anyone working at home or with a desire to do so.

Dues: $44.95 per year.

Meetings: None.

Publications: Members receive two issues each of *Homeworking Mothers Annual,* the association newsletter, and *Kids&Career,* a publication about other flexible working situations. The organization publishes *Mothers' Home BusinessPages Yearbook* and *Work-At-Home Fraud Detector.* MHBN sells home-based business books geared toward mothers; members get one free with membership.

Benefits: Merchant status and discounts from Penny Wise Office Products.

National Association for the Self-Employed

PO Box 612067 • Dallas, TX 75261-2067
phone: (800) 232-6273 • fax: (800) 551-4446
web site: http://www.nase.org

History/Mission Statement: Founded in 1981, this is the largest small-business association. The organization's goal is to help small businesses become more competitive.

Number of Members: 325,000

Eligibility: Anyone.

Dues: $72 per year.

Meetings: Annual conference.

Publications: Members receive *Self-Employed America,* a bimonthly magazine ($12 for nonmembers). The association issues dozens of publications. Some are books available at a discount to members, such as *PCs for Dummies* ($11.99). Others are produced for the organization, such as *The NASE Guide to Successful Advertising* ($5.95) and *The NASE Hiring Guide* ($5.95).

Benefits: Discounts on overnight shipping with Airborne Express; discounts on car rentals from Alamo, Hertz, and National; TaxTalk, an online consultant service to answer your tax questions; amusement-park coupons; discounts on eye exams and lenses from LensCrafters; and $10,000 common carrier accidental-death insurance free to members. Many of the guerrillas we interviewed said that they belonged in order to participate in the group health-insurance plan.

National Association of Women Business Owners
1100 Wayne Avenue, Suite 830 • Silver Spring, MD 20910
phone: (301) 608-2590 • fax: (301) 608-2596
web site: http://www.nawbo.org

History/Mission Statement: Founded in 1974 by a small group of Washington, DC businesswomen, the association propels women entrepreneurs into economic, social, and political spheres of power worldwide. The organization promotes economic development of its members and influences public policy.

Number of Members: 6,500

Eligibility: Sole proprietors, partners, and corporate owners with day-to-day management responsibility. Active members who live in a chapter area automatically must join both chapter and national. Those who do not live in a chapter area join as at-large members.

Dues: $75 per year for chapter members plus chapter dues (chapter dues vary); $120 per year for at-large members.

Meetings: Annual conference. Other meetings vary by chapter.

Publications: Monthly newsletter, *NAWBOTime,* included with membership.

Benefits: Referral service. Discounts on books and IBM products.

National Business Association
5151 Beltline Road, Suite 1150 • Dallas, TX 75240
phone: (800) 456-0440 • fax: (972) 960-9149
web site: http://www.nationalbusiness.org

> *History/Mission Statement:* This nonprofit organization was established in 1982 to support and educate small-business owners, entrepreneurs, and professionals.
>
> *Number of Members:* 40,000
>
> *Eligibility:* Self-employed individuals and small-business owners and their employees.
>
> *Dues:* $144 per year.
>
> *Meetings:* None.
>
> *Publications:* All of the following are included with membership: *National Business News* (published bimonthly); *Helpful Healthful Hotlines; Starting Your Own Business; Yellow Page Advertising: The Inside Scoop; Building Your Business: Capital Ideas;* and *Software for Your Small Business Success.*
>
> *Benefits:* Discounted long-distance telephone service; a series of computer software programs, such as First Step Business Plan; merchant status; 20 percent discount on New Horizons Computer Learning Center classes; 36 percent discount on Penny Wise Office Products; eligible for credit union membership; discounted books; 5 percent discount from Sprint PCS; discounted training classes from CompUSA; 35 percent discount on Nightingale-Conant audio- and videotapes; car-rental discounts from Alamo, Budget, and National; 20 percent discount on Choice Hotels and 10 to 30 percent discounts on other hotels; discounted movie tickets; 10 percent discounts at Jiffy Lube and Meineke Discount Mufflers; theme-park coupons; accidental-death insurance policy; and eligibility for group insurance coverage.

National Federation of Independent Businesses
53 Century Boulevard, Suite 205 • Nashville, TN 37214
phone: (615) 872-5800 • fax: (615) 872-5353
web site: http://www.NFIBOnline.com

History/Mission Statement: Founded in 1943 to influence public policy at the state and federal levels for the benefit of small and independent business owners in America.

Number of Members: 600,000

Eligibility: Owners of privately held businesses.

Dues: $100 to $1,000 per year

Meetings: Small Business Summit in Washington, DC every other year. State meetings at the discretion of state directors.

Publications: All of the following publications are included with membership: a newsletter published six times per year, a magazine published six times per year, and an issue ballot.

Benefits: Eligibility for group insurance coverage and credit card.

INDUSTRY-SPECIFIC ASSOCIATIONS

American Booksellers Association (ABA)
828 South Broadway • Tarrytown, NY 10591
phone: (800) 637-0037 • fax: (914) 591-2720
web site: http://www.bookweb.org

History/Mission Statement: Founded in 1900, the organization works toward the establishment, improvement, and maintenance of favorable trade conditions. The organization provides services that simplify daily operations, as well as conducts educational seminars on retail bookselling.

Number of Members: 6,220

Eligibility: Independent, specialty, and franchise bookstores; college and university stores; publishers; wholesalers; distributors; and others with a special interest in bookselling.

Dues: $175 per year.

Meetings: The ABA hosts a huge annual four-day convention called BookExpo America, usually held in Chicago or Los Angeles.

Publications: As you would imagine, the American Bookseller's Association publishes several books and periodicals. Some highlights: *Book-*

selling This Week, a weekly newsletter ($30 per year for members, $60 for nonmembers); *American Bookseller,* a monthly magazine ($24.95 per year for members, $49.99 for nonmembers); and *A Manual on Bookselling* ($15 for members, $25 for nonmembers). The *ABA Book Buyer's Handbook* is free and available to members only.

Benefits: Access to group health-insurance coverage, access to group business-insurance coverage, merchant status, access to ABA research surveys, and discounts on shipping.

American Institute of Certified Public Accountants (AICPA)
99 Caven Point Road • Jersey City, NJ 07305
phone: (888) 777-7077 • fax: (800) 862-5066
web site: http://www.aicpa.org

History/Mission Statement: Founded in 1887, this is one of the oldest professional associations in the United States. The organization prepares and grades the national, uniform CPA Examination for the state licensing agencies. It is responsible for establishing auditing and reporting standards, as well as overseeing the practices of its members.

Number of Members: 330,000

Eligibility: Members must be Certified Public Accountants, as well as meet stringent continuing education and hours in practice requirements.

Dues: $65 per year for new members. A complex rate structure applies to all other members.

Meetings: Annual conference.

Publications: The association publishes a lot of tax-related material. Its main publications are: the *Journal of Accountancy* ($28 per year, free with membership) and *The CPA Letter* ($20, free with membership).

Benefits: Members receive 44 percent discount on Airborne shipping, 20 percent off on Hertz Car Rental, 10 percent discount on Intuit TurboTax software, 10 percent discount on Research Institute of America's tax-research information products, and 20 percent off Xerox products.

American Society of Journalists and Authors (ASJA)
1501 Broadway, Suite 302 • New York, NY 10036
phone: (212) 997-0947 • fax: (212) 778-7414
web site: http://www.asja.org

History/Mission Statement: The ASJA seeks to elevate the professional and economic position of nonfiction writers. It provides a forum for discussion of common problems among writers and editors, and promotes a code of ethics for writers and editors.

Number of Members: 900

Eligibility: Freelance writers of nonfiction articles and books are eligible to join.

Dues: $165 per year.

Meetings: Annual convention and eight meetings per year, always held in New York.

Publications: ASJA Members' Newsletter, a monthly publication available to members only.

Benefits: The ASJA operates Dial-A-Writer, a referral service for companies seeking writers. The organization also has an editorial liaison for settling disputes.

American Society of Training and Development (ASTD)
1640 King Street, Box 1443 • Alexandria, VA 22313-2043
phone: (703) 683-8100 • fax: (703) 683-8103
web site: http://www.astd.org

History/Mission Statement: Founded in 1944 to provide leadership to individuals, organizations, and society to achieve work-related competence, performance, and fulfillment.

Number of Members: 70,000

Eligibility: Any individual who is engaged in the training and development of business, industry, education, or government employees.

Dues: $150 per year for standard individual membership, $229 per year for Membership Plus (added benefits), $75 per year for students, and $75 per year for seniors.

Meetings: Annual conference. Monthly chapter meetings in 157 areas.

Publications: The association publishes a wide range of training materials. The most popular is *Training and Development,* a monthly magazine that is free to members ($75 per year for nonmembers). Some of the other publications include: the annual *ASTD Buyer's Guide and*

Consultant Directory (free to members, $59 for nonmembers), *Human Resource Development Quarterly* ($36 for members), and *Technical Skills and Training* (eight reports per year for $50 for members, $59 for nonmembers).

Benefits: Discounts on books and access to information center services.

Independent Computer Consultants Association (ICCA)
11131 South Towne Square, Suite F • St. Louis, MO 63123
phone: (800) 774-4222 • fax: (314) 487-1345
web site: http://www.icca.org

History/Mission Statement: Established in 1976 to support the success of independent computer consultants in providing professional services to their clients. Encourages high standards of performance, increases client understanding of computer resources, and enhances recognition of computer-consulting profession.

Number of Members: 1,500 member firms

Eligibility: Membership is open to any company that provides computer consulting services publicly for a fee (member firm) or those associated with computers, such as a lawyer who specializes in computer law (associate firm). Members are registered by company, but all employees of a company are eligible for the benefits.

Dues: $175 for a one-person firm and $225 for a two- to nine-person firm. Dues are the same for both member firms and associate firms.

Meetings: Annual conference. Twenty-four chapters throughout the U.S. that meet on a monthly basis.

Publications: All of the following publications are included with the cost of membership: "Standard Form Consulting Contract," "Client Brochure," and the "Tax and Business Handbook for Consultants and Clients: A Guide for Doing Business as an Independent Consultant Under Section 1706 of the 1986 Tax Reform Act."

Benefits: A listing on the associations' web page and a link to your own page; special group rates on insurance coverage; a low-cost training lending library; discounted Airborne Express shipping; discounted long-distance telephone service; a credit card with no annual fee; discounted rates from National Credit Systems, a collections agency; 20

percent discount on hotels from Choice Hotels International; discounted subscriptions to *Contract Professional* and *Home Office Computing* magazines; and discount coupons for Avis and Hertz rental cars and Disney theme parks.

National Association of Enrolled Agents (NAEA)
200 Orchard Ridge Drive, Suite 302 • Gaithersburg, MO 20878
phone: (800) 424-4339 • fax: (301) 990-1611
web site: http://www.naea.org

History/Mission Statement: The association promotes the ethical representation of financial position of taxpayers before government agencies.

Number of Members: 10,000

Eligibility: Any individual with EA status who completes thirty hours of continuing-education credit.

Dues: $140 per year.

Meetings: Annual convention.

Publications: The *EA Journal*, a bimonthly periodical available for free to members ($48 per year for nonmembers), and *E@lert*, a biweekly newsletter free to members.

Benefits: Discounted continuing education self-study courses; 48 percent discount on long-distance telephone service with Eclipse Communications; Airborne Express discounts; car-rental discounts with Alamo, Avis, Budget, and Hertz; 15 percent discount on eyeglasses, contact lenses, and other vision-care products; cooperative *Yellow Pages* advertising; free referral hotline listing; free Internet listing; discounted web-page creation, hosting, and maintenance; access to group health and business insurance; and discounted books from Amazon.com.

National Association of Professional Organizers (NAPO)
1033 La Posada, Suite 220 • Austin, TX 78752
phone: (512) 206-0151 • fax: (512) 454-3036
web site: http://www.napo.net

History/Mission Statement: Founded in 1985.

Number of members: 1,175

Eligibility: Any individual or company doing business in the field of organizing through consulting, training, writing, speaking, and/or ancillary services.

Dues: $150 per year.

Meetings: Four-day annual conference held in a major U.S. city. Chapter meetings held monthly near Chicago, Atlanta, Los Angeles, Minneapolis, New York, Portland, Philadelphia, San Diego, San Francisco, and Washington, DC.

Publications: A newsletter six times per year that is included with membership. The organization also publishes a Resource Directory ($15) that lists organizing books, audiotapes, and videotapes created by NAPO members.

Benefits: Group insurance program and marketing assistance, including boiler plate press releases that members can customize and send to local media.

National Mail Order Association (NMOA)
2807 Polk Street NE • Minneapolis, MN 55418-2954
phone: (612) 788-1673 • fax: (612) 788-1147
web site: http://www.nmoa.org

History/Mission Statement: To provide education, information, ideas, and connectivity to small and midsized mail marketers.

Number of Members: Not available.

Eligibility: Direct mail-order marketers of products and services.

Dues: $99 per year.

Meetings: Not available.

Publications: The two main publications included with membership are: *Mail Order Digest,* a monthly periodical; and *Washington Newsletter,* a monthly publication that lists new postal rate and procedure changes.

Benefits: Telephone consultations; flat-rate group toll-free telephone-number service; merchant status; free classified ad in the association's newsletter; $50 gift certificate from Advanced Business Strategies computer-software company; and discounts from Hertz and Deluxe Business Forms.

National Speakers Association
1500 South Priest Drive • Tempe, AZ 85281
phone: (602) 968-2552 • fax: (602) 968-0911
web site: http://www.nsaspeaker.org

History/Mission Statement: The association is dedicated to advancing the art and value of experts who speak professionally.

Number of Members: 3,800

Eligibility: Individuals who have had at least ten paid speaking engagements.

Dues: $325 per year.

Meetings: The NSA holds three major workshops and a convention each year. The locations of these events vary from year to year. It also holds five educational labs per year at its headquarters in Arizona.

Publications: Members receive *Professional Speaker Magazine* ($49 subscription for nonmembers). Educational audiotapes are also available at varying prices.

Benefits: Members are eligible for group health insurance. They also receive discounts on National Car Rental and Airborne Express shipping.

Newsletter Publishers Association (NPA)
1501 Wilson Boulevard, Suite 509 • Arlington, VA 22209-2403
phone: (800) 356-9302 • fax: (703) 841-0629
web site: http://www.newsletters.org

History/Mission Statement: Founded in 1976 to further the professional, economic, and organizational interests of the members.

Number of Members: 700

Eligibility: Firms that publish for-profit, subscription-based newsletters.

Dues: Depends on revenue, starts at $395 a year.

Meetings: Two annual meetings, one in New York City and one in Washington, DC.

Publications: A biweekly newsletter, *Hotline,* included with membership, as well as an annual membership and supplier directory ($250),

Newsletter Publisher's Guidebook, and a book on newsletter publishing, *Success in Newsletter Publishing: A Practical Guide* (free to new members, $20 for existing members, $39.50 for nonmembers).

Benefits: Free study of financial and operating ratios; discounts of up to 20 percent on publishers libel insurance; six free hours yearly of prepublication counseling from a First Amendment and copyright lawyer; four free hours annually of market-related counseling; discounted books; free welcome package with several books; and discounts on travel and office supplies.

Public Relations Society of America (PRSA)
33 Irving Place • New York, NY 10003-2376
phone: (212) 995-2230 • fax: (212) 995-0757
web site: http://www.prsa.org

History/Mission Statement: Chartered in 1948, this is the world's largest organization for public-relations professionals. Members represent business and industry, counseling firms, government, associations, hospitals, schools, professional-service firms, and not-for-profit organizations. PRSA's mission is to empower public-relations practitioners to realize their full potential and to advance the practice, power, and value of public relations. PRSA has a Code of Professional Standards, backed by enforcement procedures, to which all members must adhere.

Number of Members: 19,000

Eligibility: Any individual who devotes a substantial portion of time to the paid professional practice of public relations or to the teaching or administration of a public-relations curriculum in an accredited college or university.

Dues: $175 per year ($65 initiation fee).

Meetings: Annual national conference held in the fall. Other conferences for specific interests held throughout the year.

Publications: Two magazines included with membership: *The Strategist,* a quarterly ($48 per year for nonmembers), and *Public Relations TACTICS,* a monthly ($40 per year for nonmembers).

Benefits: Access to group insurance, free career consultations, and referral service.

Small Publishers Association of North America (SPAN)
PO Box 1306 • Buena Vista, CO 81211-1306
phone: (719) 395-4790 • fax: (719) 395-8374
web site: http://www.SPANnet.org

History/Mission Statement: This association works to advance the image and profits of independent publishers through education and marketing.

Number of Members: 1,100

Eligibility: Self-publishers, small presses, and authors.

Dues: $95 per year regular, $120 per year associate vendor member.

Meetings: Annual convention.

Publications: SPAN Connection, a monthly newsletter included with membership.

Benefits: A 58 percent discount on freight shipping; merchant status; discounted cooperative advertising in large publications; discounts on subscriptions to *Publishers Weekly, Independent Publisher,* and *Publishing Entrepreneur;* a co-op booth at the BookExpo America convention for displaying books; online book emporium where members can sell their books at full retail; 10 percent discount on Avis Car Rental; discount on Luce Press Clippings service; 10 to 20 percent discount on RPS shipping; access to group publisher's liability-insurance coverage; and 36 percent discount on Penny Wise office products.

Toastmasters International
PO Box 9052 • Mission Viejo, CA 92690
phone: (949) 858-8255 • fax: (949) 858-1207
web site: http://www.toastmasters.org

History/Mission Statement: Founded in 1924, this nonprofit organization was developed to help individuals improve their public speaking and listening skills.

Number of Members: 174,900

Eligibility: Anyone over 18 years old.

Dues: $16 initial fee plus $3 per month.

Meetings: Required weekly one-hour meeting at local Toastmaster club.

Publications: Toastmaster, a monthly magazine, included with membership.

Benefits: Upon joining, new members receive a variety of manuals and resources on public speaking.

APPENDIX B | FURTHER READING

BOOKS BY TOPIC

FRUGALITY

The Complete Tightwad Gazette: Promoting Thrift as a Viable Alternative Lifestyle by Amy Dacyczyn. Villard Books, 1999. 912 pages, $19.99.

> This classic grew out of *The Tightwad Gazette* newsletter, which Dacyczyn published for six years. Among other reasons, Dacyczyn originally started the newsletter to dispel the belief that two incomes are necessary in today's society. Thus, the book is devoted to saving money in every area of life from food shopping and clothing to holidays and utilities. Though the book is not solely about managing a home business on a shoestring, Dacyczyn explains many of the principles of frugality in an entertaining way. Her essays and well-researched articles make this book a must-read for anyone who is serious about saving money.

How to Survive Without a Salary: Learning How to Live the Conserver Lifestyle by Charles Long. Firefly Books, 1996, 232 pages, $14.95.

> This book teaches the overriding concepts of what Long calls the "conserver lifestyle." This Canadian author shows readers through personal anecdotes how he and his family live well without spending a lot or working regular 9-to-5 jobs. The best parts of the book are the chapters on needs and on alternatives to buying. Both provide strong unconventional perspectives to mainstream North American culture.

231

Invest in Yourself: Six Secrets to a Rich Life by Marc Eisenson, Gerri Detweiler, and Nancy Castleman. John Wiley and Sons, Inc., 1998. 326 pages, $22.95.

> Like Dacyczyn, authors Eisenson, Detweiler, and Castleman practice what they preach and this book, at least in part, grew out of their personal experiences. The book is a blueprint for creating an overall satisfying life. Their main premise is that gaining control over your financial life will help you fulfill your goals. The six secrets are: make your own lifestyle decisions; put your family first; wherever you work, be in business for yourself; make the most of the money you bring home; turn your debts into golden investment opportunities; and map out your own financial future. The best part about this book is the wealth of telephone numbers and web-site addresses of further resources that it lists. Though the book will help anyone who wants to change his or her life, those that will benefit the most from reading it are new home-based business owners or those who would like to be.

The Simple Life: Thoughts on Simplicity, Frugality, and Living Well, edited by Larry Roth. Berkeley Books, 1998. 264 pages, $13.00.

> This compilation of essays from Amy Dacyczyn, Vicki Robin, Terri Lonier, and others will give readers a broad overview of the simplicity/ frugality movement. Topics addressed range from recycling and saving in business to the pleasures of frugality to cutting the cost of a college education. This book is interesting mainly because it gives you some insight into the lives of other frugal people and encourages you to save even more.

Your Money or Your Life: Transforming Your Relationship with Money and Achieving Financial Independence by Joe Dominguez and Vicki Robin. Viking Penguin, 1993. 336 pages, $12.95.

> This book presents some truly revolutionary ideas on how to approach money and the nature of fulfillment (how much is enough). The concept that "money is something we trade our life energy for" is enlightening. The chapters related to work and income will help guerrillas determine how much to charge for their products and services and

which projects are profitable and worthwhile. The chapter on the principles of frugality and "101 Sure Ways To Save Money" is solid. The book chronicles the journey of a half-dozen individuals on the road to financial independence. A must-read!

FURNITURE AND EQUIPMENT

Practical Home Office Solutions by Marilyn Zelinsky. McGraw-Hill, 1999. 330 pages, $22.95.

This book is geared toward home-based entrepreneurs and telecommuters alike. Written by a regular contributor to *Home Office Computing* magazine, it discusses every aspect of designing and outfitting a home office and is filled with photographs that illustrate different home offices. The book covers ergonomics, Feng Shui, and zoning laws, as well as kidproofing and petproofing. One particular chapter that will interest guerrilla savers is "A Bargain Hunter's Guide To Buying Home Office Furnishings."

HOME-BASED BUSINESS

Homemade Money: How to Select, Start, Manage, Market, and Multiply the Profits of a Business at Home, 5th ed., Revised, by Barbara Brabec. F & W Publications, Inc., 1997. 384 pages, $21.99.

This enormous book is often called the "The Home Business Bible." It is well-organized, well-researched, and clearly written. It is a wonderful primer for individuals starting home-based businesses, but it contains a lot of good tips and advice for long-time home-based professionals, too.

The Home Office Solution: How to Balance Your Professional and Personal Lives While Working at Home by Alice Bredin. John Wiley and Sons, Inc., 1998. 221 pages, $14.95.

This is an excellent book on the emotional and psychological aspects of working at home. Bredin covers how to handle distractions; cope with rejection; overcome isolation; manage time, work, and stress; and create a balance between work and home life. Bredin gives examples from real home-based businesspeople to illustrate her points.

The Home Team: How to Live, Love, and Work at Home by Scott Gregory and Shirley Siluk Gregory. Bookhome Publishing, 1999. 256 pages, $14.95.

If you run your home-based business with your significant other, this book is a must-read. The Gregorys provide a humorous approach to such issues as: who will wash the dog, who will take care of the kids, how to work out when you are working at home, and how to keep romance alive. The book includes anecdotes from the Gregorys and other couples who work at home together.

How to Raise a Family & a Career Under One Roof by Lisa Roberts. Bookhaven Press, 1997. 224 pages, $15.95.

This book discusses how to integrate a home-based business and a family. It covers how a home-based business affects children's development, the impact it will have on a marriage, and how it effects home life. It is peppered with delightful stories about Roberts' experiences as a work-at-home mother of four. The book is especially suited for mothers who are considering starting a home-based business, though experienced home-based entrepreneurs with children will enjoy it as well.

Making a Living Without a Job: Winning Ways for Creating Work that You Love by Barbara J. Winter. Bantam Books, 1993. 260 pages, $12.95.

This book is geared toward those who are toying with the idea of becoming self-employed, but contains a lot of solid information and encouragement for those who have already taken the plunge. Some of the most interesting chapters are "Creating Multiple Profit Centers," "Considering the Possibilities," and "Making the Transition," which help readers to see alternative income sources. Winter's chapter on "Enjoying Your Spaghetti Days" is a fun look at how you can live a rich life without spending a lot of money.

Mompreneurs: A Mother's Practical Step-by-Step Guide to Work-at-Home Success by Ellen H. Parlapiano and Patricia Cobe. The Berkeley Publishing Group, 1996. 314 pages, $13.00.

> This book covers all of the special issues related to being a mother and running a home-based business, particularly child care. It offers tips on time management and protecting your professional image. The book includes plenty of quotes and anecdotes from other work-at-home moms.

Working from Home: Everything You Need to Know about Living and Working Under the Same Roof by Paul and Sarah Edwards. Putnam Publishing, 1994. 448 pages, $16.95.

> This massive book lives up to its subtitle. It is detailed and well researched. It covers everything from legal and tax matters to what to look for in a fax machine.

MARKETING

6 Steps to Free Publicity: And Dozens of Other Ways to Win Free Media Attention for You or Your Business by Marcia Yudkin. NAL/Dalton, 1994. 230 pages, $11.95.

> This book provides a good overview of media opportunities and how you can go about securing them. It includes examples of press releases and pitch letters, and teaches you the pitfalls of publicity and how to avoid them.

1001 Ways to Market Your Books by John Kremer. Open Horizons, 1997. 640 pages, $27.95.

> This enormous book is written mainly for writers and small independent book publishers, but the reference information is useful for anyone who wants to generate publicity. The thousands of examples may spark some unique marketing ideas.

Guerrilla Marketing: Secrets for Making Big Profits from Your Small Business by Jay Levinson. Houghton Mifflin, 1998. 388 pages, $13.00.

This best-selling text provides a solid tutorial on how to develop a marketing plan, and an overview of more than a dozen types of marketing. The book is brimming with real-life stories that illustrate each point. Home-based guerrillas will be especially interested in the chapters titled "Secrets of Saving Marketing Money" and "Secrets of Obtaining Free Research."

Guerrilla Marketing for the Home-Based Business by Jay Levinson and Seth Godin. Houghton Mifflin, 1995. 182 pages, $13.00.

This book, tailored to the home-based guerrilla, is peppered with inspiring examples from real home-based businesspeople. It covers how to position yourself in the market, the nine secrets of direct mail, where to run classified ads and why you want to, how to generate word-of-mouth advertising, and more.

Marketing Without Megabucks: How to Sell Anything on a Shoestring by Shel Horowitz. Simon & Schuster, 1993. 384 pages, $12.00.

A reviewer from *Home Office Computing* said that, in this book, "Horowitz puts Jay Levinson's popular *Guerrilla Marketing* theory into practice by explaining, in detail, how to market." Horowitz definitely understands what it means to be a guerrilla. Some of the most interesting topics the book covers are choosing a name, developing a media list, how to call media people on the telephone, and how to design *Yellow Page* and classified ads to get maximum exposure.

Surefire Strategies for Growing Your Home-Based Business: Win More Clients, Charge What You're Worth, Collect What You're Owed, Get The Money You Need to Get Organized and Grow by David Schaeffer. Upstart Publishing Company, 1998. 208 pages, $16.95.

This book provides a good template for planning and organizing your marketing so that it is consistent. It helps readers outline a business plan and a life plan that work together, by using leading sentences such as, "If the business were operating ideally, I would . . ." and "I could improve my relationships with friends and family by . . ." The book also covers rate setting, financing, and preparing for rainy days.

MONEY MANAGEMENT

Money-Smart Secrets of the Self-Employed by Linda Stern. Random House, 1997. 288 pages, $20.00.

This money-management book covers record-keeping, fee setting, loans, taxes, insurance, retirement planning, and other financial topics. Stern writes clearly with a snappy style. The accompanying charts, such as the "Value of Business/Personal Deductions" comparison chart, are extremely informative and easy to read.

ORGANIZATION

Clutter's Last Stand by Don Aslett. F & W Publications, Inc., 1984. 276 pages, $12.99.

If you have ever given any of the following reasons for hanging onto clutter, this book is for you: "It might come in handy/I might need it someday," "I paid good money for this," "I intend to fix it," or "It is still perfectly good." In this humorous, cartoon-illustrated book, Aslett shows readers how junk robs our time and money and how to "dejunk" our lives. It is a good read, and guaranteed to change the way you look at your possessions.

PRINTING

The Complete Guide to Self-Publishing: Everything You Need to Know to Write, Publish, Promote, and Sell Your Own Book by Tom and Marilyn Ross. F & W Publications, 1994. 406 pages, $19.95.

This book is jam-packed with information on product development, design, and production. For instance, it outlines permission guidelines for using copyrighted material. It also contains extensive promotion and publicity information, such as how to develop an author's tour and sell subsidiary rights. Both authors and small publishers would benefit from reading this book.

The Self-Publishing Manual: How to Write, Print, and Sell Your Own Book by Dan Poynter. Para Publishing, 1998. 458 pages, $19.95.

If you plan to publish a book, newsletter, or booklet, this book will tell you, step by step, what to do to print and promote it. It explains all of the printing lingo, such as the difference between "saddle-stitch binding" and "perfect binding."

PERIODICALS

communication briefings. 1101 King Street, Suite 110, Alexandria, VA 22314. http://www.combriefings.com; (703) 548-3800. 12 issues (1 year) for $79.

This newsletter is a bit pricey, but is packed with solid information. There is no fluff or advertising. Articles are short and to the point. Some of the articles are original material, but many are condensed excerpts from various books and periodicals. The newsletter covers a variety of communication and managerial topics, including writing, training, listening, marketing, and customer service. Download a free sample off of the publication's web site.

Fast Company. PO Box 52760, Boulder, CO 80323-2760. http://www .fastcompany.com; (800) 688-1545. 10 issues (1 year) for $19.75.

Several guerrillas we interviewed recommended this magazine. Though it is not aimed solely at entrepreneurs, the business information is applicable. A recent issue featured articles on how to make meetings work, whether you should go to business school, and a company that helps executives foster creativity. The magazine profiles a lot of interesting businesses.

Home Office Computing. PO Box 53543, Boulder, CO 80323-3543. http:// www.smalloffice.com; (800) 288-7812. 12 issues (1 year) for $16.97.

A fantastic magazine featuring all of the technology upon which so many home-based guerrillas rely. Every issue is filled with good, clear, price-conscious recommendations on hardware and software, as well as entrepreneurial profiles and solid how-to advice.

WEB SITES

FRUGALITY

The Dollar Stretcher
http://www.stretcher.com

This site covers practically every money-saving topic you could imagine. The site is well organized and fun to read. You can also subscribe to a free, weekly online newsletter.

The Free Site
http://www.thefreesite.com

Just as the name implies, this site has links to a ton of free stuff available on the web. Download free time-management or antivirus software.

Frugal Fun
http://www.frugalfun.com

A no-frills, content-packed site with over 220 articles and book excerpts on marketing, entrepreneurship, and entertainment.

The Simple Living Network
http://www.slnet.com

This site has almost 3,000 pages of information and resources on how to live a more conscious, simpler, and healthier lifestyle. It is overflowing with articles and links to other frugality/simplicity sites. A must-see!

HOME-BASED BUSINESS

American Express Small Business Exchange

http://www.americanexpress.com/smallbusiness

> This site is a must! It contains a wealth of free information, including articles; interactive tutorials, such as "How to Write a Business Plan;" and self-tests, such as "Are You a Workaholic?" The expert advice forums allow you to ask questions with the promise that they will be answered within five business days. The featured expert on this site is Alice Bredin, author of *The Home Office Solution*, and one of the sources we interviewed for this book.

Business@Home

http://www.gohome.com

> This e-zine features articles on other work-at-home entrepreneurs, as well as tips on telecommunications, law, taxes, e-commerce, marketing, and other home-based-business-related topics.

IBM Small Business Center

http://www.businesscenter.ibm.com

> Though this site mainly promotes IBM products and services to small-business owners, it also has a Question & Answer panel, where you can submit your questions to one of half a dozen experts.

Small Business Development Center National Research Network

http://www.smallbiz.suny.edu

> Sponsored by the Small Business Administration and the New York State University system, this site is a clearinghouse for information about Small Business Development Centers throughout the country. The site also maintains useful small business links and a handful of articles.

MARKETING

Guerrilla Marketing International
http://gmarketing.com

> This site features weekly success stories from other guerrillas and arti-
> cles by Jay and other *Guerrilla* authors. Find out about Jay's speaking
> engagements and new *Guerrilla* products. Also, you can sign up for a
> free weekly online newsletter.

REFERENCE

Electric Library
http://www.elibrary.com

> This web site lists the full text of thousands of articles from 150 news-
> papers, hundreds of magazines, international newswires, and classic
> books, as well as maps and photographs. The content is updated daily.
> Free access to this site is limited; however, the $60 per year or $10 per
> month subscription fee is well worth it, especially if you are a writer
> or public-relations agent. By using this service, Kathryn has cut her
> library research time down to next to nothing, a significant time-
> savings since the nearest research library is almost thirty minutes away.

Information Please
http://www.infoplease.com

> This searchable site is a stack of reference books rolled into one. It con-
> tains a dictionary, encyclopedia, and an almanac, in addition to special
> sections on business, living, people, and science and technology.

Learn2.com
http://www.learn2.com

> This eclectic site provides step-by-step instructions on how to do just
> about anything. Learn how to avoid junk mail or calculate your utility
> costs.

WRITING AND PUBLISHING SITES

BookIdea.com
http://www.Bookidea.com

> This is an online magazine for independent book publishers and writers. It features dozens of articles on writing, publishing, and marketing topics, as well as lists of industry vendors and web site links. You can also join writing and publishing groups.

The Inkspot
http://www.inkspot.com

> This site is crammed with marketing information and articles on writing techniques. It even has a Question & Answer Forum where you can ask experts in different genres for advice. Sign up for the free weekly online newsletter.

Para Publishing
http://www.parapublishing.com

> This site was created by Dan Poynter, home-based owner of Para Publishing, and one of the experts interviewed for this book. The site has hundreds of free documents on writing, publishing, and marketing books. You could be downloading for hours.

Writer's Digest
http://www.writersdigest.com

> If you are a writer or plan to write articles to boost publicity for your business, you probably want to visit this site to check out the searchable database of writer's guidelines.

POSTAGE CHARTS FOR THE UNITED STATES AND CANADA

CHART C-1 Postage Within the U.S.

OUNCES	9″ × 12″ ENVELOPE AND APPROXIMATE NUMBER OF PAGES OF 20-POUND PAPER	FIRST CLASS POSTAGE
under 2	1 to 2	44¢*
2	3 to 8	55¢
3	9 to 13	77¢
4	14 to 19	99¢
5	20 to 25	$1.21
6	26 to 30	$1.43
7	31 to 35	$1.65
8	36 to 41	$1.87
9	42 to 46	$2.09
10	47 to 52	$2.31
11	53 to 57	$2.53
12	58 to 62	$2.75
Over 13 ounces and up to 2 pounds	over 62 pages	Use Priority Mail $3.20

*This cost includes an 11¢ fee for oversized mail that is light in weight.

CHART C-2 Postage from the U.S. to Canada

OUNCES	9″ × 12″ ENVELOPE AND APPROXIMATE NUMBER OF PAGES OF 20-POUND PAPER	FIRST CLASS POSTAGE
under 2	1 to 2	76¢
2	3 to 8	$1.00
3	9 to 13	$1.20
4	14 to 19	$1.40
5	20 to 25	$1.60
6	26 to 30	$1.80
7	31 to 35	$2.00
8	36 to 41	$2.19
9	42 to 46	$2.39
10	47 to 52	$2.59
11	53 to 57	$2.79
12	58 to 62	$3.59

See Postmaster for additional weights up to 4 pounds.

D RESOURCE DIRECTORY OF BUSINESSES

This is a directory of all of the businesses we discuss throughout the book. We have also included contact information for additional businesses that were not mentioned elsewhere in the book, but have useful products nonetheless.

ABC Pictures (photo reprints)
1867 E. Florida Street • Springfield, MO 65803-4583
phone: (417) 869-3456 • fax: (417) 869-9185
web site: http://www.abcpictures.com

Amazon.com (discounted books)
900 4th Avenue, 37th Floor • Seattle, WA 98164
phone: (800) 201-7575 • fax: none listed
web site: http://www.amazon.com

American Express (merchant status)
200 Vesey Street • New York, NY 10285
phone: (800) 528-5200 • fax: none listed
web site: http://www.americanexpress.com

American Express Optima Platinum Card (no annual fee credit card)
PO Box 31549 • Salt Lake City, UT 84131-9953
phone: (800) 782-2377 • fax: (801) 965-2885
web site: http://www.americanexpress.com/smallbusiness

American Institute of Certified Public Accountants (CPA referrals)
1211 Avenue of the Americas • New York, NY 10036
phone: (888) 777-7077 • fax: (800) 862-5066
web site: http://www.aicpa.org

AT&T Universal Business Card (Mastercard) (no annual fee credit card)
PO Box 84004 • Columbus, GA 31908-9915
phone: (800) 682-7759 • fax: none listed
web site: http://www.att.com

Barnesandnoble.com (discounted books)
308 Herrod Boulevard • Dayton, NJ 08810
phone: (800) 843-2665 • fax: none listed
web site: http://barnesandnoble.com

Borders.com (discounted books)
100 Phoenix Drive • Ann Arbor, MI 48108-2202
phone: (800) 770-7811 • fax: none listed
web site: http://borders.com

Camera World of Oregon (cameras and accessories)
700 NE 55th Avenue • Portland, OR 97213-3150
phone: (800) 695-8451 • fax: (503) 205-5901
web site: http://www.cameraworld.com

Campus Technology (discounted computer software)
751 Miller Drive, SE • Leesburg, VA 20175-8920
phone: (800) 543-8188 • fax: (703) 777-3871
web site: http://www.campustech.com

Cardservice International (credit card merchant service)
PO Box 2310 • Agoura Hills, CA 91376-2310
phone: (800) 948-6457 or (800) 456-5902 • fax: (818) 880-8393
web site: http://cardservice.com

CareerTrack (business and personal development seminars, audio-tapes, and videotapes)
3085 Center Green Drive • Boulder, CO 80301-5408
phone: (800) 488-0929 • fax: (800) 832-9489
web site: http://www.careertrack.com

Checks In the Mail, Inc. (check printing)
2435 Goodwin Lane • New Braunfels, TX 78135-0001
phone: (877) 397-1541 • fax: (800) 822-0005
web site: http://www.checksinthemail.com

Chiswick Trading, Inc. (office supplies)
33 Union Avenue • Sudbury, MA 01776-2267
phone: (800) 225-8708 • fax: (800) 638-9899
web site: none listed

Credit Union National Association (credit union referrals)
PO Box 431 • Madison, WI 53701-0431
phone: (800) 358-5710 • fax: (608) 231-5791
web site: http://www.cuna.org

Current (check printing)
Check Products Division • PO Box 19000 • Colorado Springs,
CO 80935-9000 • phone: (800) 204-2244 • fax: (800) 993-3232
web site: http://www.currentchecks.com

Defense Reutilization and Marketing Offices (military surplus furniture and equipment)
Battle Creek Federal Center: DLIS-VSS • Federal Center •
74 North Washington Street • Battle Creek, MI 49017
phone: (800) GOVT-BUY or (888) 352-9333 • fax: (616) 961-4201
web site: http://www.drms.dla.mil

Delta Publishing Group, Ltd. (discounted magazine subscriptions)
1243 48th Street • Brooklyn, NY 11219
phone: (800) SAVE-SAVE • fax: (718) 972-4695
web site: none listed

Discover NOVUS (merchant status)
4411 B West Broad Street • Columbus, OH 43228
phone: (800) 347-6673
web site: http://www.equant.com

E-stamp
2855 Campus Drive, Suite 100 • San Mateo, CA 94403
phone: (888) 272-6526 • fax: (650) 554-8455
web site: http://e-stamp.com

Fidelity Products Company (office supplies)
5601 International Parkway • Minneapolis, MN 55440-0155
phone: (800) 326-7555 • fax: (800) 842-2725
web site: none listed

Gateway (computers and accessories)
PO Box 2000 • 610 Gateway Drive • North Sioux City, SD 57049
phone: (800) 846-4208 • fax: (605) 232-2023
web site: http://www.gateway.com

Grayarc (office supplies)
PO Box 2944 • Hartford, CT 06104
phone: (800) 243-5250 • fax: (800) 292-4729
web site: none listed

Hello Direct (telephone headsets and other telephone accessories)
5893 Rue Ferrari • San Jose, CA 95138-1857
phone: (800) 444-3556 • fax: (800) 456-2566
web site: http://www.HelloDirect.com

Image Checks
PO Box 548 • Little Rock, AR 72203
phone: (800) 562-8768 • fax: (501) 455-4896
web site: http://imagechecks.com

Internal Revenue Service (tax information and assistance)
PO Box 10049, Room 10-502 • Richmond, VA 23240
phone: (800) 829-3676 (forms), (800) 829-4477 (recorded tax information),
(800) 829-1040 (help from a person) • fax: none listed
web site at http://www.irs.gov

Juno (free email)
120 West 45th Street, 15th Floor • New York, NY 10036
phone: (800) 654-JUNO • fax: (212) 597-9200
web site: http://www.juno.com

Laser Recycling Company (cartridge recycling service)
12223 W. 87th Street Parkway • Lenexa, KS 66215-2811
phone: (913) 599-3337 • fax: (913) 894-8997
web site: http://www.laserrecycle.com

MacConnection (computers and accessories)
Route 101A, 730 Milford Road • Merrimack, NH 03054-4631
phone: (888) 213-0259 • fax: (603) 423-5766
web site: http://macconnection.com

The Mac Zone (computers and accessories)
707 South Grady Way • Renton, WA 98055-3233
phone: (800) 248-0800 • fax: (425) 430-3500
web site: http://www.zones.com

Mindspring (Internet access and web-site hosting)
1430 West Peachtree Street NW, Suite 400 • Atlanta, GA 30309
phone: (800) 719-4664 • fax: (404) 287-0883
web site: http://www.mindspring.net

Nashua Corporation (buys empty printer cartridges)
44 Franklin Street • Nashua, NH 03060
phone: (800) 333-3439 • fax: (603) 880-2477
web site: http://www.nashua.com

National Association of Enrolled Agents (EA referrals)
200 Orchard Ridge Drive, Suite 302 • Gaithersburg, MO 20878
phone: (800) 424-4339 • fax: (301) 990-1611
web site: http://www.naea.org

National Association of Trade Exchanges (barter exchange referrals)
27801 Euclid Avenue, Suite 610 • Cleveland, OH 44132
phone: (216) 732-7171 • fax: (216) 732-7172
web site: http://www.nate.org

Network Solutions, Inc. (domain name registration)
505 Huntmar Park Drive • Herndon, VA 20170
phone: (888) 771-3000 • fax: none listed
web site: http://www.networksolutions.com

Nightingale-Conant (business and personal-development seminars, audiotapes, and videotapes)
7300 North Lehigh • Niles, IL 60714
phone: (800) 525-9000 • fax: (847) 647-7145
web site: http://www.nightingale.com

OfficeMax (office supplies)
3605 Warrensville Center Road • Shaker Heights, OH 44122-5203
phone: (800) 788-8080 • fax: (800) 995-9644
web site: http://www.officemax.com

Oriental Trading Company, Inc. (discounted party decorations and favors)
PO Box 3407 • Omaha, NE 68103-0407
phone: (800) 228-2269 • fax: (800) 327-8904
web site: http://www.oriental.com

Ornaal Image Works (photo reprints)
24 West 25 Street • New York, NY 10010
phone: (800) 826-6312 • fax: (212) 463-8466
web site: http://www.ornaal.com

PaperDirect, Inc. (preprinted papers)
1025 East Woodmen Road • Colorado Springs, CO 80920
phone: (800) 272-7377 • fax: (800) 443-2973
web site: http://www.paperdirect.com

Paper Showcase (pre-printed papers)
150 Kingswood Road • Mankato, MN 56001
phone: (800) 287-8163 • fax: (800) 842-3371
web site: http://www.papershowcase.com

PC Connection (computers and accessories)
Route 101A, 730 Milford Road • Merrimack, NH 03054-4631
phone: (888) 213-0259 • fax: (603) 423-5766
web site: http://pcconnection.com

Penny Wise Office Products (office supplies)
6911 Laurel Bowie Road, Suite 209 • Bowie, MD 20715
phone: (800) 942-3311 • fax: (800) 622-4411
web site: none listed. Have your modem dial (800) 752-3012

Philatelic Fulfillment Service Center (prestamped, preprinted envelopes)
United States Postal Service • PO Box 419208 • Kansas City, MO 64141
phone: (800) 782-6724 • fax: (816) 545-1212
web site: http://www.usps.gov

Quill Corporation (office supplies and cartridge-recycling service)
PO Box 94080 • Palatine, IL 60094-4080
phone: (800) 789-1331 • fax: (800) 789-8955
web site: http://www.quillcorp.com

RapidForms (office supplies)
301 Grove Road • Thorofare, NJ 08086-9499
phone: (800) 257-8354 • fax: (800) 451-8113
web site: http://www.rapidforms.com

RDS Recharging Systems (cartridge recycling service)
29 Vassar Road • Poughkeepsie, NY 12603
phone: (800) 344-9951 • fax: (914) 462-4610
web site: none listed

Service Corps of Retired Executives Association (free small-business assistance)
409 3rd Street SW, 6th Floor • Washington, DC 20024
phone: (800) 634-0245 • fax: none listed
web site: http://www.score.org

Small Business Development Centers (free small-business advice and information)
1222 North Main Street, #712 • San Antonio, TX 78212
phone: (800) 689-1912 • fax: (210) 458-2464
web site: http://www.asbdc-us.org

Small Publishers Co-Op (printing)
2579 Clematis Street • Sarasota, FL 34239
phone: (941) 922-0844 • fax: (941) 378-1583
web site: http://www.spco-op.com

Stamps.com
3420 Ocean Park Boulevard, Suite 1040 • Santa Monica, CA 90405-3035
phone: (310) 581-7200 • fax: none listed
web site: http://www.stamps.com

Staples, Inc. (office supplies)
8 Technology Drive • PO Box 5173 • Westborough, MA 01581
phone: (800) 333-3330 • fax: (800) 333-3199
web site: http://www.staples.com

The Stationery House (stationery)
1000 Florida Ave. • Hagerstown, MD 21740
phone: (800) 638-3033 • fax: (800) 554-8779 • web page:
http://www.stationeryhouse.com

The Stock Market Photo Agency (stock photography)
360 Park Avenue South, 16th floor • New York, NY 10010 •
phone: (800) 999-0800 • fax: (212) 532-6750
web site: http://www.stockmarketphoto.com

Tape Rental Library, Inc. (audiotape rentals)
One Cassette Center • PO Box 107 • Covesville, VA 22931
phone: (804) 293-3705 or (804) 263-5875 • fax: (804) 263-5543
web site: none listed

Telecommunications Research & Action Center (telephone service reports)
PO Box 27279 • Washington, DC 20005
phone: (202) 408-1130 • fax: none listed
web site: http://www.trac.org

Total Administrative Services Corp. (medical reimbursement plans)
2302 International Lane • Madison, WI 53704
phone: (800) 422-4661 • fax: (608) 241-4584
web site: http://www.plan105.com

Video Arts, Inc. (business and personal-development audiotapes and videotapes)
3083 Brickhouse Court • Virginia Beach, CA 23452
phone: (800) 285-9107 • fax: none listed
web site: http://www.videoarts.com

Viking Office Products (office supplies)
13809 South Figueroa Street • PO Box 61144 • Los Angeles,
CA 90061-0144 phone: (800) 421-1222 • fax: (800) 762-7329
web site: http://www.vikingop.com

Wholesale Supply Company (office supplies)
PO Box 23437 • Nashville, TN 37202
phone: (800) 962-9162 • fax: (800) 962-4FAX
web site: http://www.wholesalesupply.com

York Photo Labs (photo developing)

PO Box 500000 • Parkersburg, West Virginia 26102-9499

phone: (304) 424-YORK • fax: (304) 420-5600

web site: http://www.yorkphoto.com

INDEX

F

G

ABOUT THE AUTHORS

Jay Conrad Levinson is the president of his own marketing and consulting firm, Guerrilla Marketing International, and has been working from his California home for more than fifteen years. His best-selling book, *Guerrilla Marketing*, has spawned a series of *Guerrilla* books. He is the author of:

➤ *The Most Important $1.00 Book Ever Written*

➤ *Secrets of Successful Free-Lancing*

➤ *San Francisco: An Usual Guide to Unusual Shopping* (with Pat Levinson and John Bear)

➤ *Earning Money Without a Job*

➤ *555 Ways to Earn Extra Money*

➤ *150 Secrets of Successful Weight Loss* (with Michael Lavin and Michael Rokeach, MD)

➤ *Quit Your Job!*

➤ *An Earthling's Guide to Satellite TV*

➤ *Guerrilla Marketing*

➤ *Guerrilla Marketing Attack*

➤ *The Investor's Guide to the Photovoltaic Industry*

➤ *Guerrilla Marketing Weapons*

➤ *The 90-Minute Hour*

➤ *Guerrilla Financing* (with Bruce Jan Blechman)

- *Guerrilla Selling* (with Bill Gallagher and Orvel Ray Wilson)
- *Guerrilla Marketing Excellence*
- *Guerrilla Advertising*
- *Guerrilla Marketing Handbook* (with Seth Godin)
- *Guerrilla Marketing Online* (with Charles Rubin)
- *Guerrilla Marketing for the Home-Based Business* (with Seth Godin)
- *Guerrilla Marketing Online Weapons* (with Charles Rubin)
- *The Way of the Guerrilla*
- *Guerrilla Trade Show Selling* (with Mark S.A. Smith and Orvel Ray Wilson)
- *Get What You Deserve: How to Guerrilla Market Yourself* (with Seth Godin)
- *Guerrilla Marketing with Technology*
- *Guerrilla Marketing Online*, 2nd Edition (with Charles Rubin)
- *Guerrilla TeleSelling* (with Mark S. A. Smith and Orvel Ray Wilson)
- *Mastering Guerrilla Marketing*

Jay's books have been translated into thirty-one languages. He lectures worldwide on guerrilla business techniques for universities, organizations, and corporations.

Kathryn Tyler is an author and freelance writer who has worked from her home since 1993. The idea for this book grew out of an article she wrote for the September 1996 *Writers Connection*. Kathryn writes regularly for *HR Magazine* and has written for *Your Money, Woman's Day, FamilyFun, communication briefings, The Rotarian, Good Housekeeping,* and others. In addition to writing, she has taught at the University of California, San Diego; San Diego State University; and in the private sector.

Kathryn received her B.A. in English–American Literature from the University of California, San Diego in 1992 and graduated with a M.A. in English Literature from San Diego State University two years later. She lives in Michigan with her husband and children.

The authors are interested in your feedback! Please contact them via their web sites at http://gmarketing.com or http://www.kathryntyler.com.